Slavery and Europe

The question of the impact of slavery has gained new importance in debates on the history of economic development, capitalism and inequality. This edited volume explores how Atlantic slave-based economic activities and their spin-offs have contributed to the economic development of Europe.

The contributions to this volume each provide new data and methods for assessing the impact of Atlantic slavery, the slave trade and slave-related economic activities on Europe's economic development. It traces this impact across Europe, from maritime and colonizing regions to landlocked regions, of which, the ties to the Atlantic slavery complex might seem less obvious at first glance. Together the studies of this volume indicate that slavery and colonialism played a pivotal role in the rise of Europe and globally diverging economic fortunes.

The chapters in this book were originally published as a special issue of the journal *Slavery & Abolition*.

Tamira Combrink is Lecturer in History and Research Fellow at the International Institute of Social History (Netherlands Royal Academy of Arts and Sciences).

Matthias van Rossum is Senior Researcher at the International Institute of Social History (Netherlands Royal Academy of Arts and Sciences), and specialized in global labour history and the history of slave trade and slavery. He is Co-leader of *Exploring Slave Trade in Asia* and Leader of GLOBALISE, research infrastructure projects that explore histories of slavery and colonialism.

Routledge Studies in Slave and Post-Slave Societies and Cultures
Edited by Gad Heuman

After Slavery
Emancipation and its Discontents
Edited by Howard Temperley

Rethinking the African Diaspora
The Making of a Black Atlantic World in the Bight of Benin and Brazil
Edited by Edna G. Bay and Kristin Mann

Representing the Body of the Slave
Edited by Jane Gardner and Thomas Wiedemann

Structure of Slavery in Indian Ocean Africa and Asia
Gwyn Campbell

Abolition and Its Aftermath in the Indian Ocean Africa and Asia
Gwyn Campbell

Resisting Bondage in Indian Ocean Africa and Asia
Edited by Edward A. Alpers, Gwyn Campbell and Michael Salman

Representations of Slave Women in Discourses on Slavery and Abolition, 1780–1838
Henrice Altink

Popular Politics and British Anti-Slavery
The Mobilisation of Public Opinion against the Slave Trade 1787–1807
J.R. Oldfield

Motherhood, Childlessness and the Care of Children in Atlantic Slave Societies
Edited by Camillia Cowling, Maria Helena Pereira Toledo Machado, Diana Paton and Emily West

Slavery and Europe
Exploring the Economic Impact of Atlantic Slavery
Edited by Tamira Combrink and Matthias van Rossum

For more information about this series, please visit: www.routledge.com/Routledge-Studies-in-Slave-and-Post-Slave-Societies-and-Cultures/book-series/RSSPSS

Slavery and Europe

Exploring the Economic Impact of Atlantic Slavery

Edited by
Tamira Combrink and Matthias van Rossum

LONDON AND NEW YORK

First published 2023
by Routledge
4 Park Square, Milton Park, Abingdon, Oxon, OX14 4RN

and by Routledge
605 Third Avenue, New York, NY 10158

Routledge is an imprint of the Taylor & Francis Group, an informa business

British Library Cataloguing-in-Publication Data
A catalogue record for this book is available from the British Library

ISBN13: 978-1-032-16360-4 (hbk)
ISBN13: 978-1-032-16365-9 (pbk)
ISBN13: 978-1-003-24821-7 (ebk)

DOI: 10.4324/9781003248217

Typeset in Minion Pro
bycodeMantra

Publisher's Note
The publisher accepts responsibility for any inconsistencies that may have arisen during the conversion of this book from journal articles to book chapters, namely the inclusion of journal terminology.

Contents

Citation Information

The following chapters were originally published in the journal *Slavery & Abolition*, volume 42, issue 1 (2021). When citing this material, please use the original page numbering for each article, as follows:

Chapter 2
The profits of the Portuguese–Brazilian transatlantic slave trade: challenges and possibilities
Filipa Ribeiro da Silva
Slavery & Abolition, volume 42, issue 1 (2021) pp. 77–104

Chapter 3
Governance, value-added and rents in plantation slavery-based value-chains
Klas Rönnbäck
Slavery & Abolition, volume 42, issue 1 (2021) pp. 130–150

Chapter 4
Slavery and the Dutch economy, 1750–1800
Pepijn Brandon and Ulbe Bosma
Slavery & Abolition, volume 42, issue 1 (2021) pp. 43–76

Chapter 5
Slave-based coffee in the eighteenth century and the role of the Dutch in global commodity chains
Tamira Combrink
Slavery & Abolition, volume 42, issue 1 (2021) pp. 15–42

Chapter 6
A cloth that binds: new perspectives on the eighteenth-century Prussian economy
Anka Steffen
Slavery & Abolition, volume 42, issue 1 (2021) pp. 105–129

Chapter 7
How important was the slavery system to Europe?
Guillaume Daudin
Slavery & Abolition, volume 42, issue 1 (2021) pp. 151–157

Chapter 8

The value of figures
Pepijn Brandon
Slavery & Abolition, volume 42, issue 1 (2021) pp. 158–164

Chapter 9

Revisiting Europe and slavery
Sven Beckert
Slavery & Abolition, volume 42, issue 1 (2021) pp. 165–178

Notes on Contributors

Sven Beckert is Professor at Harvard University, Department of History, USA.

Ulbe Bosma is Senior Researcher at the International Institute of Social History, Amsterdam, the Netherlands, and Professor of International Comparative Social History at the VU Amsterdam.

Pepijn Brandon is Senior Researcher at the International Institute of Social History, Amsterdam, the Netherlands, and Assistant Professor of Economic and Social History at the VU Amsterdam.

Tamira Combrink is Lecturer in History at Leiden University, the Netherlands, and Research Fellow at the International Institute of Social History (Netherlands Royal Academy of Arts and Sciences), Amsterdam, the Netherlands.

Filipa Ribeiro da Silva is at the International Institute of Social History (IISH), Amsterdam, the Netherlands.

Guillaume Daudin is Professor at the Université Paris-Dauphine, Université PSL, LEDA, CNRS, IRD, DIAL, Paris, France.

Klas Rönnbäck is Professor in Economic History at the Department of Economy and Society at the University of Gothenburg, Sweden.

Anka Steffen is PhD Candidate at the European University Viadrina, Frankfurt (Oder), Germany.

Matthias van Rossum is Senior Researcher at the International Institute of Social History (Netherlands Royal Academy of Arts and Sciences), Amsterdam, the Netherlands.

Foreword

How important were the transatlantic slave trade and slavery to the economic development of Europe? Many historians will answer: That importance was marginal. A recent encyclopaedia article states for example: "The notion that the Atlantic slave trade was of major importance to European economic development has been abandoned today."[1]

The authors of the present wonderful collection show that such a conclusion is the result of sloppy thinking. The weakness of the reasoning behind it is that only two aspects of slavery and the slave trade are considered: the money earned by selling people bought in Africa across the ocean at a profit, and the profit made by the labour of the enslaved in the Americas for the plantation owners there. But in reality the matter is more complicated.

It already starts with the journey of the slave trader and his crew from Europe to Africa to buy his human commodities. His ship must first be built and supplied, not only with provisions for the crew, but also with goods to trade on the African coast and the buoys and chains necessary to control the enslaved during the voyage across the ocean; and of course food and drink to keep the "merchandise" alive during that journey. The construction and equipment of such a ship was a costly affair, and it could take up to a year for a ship to return to its home port. The required capital came about through contributions from associates and loans from bankers and others.

The enslaved aboard the ship—the "cargo"—were vulnerable; on average, about fourteen percent did not make it across, due to illness, suicide, or violence. Ships could also be damaged or even wrecked. In order to make the risk manageable, the slave traders concluded contracts with insurers.

In the Americas, the enslaved were sold, directly or through middlemen, and employed as domestics or as labourers on the sugar, coffee, and cotton plantations. Before the plantation owners could put their "personnel" to work, they obviously had to make investments; they were forced to acquire land, build sugarmills, etc. They also had to make sure that the enslaved had clothes (and sometimes shoes) - goods usually bought elsewhere, often through long-distance trade.

The cash crops produced were then sold to a trader who transported them to Europe, where they were further processed in sugar refineries, cottage industries, and factories, and resold.

In other words, the slave trade and slavery have a much greater impact on the international economy than meets the eye. Hundreds of thousands of artisans and wage earners in Europe and its settler colonies, and a large number of East European serfs were involved. There was therefore also a clear, but complicated, multiplier effect: expenditure incurred by slave traders and slave owners also generated additional income elsewhere beyond the initial spending.

It is remarkable that this insight has eluded most historians for so long. Its neglect also had political consequences. For while almost everyone realizes that slavery was a human drama of enormous proportions, looking only at the immediate aspects it seemed as if slavery and the slave trade were relatively insignificant *economically*.

The chapters collected here mark a turning point in the economic historiography of Atlantic slavery and the slave trade. They explore the important aspects of this problem. They form fragments of a larger puzzle, the contours of which are already becoming visible. They thus contribute substantially to a necessary reorientation. As Eric Williams wrote in the last lines of his *Capitalism and Slavery*: "The historians neither make nor guide history. Their share in such is usually so small as to be almost negligible. But if they do not learn something from history, their activities would then be cultural decoration, or a pleasant pastime, equally useless in these troubled times."

Marcel van der Linden
Amsterdam, October 2021

Note

1. Guy Saupin, "The Return Effects of the Atlantic Slave Trade in Europe," *Encyclopédie d'histoire numérique de l'Europe* [online], published on 22/06/20, consulted on 03/10/2021. Permalink: https://ehne.fr/en/node/12272. Compare e.g. David Eltis and Pieter C. Emmer, "More Than Profits? The Contribution of the Slave Trade to the Dutch Economy: Assessing Fatah-Black and Van Rossum," *Slavery and Abolition*, 37:4 (2016), 724–35, at 724: "the impact of the slave trade on the Dutch economy was minimal".

Introduction

Introduction: the impact of slavery on Europe – reopening a debate

Tamira Combrink and Matthias van Rossum

This volume questions how slave-based economic activities and their spinoffs have contributed to the economic development of Europe. The question of the impact of slavery has gained new importance in debates on the history of economic development, capitalism and inequality.[1] Whereas the debate on the role of slavery in European capitalist development originally focused on the Williams thesis, targeting especially the link between the profits of the slave trade and industrialisation, subsequent studies have targeted the wider economic impact of early modern slavery-related activities on both Europe and the Atlantic world, moving the debate beyond the restricted focus on profits and profitability.[2] Emphasising the strategic role of the slave trade and slavery-related commodity chains, several new research initiatives in different national and historiographic contexts have started to explore different elements of the role slavery played in economic relations between Europe and its colonies.[3] This volume contributes to this reconsideration of the relation between Europe and slavery. It argues that it is time to readdress our assessment of how the impact of slavery can be measured. In doing so, this volume brings together a collection of articles that each provides new data and considerations for assessing the impact of slavery, the slave trade and slave-related economic activities on the economic development of regions across Europe. Together the articles indicate that slavery and colonialism played a pivotal role in the rise of Europe and in globally diverging economic fortunes.

Deep entanglements: Europe and slavery

Academic interest in the economic importance of slavery across history is part of a wider development in re-examining the history and meaning of slavery and its legacy in relation to European histories and identities. Since 2010, museums in particular have started reflecting on their collections and links to or origins in colonial expropriation, violence and slavery.[4] These re-examinations are not just increasing in number or reviving interest in histories that thus far have been dealt with far too little, but more importantly they are part of and contributing to the improvement, or perhaps even transformation, of our understanding of the dynamics and impact of slavery. The slavery exhibition organised by the

Dutch national Rijksmuseum in Amsterdam in 2021, for example, challenges a long-standing tradition of portraying 'Dutch' national self-imagery centred around ideas of tolerance, enlightenment and science, while simultaneously for the first time bringing together in one integrated public narrative the understudied history of slavery and the slave trade in the early modern Dutch colonial world in the Indian Ocean and Indonesian Archipelago with the traditionally more dominant Atlantic history.[5]

A wider wave of initiatives explores the history and legacy of slavery by making it visible, showing its past and present centrality by uncovering its pervasive and widespread presence in material, visual, cultural and urban contexts. In so doing, these initiatives challenge the still deeply engrained notion that the history of slavery was an 'overseas' history, and that slavery only affected, and took place in, the world outside Europe. This trope facilitated the widespread exclusion of slavery from official and dominant narratives on national histories that are still visible across Europe, but that are now increasingly questioned. The widespread public attention has been sparked especially by projects such as the compensation database tracing the legacies of British slave-ownership,[6] but many more initiatives expand well beyond the confines of academia, for example, in the mapping of the visual and material legacy of slavery in cities in the Netherlands and the US or in the collection of new bodies of knowledge.[7] Inspired by US initiatives revisiting the ties of slavery to universities and cities in the North, cities across Europe have begun to examine their links to slavery and the slave trade from an urban perspective.[8]

These public initiatives to make the historical connections of slavery tangible and explore them from hitherto underrepresented angles have in turn fuelled new academic questions.[9] The question of contemporary knowledge as well as the visibility of slavery in early modern Europe, for example, has stimulated a rising interest in the understudied history of the lives and experiences of enslaved people from the Atlantic, Indian Ocean and Indonesian archipelago worlds who were taken to Europe. Roughly one-fifth of the population of the city of Lisbon consisted of people of colour in the eighteenth century.[10] In Germany, Scandinavia and the Netherlands, research indicates that the presence of enslaved individuals was far more widespread at royal courts and in elite households than previously thought, but was at the same time certainly not limited to the estates of nobility, patricians and the richest merchants. An early 'black' presence in northern Europe was not as extensive as in southern Europe, but did lead to modest communities in places such as London and Amsterdam from the early seventeenth century onwards.[11] Despite classic dogmas that tend to associate Europe with the history of freedom and civil rights, and despite claims that 'any slave who touched foot on French soil' would be freed, studies also indicate that enslaved people brought to France, the UK or the Dutch Republic were mostly not freed, but remained under the control of their masters and in the positions of unfreedom. The dogma that there was 'no slavery' in northwestern Europe thus does not hold up, since slavery existed at least in practice and often even in law. In the context of Amsterdam, for example, the practice of slavery was even confirmed by law as late as 1776.[12] The social, cultural and economic connections between Europe and slavery were thus much deeper and more complex than its involvement in regimes of overseas colonial exploitation alone.

The mapping and re-examination of the historical links between cities and slavery also forces historians to face up to specific terrains of historical enquiry that have hitherto remained relatively understudied. Despite the large bodies of knowledge on early modern elites, urban governance and the networks of merchants active in overseas trade from northern European cities, for example, thus far little systematic effort has been made to connect these to the early modern economics and politics of slavery and the slave trade. Here the 'urban' perspective thus opens up new terrains of research. The case of Amsterdam could again be telling. Only recently has its fundamental role in governing Atlantic colonies such as Surinam attracted the interest of historians.[13] The role of the city in shaping other colonies such as Nieuwer-Amstel remains relatively unexplored.[14] The same can be said for the even more prominent role of the city in the highly aggressive politics of colonial expansion of the Dutch East India Company (VOC) in the first decades of the seventeenth century, despite the fact that the latter resulted in the establishment of a Dutch empire throughout Asia to which an estimated 660,000–1.14 million enslaved Asians and Africans were transported over the course of the seventeenth and eighteenth centuries.[15]

An economic view: Europe, connections and comparisons

These re-examinations along a wide spectrum of routes are necessary to understand the complex and diverse ways in which slavery, the slave trade and wider regimes of colonial coercion and exploitation have impacted both the non-European world and Europe itself. At the same time, however, knowledge is not only advanced by embracing and adjoining the complementary insights of different approaches – a certain focus is instrumental and even needed, perhaps, to advance our insight into specific central research questions. This thematic volume takes the latter as its point of departure.

This volume aims to further the debates on slavery, early modern globalisation and economic development by bringing together new research based on a global-comparative perspective. It builds upon the conference session *Europe and Slavery. Estimating the share of slave-based activities in European economies, 1500–1850* (WEHC 2018, Boston), which was organised as a follow-up to the conference session *Global Impact of Slave Trade and Slavery* (WEHC 2015, Kyoto). Central to the Boston session and its discussions were the recently (re)discovered method of *global value chain analysis*, indicating the economic and financial links between different stages of investment, manufacture, trade and consumption (see, for example, the focus on *global value chains* by the

World Trade Organization in its 2014 annual report).[16] The global commodities and their chains of production and trade driving early modern expansion are a reminder that there are long-lasting and global histories behind contemporary commodity chains.

The 'flavour makers' and stimuli that emerged in the early modern era, such as the wide range of spices, sugar, tobacco, coffee and tea, did not merely connect different ends of the world through patterns of trade or emerging consumption cultures, but had deep, lasting and increasingly transformative effects, not only in the Atlantic but also in South and Southeast Asia.[17] Historians of work and labour relations are now increasingly trying to understand how the connections set in motion through these early modern global commodity chains transformed, transplanted and expanded often coercive labour regimes in and between different localities. The effects could be highly uneven between different parts of the commodity chains and the regions where these were based.[18] Similarly, for the history of economic development, we can take from this lesson that we should be more attentive to the role played by colonial trade and related activities – quantitatively and qualitatively – in the (mis)fortunes of and inequalities between different societies.[19] Global value chain analysis can be useful for historians as a way to improve our understanding of global links in economic development. It brings to mind and enables us to trace both forward and backward linkages of slave-based colonial production, thus indicating that such commodities were not only related to the (overseas) sites and stages of production, but to the wider worlds of provisioning, transport and consumption. This reconnects the global history of (colonial) coerced labour to the regional histories of economic development in Europe, with direct ties ranging from the production and delivery of slave-ship victuals to the development of extensive distribution networks of colonial groceries through bakeries and home-run coffee shops.

Considering the dynamics and impact of the global connections that flowed from the early modern slavery complex, this volume argues for making the impact of slavery and the slave trade on the development of the European economy into a field of more thorough and systematic interrogation. This volume thus stresses connections and shows the impact of slavery. It shows that the slave trade and slave-related economic activities not only led to coercion and extraction in colonial contexts, but through global commodity chains created an economic impact that resulted in higher gains in the metropole and to overall contributions that mattered significantly in the economies of Europe. The contributions published in this volume do not provide the final answers but must be seen as a first step towards the more systematic, comparative and connecting international research agenda for exploring and discussing the economic impact of slavery in different parts of the world called for by this volume.

We have chosen to start this exploration with a comparative approach, covering both regions that were at the forefront of European imperial expansion and that laid the basis for overseas slave-based production, as well as regions that may seem to have been less directly involved. This first step focusses on comparisons of the impact of the Atlantic slavery system on Europe in the early modern period, mostly the eighteenth century, because of its central role in debates on global economic divergence, colonialism and inequality. Taken together, the studies in this volume challenge the persistent notion of the 'marginality' of slavery and the slave trade, and especially their economic gains, to the economic history and development of Europe. This contribution is all the more urgent considering the resurgence across the globe of narratives that recycle the claims of European (enlightened) exceptionalism and cultural, economic and institutional superiority.[20]

Of course, early modern Europe was not the only time and place that depended heavily on slave-related economic activities. Slavery was at the core of European society and economic development from at least the time of the Roman Empire, and this remained the case in the Mediterranean until the nineteenth century. And slavery existed outside Europe and outside European colonies as well. And, as is discussed in some of the contributions in this volume, slave-related commodity chains generated their own dynamics and impacts in West Africa and the Americas. At the same time, the impact of slavery was not uniform across Europe. Different regions were connected to the Atlantic slavery system in different ways. This is most clear, of course, in comparisons between landlocked Europe and maritime regions, but is also an important factor to keep in mind when comparing the different European maritime empires. The historiographic dominance of the British case has in that respect not been helpful in coming to terms with the differences in the multiple European imperial circuits, and has perhaps played a role in the relative late rediscoveries of, and attention to, overseas trade circuits outside the control of the European metropole (for example, between West Africa and Brazil, or the intra-American trade); the importance of inter-imperial connections; and the differences in the structure of Iberian, Dutch, French and Scandinavian imperial involvement.[21] And to further complicate this picture, the slavery-related commodity chains that connected different parts of the world did not exist in isolation, but were continuously interlocked in complex constellations of interdependence, complementarity and competition in the stages of consumption, transport, refinement and production. Again, these interactions cut right through the boundaries of nations and empires. All these considerations, however, do not inflate the relevance of assessing the importance of slavery to European economic development and to its acceleration in a period of global economic divergence.

This volume thus brings together the research from authors who were each asked to contribute to a collective attempt to assess the role of slave-based economic activities in the wider economies of European regions. We asked authors to contribute by exploring ways in which they could provide information on national economies as a whole or on specific sub-regions, identifying slavery-related trade and industries, indicating the size of such industries and branches of trade where possible and estimating their role in relation to economies at large (for example, through indicators on the value of economic performance [GDP], the size of trade, economic growth or employment figures, etc.). The national or regional levels and the quantitative approach were instrumental in our aim to develop more systematic comparative insights. This open quantitative and comparative set-up thus served to facilitate comparisons for assessing the importance of slavery for societies across time and space, irrespective of whether the slavery itself was based in that society or it was externalised and overseas. By raising awareness of (global) value or commodity chain approaches we hoped we could also provide a way of highlighting the interconnections and intertwinements between political and economic clusters. The collection could thus at the same time provide a starting point for further exchange and discussion on the methodologies used. The discussion at the Boston roundtable suggests that this may have succeeded, and we support the idea that the next steps would be to further develop quantifications, methods and connections in future research.

Several lessons for ways forward

The approach taken here does not mean we think we should limit research to the now for practical means chosen set-up. Rather, we hope that this modest comparative, still very much national structure-oriented, quantitative exercise provides a contribution to a much broader reinvigoration of the debate on the question of the impact of slavery. We believe that, at this stage, a focused and collective quantitative approach is needed to further our understanding, but we do not contend that this should be the only way forward. To further our insights, it should in fact be accompanied by qualitative approaches to the economic, institutional, political, cultural and social dimensions of these histories.

The *complementarity* of insights gained from different methods and thematic domains, however, is not the only issue that requires our immediate attention. The contributions to this volume also provide important reminders that it is of key importance to consider both the *scope* and *scale* of our future historical enquiries. While it is clear that slavery was not only an 'overseas' history, it is simplistic to analyse the impact of slavery along rigid lines (Europe–Atlantic, or Global North–Global South). The attempt to reconnect and reintegrate Europe in the analysis of the history of slavery and the impact of slavery, especially when we try to understand these through the transformations and connections forged by commodity chains, reminds us of the complexities that mark these histories of coercion and exploitation. We can take several lessons from the current state of historiography.

First, it is important to not oversimplify or even reify the (national) entities needed in the course of our analytical exercises, but to bring to light the complexities of the political-economic structures that moulded or attempted to steer control of flows of trade, production and consumption along increasingly national and imperial lines. Neither these structures nor their boundaries were stagnant, and – just as important – they were continuously influenced by economic and political elites that were to be found not only in the metropole but also in Brazil, Surinam and North America. Moreover, these often 'national' imperial projects stood in complex interplay with legal and illegal trade across imperial and national borders and inter-imperial collaborations and connections. And in the new-found states created in Atlantic colonies that broke away from European metropoles, except if their revolts were led by slaves demanding their freedom, as in the case of Haiti, slave-based production regimes generally continued or even accelerated, as was the case in the US (until 1865) and Brazil (1888).

Second, this means that – although this volume again revisits the connections between the Atlantic and Europe – the history of (colonial) commercial slavery was not confined to the Atlantic. Its scope was much *wider*, including the Indian Ocean and Indonesian Archipelago worlds,[22] and it was continuously *related to* and *interacting with* the broader histories of coercion and colonial exploitation, both in the Atlantic and elsewhere. In particular, the histories of the development of the 'corvée' and 'cultivation' systems in South and Southeast Asia, but also the early Asian histories of contract migrant labour and colonial carceral regimes are important reminders that colonial coercive labour regimes spread throughout the world in a variety of forms, and that these regimes of coercion would in an early stage start to transform the global countryside beyond the Atlantic realm already in the early modern period.[23] The experiences and labour regimes of these other regimes of colonial exploitation increasingly started to feed into the Atlantic world in response to the nineteenth-century abolitions of slave trading and slavery. In order to improve our understanding of the Atlantic slavery complex, its transformations and its aftermath, we thus need to improve our understanding of (colonial) coercion and exploitation elsewhere in the world, especially in the wider Indian Ocean and Indonesian Archipelago worlds.

In better understanding the impact of these global histories of coercion, *scale* matters. First, in discussing 'regimes', 'systems' or 'chains' it is important to recall that a real understanding of what such abstractions implied in terms of coercive practices, social relations or other effects for the people involved can only come from testing how these abstractions functioned in everyday life contexts.[24] Second, recent studies, including those in this volume, indicate the concentrated and sometimes very high local impact of the spoils of slave-related commodity chains, with the local economies of some cities heavily dependent on economic activities related to slavery-related industries. The economies of port cities such as Flushing (Vlissingen), Nantes and Liverpool, for example, were deeply connected to the slave trade and its provisioning. It is clear that other cities, such as Amsterdam, London or Bristol, not only profited from the slave trade, but also from the wide range of slavery-related provisioning and (re)processing industries, trade and other economic activities, for example, banking, insurance, sugar, coffee and even glass bead trades. The contributions to this volume point out not only that this mattered at a national level (the Dutch Republic, Portugal, the UK), but that the impact could be much deeper at the regional and urban level (for example, for Holland, or Amsterdam and London) and that both the connections and impact stretched far into European hinterlands (Silesia) as well as back across the Atlantic (Brazil). Our quest for measuring impact should, in future research, thus not be guided by methodological nationalism, but steered by the search for the key levels if we are to make sense of the role and impact of slavery – this should be both quantitative (focusing on the importance of specific sectors) and qualitative (focusing on political-economic regimes that were consciously nurtured and shaped by elites of merchants and rulers).

Slavery's impact across Europe – first assessments

This volume attempts to assess the impact of slavery and slavery-related economic activities on Europe, with its collection of articles covering the ways of assessing the role and weight of slave-based colonial activities for Portugal and Brazil (Filipa Ribeiro da Silva), the sugar value chain for Great Britain (Klas Rönnbäck), the coffee trade (Tamira Combrink) and the wider Atlantic slave-based economy for the Dutch Republic (Pepijn Brandon and Ulbe Bosma) and linen production for Silesia (Anka Steffen). Expanding on very unevenly developed historiographies, the contributions collectively expose not only the importance of the Atlantic slave-related commodity chains of trade, production and services for the early modern European economy, but also these forged connections that reached far beyond the European metropoles, into European hinterlands as well as across different Atlantic colonies, which at times played pivotal roles in shaping larger political and economic developments.

For the Dutch Republic, Tamira Combrink shows in her contribution how the commodity chain of slave-produced coffee was important in re-orienting the Dutch economy from the Baltic and Mediterranean to the Rhine and the German hinterland, with the coffee trade rising 'from very little' to a share of '9.5% of the total trade value' of the Dutch Republic in the second half of the eighteenth century. These studies on the Dutch case contribute to a reviving debate on the impact of the slave trade and slavery to the wealth of the Netherlands. Earlier studies that stirred up the Dutch debate employed an approach focusing on the 'gross margin' or 'impact' of the slave trade, and indicated that this single industry – despite earlier claims that it was an unprofitable business – already contributed up to 0.5% to the economy of the entire Dutch Republic (Van Rossum and Fatah-Black), with one-tenth or even one-third of the economies of specific port cities such as Middelburg and Flushing arising from economic activities related to the slave trade (De Kok).[25] In 2012, Van Rossum and Fatah-Black therefore called for 'further reconstructions of the size and impact of other elements of the Atlantic system' in order to 'provide new insights for the debate on the role of slavery and the related economic activities in the trans-Atlantic trade system and the influence on the development of early modern Europe'.[26] In their contribution in this volume, Pepijn Brandon and Ulbe Bosma take up this call and expand on this approach, calculating the contribution of slave-based activities to the GDP of the Dutch Republic (5.2%) and the province of Holland (10.36%) around 1770.

Of course, the implications of such basic assessments are often challenged by questioning whether specific percentages should not be considered small rather than large. Some examples could provide a clear point of reference to the importance of these indications of the slavery-related contributions to early modern economy. In 2006, on the eve of the globally disruptive financial crisis of 2007–08, it was calculated that the gross value added of the entire 'financial and insurance services' was 7.7% of the UK's GDP and 7.5% of the US's GDP.[27] This comparison provides two clear arguments as to why the impact was significant. First, these sectors were considered too big to fail, as indicated in the 2007–08 crisis with massive bailouts and the subsequent deep economic downturn. Second, as with the financial sector, the early modern Atlantic slave-related trade and economy was deeply connected to a myriad of other sectors, from supplying, processing and servicing industries. The Dutch Republic was obviously not alone in its strong reliance on slavery and slave-based economic activities, and these studies join a wider landscape of new research that suggests the importance of slavery for different parts of Europe.

For Great Britain, recent estimates suggest that economic activities relating to the Atlantic slavery complex reached as much as 11% of the entire British economy by the early nineteenth century (Klas Rönnbäck).[28] In his contribution to this volume, Rönnbäck illuminates the importance and impact of the sugar value chain to the British economy, with the sugar-refiners in Britain being the main beneficiaries of British protectionist policies. The value of slavery-based colonial economic activity has been measured for other parts of northwestern Europe as well. In an earlier study, Rönnbäck concluded that at the end of the eighteenth century, the 'three small islands of the Danish West Indies', with a population of only 1% of the Danish empire, contributed a net profit equal to some 5% or 6% of the total public revenue of Denmark proper, which 'was repatriated straight into the coffers of the Danish Kingdom'.[29] For the major German port city of Hamburg, representing 'about 70 per cent of all overseas imports' of present-day middle and northern Germany, Ulrich Pfister calculated that the value of colonial commodities in the total record of trade imports rose from around 47% in the 1730s to almost 72% in the 1790s. The two major slavery-produced commodities of sugar and coffee accounted for 39.1% of total imports into the city in the 1730s, but this figure rose to 62.3% in the 1790s.[30]

The contributions of this volume confirm that the impact of slavery-related economic activities was not confined to the European maritime colonial nations, and that much more research is needed to create a comprehensive insight into the complex connections between and impacts on different parts of the European continent. For Portugal it has been estimated that the overseas empire contributed 'around 20 percent' to Portugal's per capita income.[31] In her contribution on the Portuguese empire, Filipa Ribeiro da Silva brings the complex links between Portugal and Brazil to the fore, making it clear that the slave trade and slavery-related economic activities clearly affected both sides. She calls to reconsider our methods of assessing the multi-directional relationship and the gains that were found both in Europe and in the colonies. Anka Steffen integrates the history of Silesian linen production into that of Western Europe and its history of slavery in the Atlantic. She estimates that the production of linen for the Atlantic slavery complex accounted for some '15% of the total value of all manufactures produced in the Prussian state' at the end of the eighteenth century. In this way, she brings the history of the European 'hinterland' into the analysis of the history of slavery, while simultaneously asking whether the labour-intensive orientation of economies in Eastern European regions might have favoured capital-intensive developments in the Western parts of the continent.

To conclude, the implications of the contributions in this volume for our understanding of the impact of slavery on European economic development, as well as for the direction of future debates and research, are discussed in a roundtable with essays by three special experts in the fields of the history of slavery, early modern economic development and capitalism. These contributors to the roundtable have taken it upon themselves not only to reflect on the contributions and implications of this volume, but also to debate what direction future research should take. Guillaume Daudin argues for an approach that focuses more on economic theory and the development of counterfactuals to assess the role and significance of the slave trade and slave-based activities. Pepijn Brandon encourages to continue the quantitative reconstructive approaches that have been given a new impulse with research on the impact of the slave trade and the Atlantic slavery complex in, for example, the UK (Rönnbäck) and the Dutch Republic (following Van Rossum and Fatah-Black, De Kok et al.).[32] Sven Beckert warns against a-historic counterfactuals and against approaches that take too exclusively quantitative directions, and points out the importance of the wider roles of slavery and colonial exploitation.

We embrace these pointers towards future research, although our suggestion here is to avoid easy counterfactuals and fragmented research agendas, as these could disguise the specific strategic role of coerced mobilisation, transplantation and coercion of people in early modern and later economies. Slavery and the slave trade were part of the larger structures of political-economies (or modalities of domination and dependence) of which we can only improve our understanding if we reconstruct their roles and effects through systematic (quantitative with qualitative), comparative and connecting global approaches.

Funding

This volume was the result of the conference session *Europe and Slavery. Estimating the share of slave-based activities in European economies, 1500–1850* at the World Economic History Conference in Boston in 2018. This was organised by the editors as part of their research efforts for the respective projects *Slaves, commodities and logistics. The direct and indirect, the immediate and long-term economic impact of eighteenth-century Dutch Republic transatlantic slave-based activities*, NWO Project Number 360-53-170 (principal applicants Marcel van der Linden, Karel Davids and Henk den Heijer) and *Between local debts and global markets: Explaining slavery in South and Southeast Asia 1600–1800* (Matthias van Rossum, NWO Veni Grant, 2016–19) funded by the Dutch Council of Scientific Research (NWO).

Notes

1. E.g. Sven Beckert, *Empire of Cotton: A Global History* (New York: Alfred A. Knopf, 2014).
2. Eric Williams, *Capitalism and Slavery* (Chapel Hill: University of North Carolina Press, 1944). On the economic impact of slavery on the Atlantic: Richard B. Sheridan, 'The Wealth of Jamaica in the Eighteenth Century', *Economic History Review* 18:2 (1965), 292–311; Barbara L. Solow and Stanley L. Engerman (eds.), *British Capitalism and Caribbean Slavery* (Cambridge: Cambridge University Press, 2004), 11; Herbert S. Klein, *The Middle Passage: Comparative Studies in the Atlantic Slave Trade* (Princeton, NJ: Princeton University Press, 1978); Henry A. Gemery and Jan S. Hogendorn (eds.), *The Uncommon Market. Essays in the Economic History of the Atlantic Slave Trade* (New York: Academic Press, 1979). On the impact of slavery on Europe: Robin Blackburn, *The Making of New World Slavery: From the Baroque to the Modern, 1492–1800* (New York: Verso, 1997); Gad Heuman and James Walvin, 'The Atlantic Slave Trade: Introduction', in Gad Heuman and James Walvin (eds.), *The Slavery Reader* (London and New York: Routledge, 2003), 3–10; Klas Rönnbäck, 'Who Stood to Gain from Colonialism? A Case Study of Early Modern European Colonialism in the Caribbean', *Itinerario* 33:3 (2009), 135–54; Matthias van Rossum and Karwan Fatah-Black, 'Wat is winst? De economische impact van de Nederlandse trans-Atlantische slavenhandel', *TSEG/ Low Countries Journal of Social and Economic History* 9:1 (2012), 3–29; Karwan Fatah-Black and Matthias van Rossum, 'Beyond Profitability: The Dutch Transatlantic Slave Trade and Its Economic Impact', *Slavery & Abolition* 36:1 (2015), 63–83; Gerhard de Kok, 'Cursed Capital: The Economic Impact of the Transatlantic Slave Trade on Walcheren around 1770', *TSEG/ Low Countries Journal of Social and Economic History* 13:3 (2016), 1–27; Klas Rönnbäck, 'On the Economic Importance of the Slave Plantation Complex to the British Economy during the Eighteenth Century: A Value-Added Approach', *Journal of Global History* 13:3 (2018), 309–27; Pepijn Brandon and Ulbe Bosma, 'De betekenis van de Atlantische slavernij voor de Nederlandse economie in de tweede helft van de achttiende eeuw', *TSEG/ Low Countries Journal of Social and Economic History* 16:2 (2019), 5–46.
3. For example, the Dutch NWO-project *Slaves, commodities and logistics*, IISH and Leiden University, 2014–19; the German DFG-project *The Globalized Periphery,*

Europa-Universität Viadrina, 2015–17; Cátia Antunes, *Exploiting the Empire of Others*, NWO Vici Grant, 2020–25.

4. With varying initiatives in, for example, France, Germany, Belgium, the UK and the Netherlands.
5. The regular exhibition displays of the Rijksmuseum, in fact, still strongly supports this national self-imagery. More information on this exhibition: https://www.rijksmuseum.nl/en/slavery.
6. See for example: https://www.ucl.ac.uk/lbs/.
7. See for example: https://mappingslavery.nl/; http://www.theblackarchives.nl/; Nancy Jouwe, Wim Manuhutu, Matthias van Rossum and Merve Tosun (eds.), *Slavernij herbezien: Visuele bronnen over slavernij in Azië / Re-visualising Slavery: Visual Sources on Slavery in Asia* (Amsterdam and Seattle, WA: LM Publisher and University of Washington Press, 2021).
8. See for example: http://www.slaveryinnewyork.org/; http://www.harvardandslavery.com/wp-content/uploads/2011/11/Harvard-Slavery-Book-111110.pdf . European examples: Glasgow, Liverpool, Rotterdam, Amsterdam, Utrecht and The Hague.
9. For example, revisiting the relation between Europe and the Atlantic, see e.g. Felix Brahm and Eve Rosenhaft, (eds.), *Slavery Hinterland: Transatlantic Slavery and Continental Europe, 1680–1850* (Woodbridge: Boydell & Brewer, 2016).
10. James H. Sweet, 'The Hidden Histories of African Lisbon', in Jorge Canizares-Esguerra, Matt D. Childs and James Sidbury (eds.), *The Black Urban Atlantic in the Age of the Slave Trade* (Philadelphia: University of Pennsylvania Press, 2013), 233–47, 237; Erin Kathleen Rowe, *Black Saints in Early Modern Global Catholicism* (Cambridge: Cambridge University Press, 2019).
11. Norma Myers, *Reconstructing the Black Past: Blacks in Britain 1780–1830* (London: Routledge, 2013); Rebekka von Mallinckrodt, 'There Are No Slaves in Prussia?', in Brahm and Rosenhaft, *Slavery Hinterland*, 109–32; Dienke Hondius, *Blackness in Western Europe: Racial Patterns of Paternalism and Exclusion* (London: Routledge, 2017); Mark Ponte, '"Al de swarten die hier ter stede comen": Een Afro-Atlantische gemeenschap in zeventiende-eeuws Amsterdam', *TSEG/ Low Countries Journal of Social and Economic History* 15:4 (2018), 33–62.
12. Sue Peabody, *There Are No Slaves in France: The Political Culture of Race and Slavery in the Ancien Régime* (Oxford: Oxford University Press, 1996); Samuel L. Chatman, '"There Are No Slaves in France": A Re-Examination of Slave Laws in Eighteenth Century France', *The Journal of Negro History* 85:3 (2000), 144–53; Sue Peabody and Keila Grinberg (eds.), *Free Soil in the Atlantic World* (London: Taylor and Francis, 2016) – based on special issue *Slavery & Abolition: A Journal of Slave and Post-Slave Studies* 32:3 (2011); Karwan Fatah-Black and Matthias van Rossum, 'Slavery in a 'Slave Free Enclave'? Historical Links between the Dutch Republic, Empire and Slavery, 1580s–1860s', *Werkstatt Geschichte* 66–67 (2015), 55–74, 67.
13. Karwan Fatah-Black, *Sociëteit van Suriname – 1683 – 1795: Het bestuur van de kolonie in de achttiende eeuw* (Zutphen: Walburg Pers 2019).
14. Andrea Mosterman, 'Nieuwer-Amstel, Stadskolonie aan de Delaware', in Pepijn Brandon, Guno Jones, Nancy Jouwe and Matthias van Rossum (eds.), *De slavernij in Oost en West: Het Amsterdam onderzoek* (Amsterdam: Spectrum, 2020).
15. Matthias van Rossum, *Kleurrijke tragiek. De geschiedenis van slavernij in Azië onder de VOC* (Hilversum: Verloren, De Zeven Provinciën reeks, 2015). For example, there is the outspoken role of contra-remonstrant Reynier Pauw, who led the Amsterdam city council from 1611, and was a major figure amongst the *bewindhebbers*

that appointed Jan Pietersz Coen to ensure a more aggressive expansion politics. See Matthias van Rossum, 'Van Amsterdam naar Azië: slavernij en de VOC', in: Brandon, Jones, Jouwe and Van Rossum, *Amsterdam en de slavernij*.

16. See: Deborah K. Elms and Patrick Low (eds.), *Global Value Chains in a Changing World* (Geneva 2013); https://www.wto.org/english/res_e/booksp_e/aid4tradeglobalvalue13_intro_e.pdf
17. Maxine Berg (ed.), *Goods from the East, 1600-1800: Trading Eurasia* (Houndmills: Palgrave Macmillan, 2015).
18. See e.g. Matthias van Rossum, 'Labouring Transformations of Amphibious Monsters – Globalization, Diversity and the Effects of Labour Mobilization under the Dutch East India Company (1600–1800)', *International Review of Social History* s64 (2019), 19–42; Christian G. De Vito, Juliane Schiel and Matthias van Rossum, 'From Bondage to Precariousness? New Perspectives on Labor and Social History', *Journal of Social History* (online preview: 22 August 2019), https://doi.org/10.1093/jsh/shz057.
19. Jan Luiten van Zanden and Pim de Zwart, *The Origins of Globalization: World Trade in the Making of the Global Economy, 1500–1800* (Cambridge: Cambridge University Press, 2019).
20. Pepijn Brandon and Aditya Sarkar, 'Labour History and the Case against Colonialism', *International Review of Social History* 64:1 (2019), 73–109.
21. Christopher Ebert, *Between Empires: Brazilian Sugar in the Early Atlantic Economy, 1550–1630* (Leiden: Brill, 2008); David Richardson and Filipa Ribeiro da Silva (eds.), *Networks and Trans-cultural Exchange: Slave Trading in the South Atlantic, 1590–1867* (Leiden: Brill, 2014); Cátia Antunes and Amélia Polónia (eds.), *Beyond Empires: Global, Self-Organizing, Cross-Imperial Networks, 1500–1800* (Leiden: Brill, 2016); Bram Hoonhout, *Borderless Empire: Dutch Guiana in the Atlantic World, 1750–1800* (Athens, OH: University of Georgia Press, 2020).
22. New research agendas are developing for these regions, focusing on furthering comparisons, case studies and the development of quantifications based on better use of the wealth of available sources and data. Titas Chakraborty and Matthias van Rossum, 'Slave Trade and Slavery in Asia – New Perspectives', *Journal of Social History* 54:1 (2020), 1–14.
23. E.g. Jan Breman, *Mobilizing Labour for the Global Coffee Market: Profits From an Unfree Work Regime in Colonial Java* (Amsterdam: Amsterdam University Press 2015); Clare Anderson (ed.), *A Global History of Convicts and Penal Colonies* (London: Bloomsbury, 2018); Van Rossum, 'Labouring Transformations'; Matthias van Rossum, 'The Carceral Colony – Colonial Exploitation, Coercion, and Control in the Dutch East-Indies, 1810s–1940s', *International Review of Social History* s63 (2018), 65–88; Matthias van Rossum and Merve Tosun, 'Corvée Capitalism – the Dutch East India Company, labour Regimes and (Merchant) Capitalism in Early Modern Asia', *Journal of Asian Studies* (2021), First View: https://doi.org/10.1017/S0021911821000735.
24. E.g. Clare Anderson, *Subaltern Lives: Biographies of Colonialism in the Indian Ocean World, 1790–1920* (Cambridge: Cambridge University Press, 2012); Matthias van Rossum, 'Redirecting Global Labor History?', in Cátia Antunes and Karwan Fatah-Black (eds.), *Explorations in History and Globalization* (London: Routledge, 2016), 47–62.
25. Van Rossum, Fatah-Black, 'Wat is winst?' [translated as 'Beyond Profitability']; De Kok, 'Cursed Capital'.

26. Fatah-Black and Van Rossum, 'Beyond Profitability', 80.
27. Sources: Bureau of Economic Analysis, https://www.bea.gov/, consulted March 2020; Chris Rhodes, *Financial Services: Contribution to the UK Economy*, Commons Library Briefing no. 6193, 31 July 2019, www.parliament.uk/commons-library.
28. Rönnbäck, 'On the Economic Importance'.
29. Rönnbäck, 'Who Stood to Gain', 144–5.
30. Ulrich Pfister, 'Great Divergence, Consumer Revolution and the Reorganization of Textile Markets: Evidence From Hamburg's Import Trade, Eighteenth Century', *Economic History Working Papers*, London School of Economics and Political Science (LSE), no. 266, 2017.
31. Leonor Freire Costa, Nuno Palma and Jaime Reis, 'The Great Escape? The Contribution of the Empire to Portugal's Economic Growth, 1500–1800', *European Review of Economic History* 19 (2014), 1–22.
32. Rönnbäck, 'On the Economic Importance'; Van Rossum, Fatah-Black, 'Wat is winst?' [translated as 'Beyond Profitability']; De Kok, 'Cursed Capital'; Tamira Combrink, 'From French Harbours to German Rivers: European Distribution of Sugar by the Dutch in the Eighteenth Century', in Maud Villeret and Marguerite Martin (eds.), *La diffusion des produits ultra-marins en Europe (XVI*[e]*-XVIII*[e] *siècles)* (Rennes: Presses universitaires de Rennes, 2018); Brandon and Bosma, 'De betekenis van de Atlantische slavernij'.

Explorations

The profits of the Portuguese–Brazilian transatlantic slave trade: challenges and possibilities

Filipa Ribeiro da Silva

ABSTRACT
Together, Portugal and Brazil were the second biggest players in the transatlantic slave trade. However, we still know little about the profits generated by the slave trade and by the activities carried out by slaves within the Portuguese Empire – in particular in the Atlantic world. In other words, who were the various groups benefiting from those profits and where was the capital obtained invested and/or reinvested? In this article, we present preliminary estimates of gross profits generated by the Portuguese Brazilian participation in this business and discuss the methodological challenges faced to calculate the net profits of Portuguese–Brazilian participation in the slave trade as well as in assessing the weight of slave-based produce in the economies of Portugal, and Brazil. The first part of our study relies mainly on the data available in the Transatlantic Slave Trade Database, evidence gathered from several Portuguese archives, and the slave prices' series built by David Richardson and David Eltis *et al* for West and West Central Africa and the Brazilian slave prices series built by Laird Bergad. The second part will be based on the vast body of literature and source materials available in Portuguese, English and other languages on the topic.

Introduction

Since the 1950s, a vast body of literature on the transatlantic slave trade has been published. This scholarship has shed new light on the volume of trade, main routes, regions of embarkation and disembarkation, and living conditions and slave mortality rates in the Middle Passage.[1] This historiography has also helped to make known the territories and main players involved in this commerce, as direct and/or indirect investors and profiteers.[2] Research on the transatlantic slave trade has also sparked an important debate concerning the role of the slave trade, slave-based activities and slave produce in the process of industrialisation and enrichment of the European countries involved both in this business and in the process of empire building, which was also partially based on slave labour. Started by Eric Williams in 1938, this discussion has been very heated until the present. Most of the debate has focused on Britain, but recently scholars have started to address the questions raised by Williams in relation to other countries involved in the transatlantic and slave-based colonial economies, but for which a direct link between slave trade, slavery, industrialisation and the development of modern capitalism cannot be immediately established.[3] This has been, for instance, the case for the Netherlands – the fourth major player in the transatlantic slave trade, according to the data available in the Transatlantic Slave Trade Database (TSTD) – which was engaged in slave trading and held slave-based colonies, but where industrialisation took place rather late.[4]

Together, Portugal and Brazil were the second biggest players in the transatlantic slave trade. By the mid-eighteenth century, Brazil was probably one of the largest slave-based economies in the Americas, where most of the produce resulted entirely or partially from slave labour. In the past three decades, scholars in Brazil, Portugal and elsewhere have shown a growing interest in the study of Portuguese–Brazilian participation and investment in the transatlantic slave trade, and the role slave labour has played in the economies of Brazil, and to a lesser extent Portugal.[5] Although, by now, we have a comprehensive knowledge of the numbers, circuits, regions and main ports involved, and the intricate bureaucratic and financial schemes that supported this business, we still know little about the profits generated by the slave trade and by the activities carried out by slaves within the Portuguese Empire – in particular in the Atlantic world. In other words, who were the various groups benefiting from those profits and where was the capital obtained invested and/or reinvested?

Since the mid-nineteenth century, historians, economists and social scientists in Portugal and elsewhere have been busy discussing the economic situation of Portugal and its colonial empire, and as a result an extensive body of literature has been produced debating Portuguese economic backwardness in comparison to other European countries and the causes of late development and industrialisation.[6] In recent years, much progress has been made, especially by Freire, Palma and Reis, and Castro Henriques, in challenging the idea that Portugal was a poor and backward country before the nineteenth century.[7] According to these studies, the empire only seemed to contribute about 20% of Portuguese metropolitan economic growth. Pedreira, in contrast, argued in an earlier study that the empire was always very costly to the metropole and a substantial part of the profits generated by the colonial economy was reinvested within the empire and never found its way to the metropole.[8] A detailed analysis of the profits derived from the Portuguese–Brazilian participation in the transatlantic slave trade will show their role in the development of the metropolitan and colonial economies, in particular Brazil's, as well as the spill over effects of this commerce on different economic activities in Portugal, the empire and beyond.

In this article, we will address these questions in three steps. We will start by giving a brief overview of Portuguese–Brazilian involvement in the transatlantic slave trade, including the main figures in the trade, the main regions and places of embarkation and disembarkation, highlighting major shifts over time. This will be followed by our preliminary estimates of gross profits generated by early and subsequent Portuguese–Brazilian participation in this business. We will conclude by discussing the methodological challenges faced in calculating the net profits from Portuguese–Brazilian participation in the slave trade and in assessing the slave-based contribution to the economies of Portugal and Brazil. The first part of our study relies mainly on the data available in the TSTD, evidence gathered from several Portuguese archives and the slave prices series built by David Richardson, David Eltis *et al.* for West and West Central Africa, including slave prices from Portuguese source materials, mainly the data gathered by Joseph Miller.[9] For the slave prices in Brazil, we use the series built by Laird Bergad.[10] The second part of the article is based on the vast body of literature and source materials available in Portuguese, English and other languages on the topic.

Portuguese–Brazilian participation in the transatlantic slave trade

Let us begin by looking at the Portuguese–Brazilian participation in the transatlantic slave trade. As early as the fifteenth century, Portuguese merchants opened the first Atlantic slave trade circuits, which linked Western Africa to Europe. Portuguese merchants were also responsible for opening up the first transatlantic slave trade circuits in the following century. Together with Brazil-based merchants, they were the ones who remained in business the longest until as late as the mid-nineteenth century. According to the data available in the TSTD, Portuguese–Brazilian merchants transported more than 3.5 million slaves across the Atlantic in the early modern period, and given the scarcity of Portuguese source material it is likely that this number was higher. From the early sixteenth century, the number of enslaved Africans transported to the Americas notably increased, and this continued for as long as the trade took place.

During the sixteenth century, Senegambia was the main region of embarkation on the West coast of Africa for the Portuguese merchants who were engaged in the transatlantic slave trade, followed by the Bight of Biafra and the Gulf of Guinea Islands.[11] In the course of the seventeenth century, although Senegambia continued to play an important role in the Atlantic slaving business of Brazil-based Portuguese merchants, West Central Africa, in particular Angola, emerged as the main supplying region. West Central Africa, especially the coastal region south of the Congo River, retained this leading position during the eighteenth and nineteenth centuries, with the number of slaves embarking in the ports of the region – Luanda and Benguela being the most important ones – increasing considerably. The trade reached its peak between 1801 to1825, when more than 600,000 slaves departed from this region.[12] Despite the abolition of the slave trade in the northern hemisphere and British efforts to suppress similar activities in the South Atlantic, the trade continued well into the nineteenth century (see Table 1).[13] During the same period, the slave trade grew in complexity, with the development of trade between Brazil (as well as several French colonies) and East Africa, in particular Mozambique.[14]

From the sixteenth century, the demand for slave labour increased as various economic activities developed in different regions. These included mining activities in mainland Spanish America, which continued in the late seventeenth and early eighteenth century in Brazil (mainly after the 1690s), and agriculture, in particular the production of cash crops in Brazil as well as in the Caribbean Islands and certain regions of mainland Spanish America. This growing demand led Portuguese–Brazilian merchants to diversify their African slave-supplying regions. As a result, the eighteenth century witnessed the growing presence of Portuguese–Brazilian merchants in Senegambia, the Gold Coast, the Bight of Biafra and the Gulf of Guinea Islands, and especially in the Bight of Benin. The so-called *Costa da Mina* became the second biggest slave-supplying market in Africa for Portuguese–Brazilian merchants.[15] Even Mozambique, located in South-East Africa and integrated in the Indian Ocean maritime system, became part of the slave trading networks of Portuguese–Brazilian merchants, especially after the 1750s, feeding into the growing demand for slave labour in the Americas (see Table 1).[16] Thus, during the last two centuries of the transatlantic slave trade, Portuguese–Brazilian merchants used several markets located in different African regions in order to cater to the American labour demand.

In the Americas, Portuguese and later also Brazil-based merchants supplied various slave labour markets in the Americas simultaneously. Some of these slave labour markets were located in regions that fell under the jurisdiction and sphere of influence of the Portuguese Crown, while others fell outside. In fact, during the sixteenth century, Portuguese merchants catered mainly to the Caribbean Islands, while during the following century Spanish America became their main market (see Table 2).[17]

Only in the last quarter of the seventeenth century did the Brazilian economy start to be the principal consumer of slave labour catered for by Portuguese–Brazilian merchants, for whom Brazil remained the main market in the following centuries.[18] There was, therefore, an important shift in the trading patterns of Portuguese–Brazilian merchants in this period. They became busy supplying the colonial spaces controlled by Portugal, as other Europeans started to do in the seventeenth century with regard to their own colonies (see Table 2). This might be related to the interests of those people who were involved in the trade, who were increasingly based in Brazil rather than in Portugal. During

Table 1. Slaves embarked in Portuguese-Brazilian ships per regions of embarkation, 1514–1854.

Periods/Regions of Embarkation	Spain	Senegambia and offshore Atlantic	Sierra Leone	Windward Coast	Gold Coast	Bight of Benin	Bight of Biafra and Gulf of Guinea islands	West Central Africa and St. Helena	Southeast Africa and Indian Ocean islands	Other Africa	Asia & Africa	Total
1514–1525							300	624				924
1526–1550							1,393	250		262		1,905
1551–1575		763					812			262		1,837
1576–1600	183	10,982					2,451	14,272				27,888
1601–1625		10,465				1,822	2,275	57,169		1,333		73,064
1626–1650		8,674				404	676	37,474				47,228
1651–1675		2,925					54	9,879	301			13,159
1676–1700		2,360			1,390	45,000	9,222	22,284	763			81,019
1701–1725		2,854		2,803	21,009	147,684	16,005	50,283	2,021	1,451		244,110
1726–1750		5,727			23,225	177,520	9,275	231,572		1,471		448,790
1751–1775		22,157	40		2,176	134,790	2,410	214,462	1,938			377,973
1776–1800		30,961	42		384	138,183	6,916	301,261	5,719	1,796		485,262
1801–1825		36,821	390	382	2,272	141,729	56,403	696,684	138,945	8,098		1,081,724
1826–1850		6,391	13,130	1,457	1,160	68,970	24,457	492,175	136,528	3,677	490	748,435
1851–1854						696		1,065	1,993			3,754
Total	183	141,080	13,602	4,642	51,616	**856,798**	132,649	**2,129,454**	**288,208**	18,350	490	**3,637,072**

Source: TSTD, accessed 17 May 2015.

Table 2. Slaves disembarked by Portuguese-Brazilian ships per region of disembarkation, 1514–1854.

Periods/Regions of Disembarkation	Europe*	Mainland North America	Caribbean	Spanish American Mainland	Brazil	Africa	Other	Total
1514–1525	464		251					715
1526–1550			781				544	1,325
1551–1575			633	305	332			1,270
1576–1600	130		1,380	24,504	249		336	26,599
1601–1625	85		4,378	48,307	750		336	53,856
1626–1650			726	26,655	8,132		810	36,323
1651–1675	42		1,601	5,275	4,838	174	331	12,261
1676–1700			557	2,252	69,658			72,467
1701–1725	158		263		210,308			210,729
1726–1750	803			1,582	373,132			375,517
1751–1775	965		100	208	321,845	308		323,426
1776–1800			604	1,809	416,888	324		419,625
1801–1825		885	9,196	4,964	937,992	17,220	473	970,730
1826–1850			93,052	1,737	649,017	48,825		792,631
1851–1863			7,322		2,531	55		9,908
Total	2,647	885	**120,844**	**117,598**	**2,995,672**	66,906	2,830	3,307,382

Source: TSTD, accessed 17 May 2015.

Observations: Europe*: The number of enslaved Africans registered in the TSTD as disembarking in Europe is rather low. This might be because slave voyages heading to Europe were under-registered, since the main aim of the dataset was to record transatlantic journeys. A note of caution is therefore necessary here, and those interested in slave trading to Europe should look for further evidence elsewhere, including the vast body of secondary literature. See e.g. Jorge Fonseca, *Escravos no sul de Portugal (Séculos XVI–XVII)* (Lisbon: Editora Vulgata, 2002). *Idem*, *Escravos e Senhores na Lisboa Quinhentista* (Lisbon: Edições Colibri, 2010).

the same period, as several authors have shown, Brazil and its ports became important points of departure for slave voyages. In this respect, the participation of Portuguese–Brazilian merchants in the transatlantic slave trade has a peculiar feature that is not found among other European slavers. In contrast to other European states, the Portuguese Crown made it legally possible for merchants based in Brazil and other possessions within the Portuguese Atlantic Empire, namely in Africa, to engage in slave trading activities without the direct involvement of the metropolis.[19]

It must also be noted that during the same period Portuguese–Brazilian merchants continued to cater to other regions in the Americas that were not part of the Portuguese Empire, including the Spanish American mainland and the Caribbean islands. This ability to cater to markets outside the Portuguese Crown's sphere of influence is an important feature of Portuguese–Brazilian participation in the transatlantic slave trade. As we will briefly highlight in the following sections, this has implications for an analysis of the regions and people in Africa, the Americas and Europe who profited from the Portuguese–Brazilian slave trade. It also has repercussions for any future research that aims to assess economic development that was driven by profits from Portuguese–Brazilian participation in the transatlantic slave trade and its related slave-based activities. These last two points bring us to two important questions: how much profit was generated by Portuguese–Brazilian participation in this business, and what forms did this profit take?

Preliminary estimates of Portuguese–Brazilian gross earnings in the slave trade

In order to estimate gross profit in a certain business, it is essential to know how much is spent on a product, how much the product is sold for and how much was invested in costs associated with transport and transactions; in other words, purchasing prices, sale prices and transaction and transport costs. Portuguese source materials pose some challenges to scholars interested in examining this subject and aiming to estimate the gross and net profits of the Portuguese–Brazilian participation in the transatlantic slave trade, as there is no complete series of slave purchasing and selling prices, and no serial data on costs.

In order to overcome this problem, and in an attempt to offer a preliminary informed estimate of the gross profits generated in this trade, we have adopted the following procedure. To estimate the gross profit over time, we have used the total number of slaves who embarked in the various regions of Western Africa and were transported to the Americas by ships sailing under the Portuguese–Brazilian flag, as defined in the TSTD, and the price series of slave purchase in West and West Central Africa covering the period 1681 to 1810, gathered by David Richardson and David Eltis, including not only English sources, but also information gathered by Joseph Miller for the Portuguese South Atlantic.[20]

In addition to this, we have used the price series of male slave sales in Minas Gerais (Brazil) between 1715 and 1833 that was gathered by Laird W. Bergad.[21] On the basis of these, we have calculated the average price for each five-year period in Portuguese *réis* and converted them to sterling. The gross profit was then calculated by multiplying the number of slaves who embarked each five years against the five-year average slave selling prices in Minas Gerais. Additionally, we have compared over-time trends in purchasing and selling prices on the African and American coasts of the Portuguese South Atlantic. The average purchase prices in West Central Africa for five-year periods between 1811 and 1855 were calculated on the basis of the last known average prices for 1806 to 10. Regarding the use of sale prices of male slaves in Minas Gerais to calculate the gross profit, it must be noted that these prices were higher than in the first port of slave disembarkation in Brazil. For 1749, Gustavo Acioli gives a price of 102,500 réis for a male slave sold in Pernambuco.[22] If we compare this price with the average for Minas Gerais in the same period, there is a difference of about 40%, indicating the higher slave resale and import costs in the Brazilian inland markets. Therefore, it is likely that our estimate of gross profits is a bit on the high side. On the other hand, we did not account for the gross profit obtained from the illegal slave trade, which has been estimated at roughly 30%. If we take this aspect into consideration, our estimates, even though calculated with Minas Gerais prices, would not be too far-fetched.

According to our estimates for the period 1715 to 1833, Portuguese–Brazilian participation in the transatlantic slave trade generated an estimated gross profit of about £95 million (see Figures 1 and 2 and Appendix 1).[23] The bulk of these gains were obtained in the nineteenth century during the peak period of this trade and in the first half of the eighteenth century, when the differential between purchase prices in West Central Africa and sale prices in Minas Gerais was at its highest (see Figure 3 and Appendix 1).

How do Portuguese–Brazilian gross profits compare with those of the English and the Dutch? According to Anstey's estimate, English participation in the slave trade between 1761 and 1807 generated a gross profit of £49 million. In 1761–1810, Portuguese–Brazilian slave trading yielded a profit of about £19 million. Thus, the Portuguese–Brazilian slave trade seems to have generated lower gross profit margins than English slave trading in a similar period. As for the Dutch role in the transatlantic slave trade, Fatah-Black and Van Rossum have estimated that the gross profit margin for the entire period of Dutch activities (1595–1829) was about 23–79 million guilders, about £5.4–6.8 million.[24] Gross profits from Portuguese–Brazilian slaving activities appear to have been higher.

The differences found in estimated gross profit margins for Portuguese-Brazilians, English and Dutch can be explained by at least four possible factors. First, they may be simply the result of under-registration of voyages for each

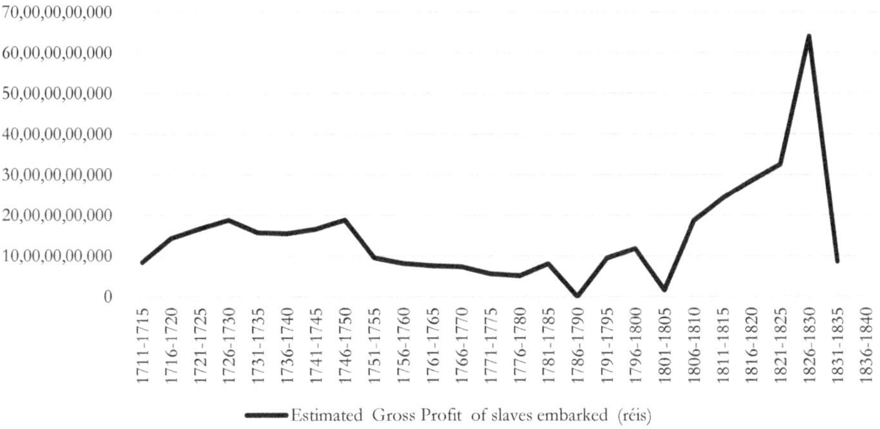

Figure 1. Estimated gross profit of slaves embarked by Portuguese-Brazilian traders, 1711–1835 (réis).

Sources and Notes: Total slaves embarked and total slaves disembarked – TSTD, accessed 17 May 2015. Average price per five-year periods calculated by the author on the basis of the slave purchasing price series for western Africa concerning 1681–1698 and 1699–1807, published by David Eltis, *The Rise of African Slavery in the Americas* (New York: Cambridge University Press, 2000), 293–7, and by David Richardson, 'Prices of Slaves in West and West-Central Africa: Toward an Annual Series, 1698–1807', *Bulletin of Economic Research* 43 (1991): 21–56. Together, these two datasets of slave prices have also been based on an article by David Eltis, 'The Slave Trade & Commercial Agriculture in an African Context', in *Commercial Agriculture, the Slave Trade & Slavery in Atlantic Africa,* eds. Robin Law, Suzanne Schwarz and Silke Strickrodt (Woodbridge: James Currey, 2013), 28–53. In addition to these, we have also based our calculations on the slave selling price series for Minas Gerais concerning 1711–1833 published by Laird W. Bergad, *Slavery and the Demographic and Economic History of Minas Gerais, Brazil, 1720–1888* (New York: Cambridge University Press. 1999).

flag in the TSTD. The risk of under-registration is especially high in the case of the Portuguese–Brazilian voyages, given the poor quality of source materials and the absence of information for specific periods. This may help to explain the differences in gross profits between Portuguese–Brazilian and English

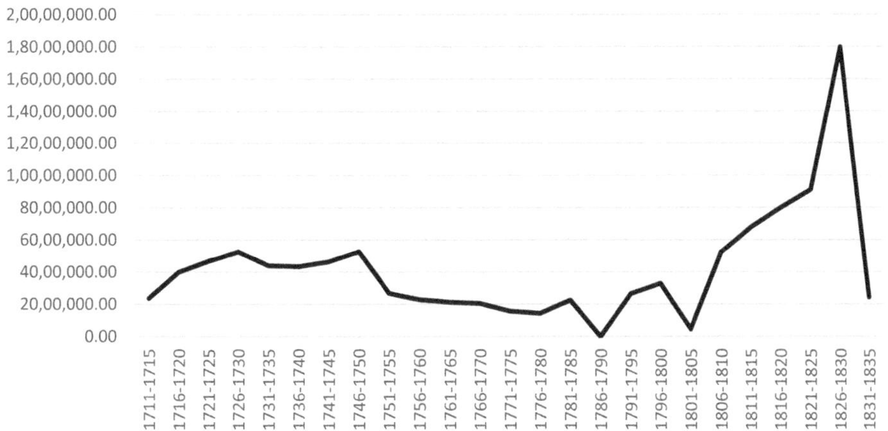

Figure 2. Estimated gross profit from slaves embarked by Portuguese-Brazilian traders, 1711–1835 (sterling) (exchange rate 3565 réis = 1 pound sterling).

Sources and Notes: see Figure 1.

Figure 3. Average slave prices in West Central Africa (WCA) versus sale prices of male slaves in Brazil (Minas Gerais), 1711–1835.

Sources and Notes: see Figure 1.

trade. Secondly, the number of slaves embarked and disembarked by the three nations, the volume of business, also seems to have played a role in these results. Here again, under-registration impacts directly on the results. Thirdly, differences in transport costs and related shipping expenses play a role. The latter is directly related to net profit margins.

Estimating net profits in the Portuguese–Brazilian slave trade: challenges and possible solutions

Estimating the net profits of the Portuguese–Brazilian transatlantic slave trade is a more complex operation than attempting to calculate gross profits and therefore poses a series of challenges to economic historians. We can identify at least four main obstacles: the logistical organisation of the Portuguese–Brazilian slave trade, namely the multitude of routes operated by these merchants; the political economy of the Portuguese–Brazilian slave trade, including the relationship between the state (the Portuguese Crown) and the private merchants involved in this business, either operating single-handedly, in partnership and consortia or in state-chartered joint stock commercial companies, as well as the multitude of players involved in this commerce; the complex relationship between the Portuguese metropolitan and colonial economies (in particular Angola and Brazil) in terms of slave trading and slave-based production and the investment of returns from these two activities; and the complex and multidirectional relationship of Brazilian slave-based colonial economic production with various countries other than Portugal.

These four obstacles have direct implications not only for any attempt to estimate net profits from slave trading and slave-based economic activities, but also in assessing the role and impact of these activities in the Portuguese metropolitan economy as well as in the economies of the major suppliers and consumers of enslaved African labour in the Portuguese Atlantic – Angola and Brazil. The obstacles also raise an important set of questions that have to be answered in order to disentangle and understand the workings of the Portuguese–Brazilian slave trade and slave-based economic activities. What were the net profits at various points in the slave trading chain? Who obtained net profits and in what kind of activity? Did profits from the slave trade and slave-based activities in the Portuguese Atlantic contribute to the development of the Portuguese economy and/or the development of the Brazilian colonial economy? And who were the main importers of Brazilian slave-based produce?

The logistical organisation of the Portuguese Brazilian transatlantic slave trade

Unlike those of the English, French and Dutch, Portuguese–Brazilian slave trading voyages did not always follow the classical triangular trade model. Triangular trade certainly dominated in the Portuguese Atlantic slave trade in the fifteenth and sixteenth centuries, but as early as the 1590s, other trade circuits started to emerge. Most of these new commercial routes were bilateral in nature, connecting Brazilian ports directly to African ports without touching Portugal. In the late sixteenth and early seventeenth centuries, most of these Brazil-bound trade voyages headed to Angola, in West Central Africa, and over time a growing number also sailed to the so-called *Costa da Mina* (present-day Gulf of Benin). Similar direct routes also developed between the region of Senegambia and Guinea-Bissau and the Spanish Americas, as well as between São Tomé and the Spanish Americas.

First, the emergence of these bilateral slave routes meant separation of the trade carried out from the metropole and the trade carried out from the colonies, Brazil and Angola being the two most important nodes in intra-imperial commerce. Secondly, the development of these bilateral slave routes contributed to the development of trading communities on both sides of the Portuguese-speaking South Atlantic. These communities had connections with the Portugal-based merchants, but at the same time had goals and strategies of their own, not always coincident with those of the metropolitan mercantile community. Thirdly, the rise of these bilateral slave routes had implications for the economy of the regions involved, as ships were outfitted and loaded with exchange goods locally. Important shares of the products used to outfit the vessels as well as for barter on the African coast to acquire slaves were produced in the colony and not in the metropole.

Fourthly, the development of bilateral slave trading routes between Brazil and various ports of Atlantic Africa, in particular those falling outside the sphere of influence and effective control of the Portuguese Crown (such as the Costa da Mina), gave Portuguese–Brazilian slave traders the possibility of trading with other Europeans involved in the slave trade, such as the English,

French and Dutch. This situation was common in the Bight of Benin and granted these European powers access to several slave-produced Brazilian goods, including gold, Brazilian distilled alcoholic beverages produced from sugar cane (*jeribita, aguardente* and *cachaça*) and tobacco (the production of this employing a smaller share of slave labour as tobacco was often grown by small farmers). These early commercial contacts between Brazil-based merchants and European powers would continue in the late eighteenth and nineteenth centuries, although by then these European merchants would import Brazilian slave-based produce directly from the colony, as we will discuss in more detail later.

Despite these developments in the South Atlantic, Portugal-based merchants continued to be heavily involved in the slave trade, in many cases following triangular trade routes. But these did not always follow the same patterns as English, French and Dutch routes. In many cases, Portugal-based merchants sailed first to Brazil and from there headed to Africa, returning to Brazil once again before sailing back to Europe.

Consequently, the Portuguese–Brazilian slave trade was carried out across a wide array of routes that more often than not did not start or end in Portugal. The existence of this complex network has implications for any attempt to calculate the net profits of the Portuguese–Brazilian participation in the slave trade. Various micro-studies for specific slave voyages in defined regions and periods suggest that net profit margins varied according to route and period (see Table 3).

Any attempt to assess or estimate the net profits obtained in the Portuguese–Brazilian slave trade needs to take into account the number of slaves who embarked and disembarked on each of these routes, the different costs of ship outfitting, acquisition of the bartering cargo and payment of the crew, as well as the expenses associated with the risks of the sea and the price of slaves at port of purchase and sale. Sources with data that allow these

Table 3. Variations in net profit margins in Portuguese-Brazilian slave voyages over time and according to trade routes (some examples).

Year	Route	Average Net Profit Margin from slave voyages(%)	Source
1749	Recife–Costa da Mina (present-day Bight of Benin)	3–4	(a)
1759–1775	Lisbon–Angola–Pernambuco-Lisbon (CGPP)	12–16	(b)
1804	Luanda (Angola)–Rio de Janeiro	8	(d)
1810–1820	Rio de Janeiro–Angola–Rio de Janeiro	19,2	(c)

Sources: (a) Gustavo Acioli Lopes, 'O Negócio da Costa da Mina e o Comércio Atlântico: Tabaco, Açúcar, Ouro e Tráfico de Escravos: Pernambuco (1654–1760)', PhD dissertation, University of São Paulo, Brazil, 2008, 163–8.; (b) Maximiliano M. Menz, 'A Companhia de Pernambuco e Paraíba e o funcionamento do tráfico de escravos em Angola (1759–1775/80)', *Afro-Ásia* 48 July/December (2013).; (c) Manolo Florentino, *Em Costas Negras* (São Paulo: Companhia das Letras, 1997), 160–9.; (d) Maximiliano M. Menz, 'From the Sea to the Hinterland: Profits and Risks in the Slave Trade from Angola, c. 1740–1807', unpublished paper presented at the IISH Lecture Series (April 2019).

Notes: CGPP: Companhia Geral de Paraíba e Pernmabuco: General Company of Paraiba and Pernambuco.

calculations to be made are limited. However, studies of specific voyages on certain routes and during key chronological periods can help us to determine average net profit margins for the various routes on which the Portuguese–Brazilian merchants operated over time.

The political economy of the Portuguese–Brazilian transatlantic slave trade

The organisation of the Portuguese–Brazilian slave trade in multidirectional commercial routes poses the researcher interested in examining this trade, and its economic outputs and impact, a wide number of problems when it comes to the study of the political economy of this trade, the net profits obtained and their investment. In the English, French and Dutch cases, it is relatively straightforward to identify the participants in the transatlantic slave trade, as credit providers, merchants, ship outfitters, captains and ship owners were based in Europe and more often than not had their agents travel on board the ships to conduct trade in Atlantic Africa. English, French and Dutch commercial companies had representatives or officials in Africa, and they provided European ships with commodities and slaves. The latter were sold in the American colonies mainly to planters, often on credit and/or in exchange for slave-produced commodities, such as sugar and cotton. These were then transported to Europe and there processed by existing proto-industries and developing new industries, being resold in retail markets throughout the continent, with returns staying and being reinvested mainly in Europe. Given the triangular nature of the trade, the participants in these voyages more often than not remained the same throughout each voyage and were involved in the entire venture: often it was only with the return of the vessels to Europe that they would be paid. European states (Britain, France and the Dutch Republic) seem to have had limited powers to intervene in the trade, as monopoly rights over trade and the management of colonial territories were often granted to chartered companies.

In the Portuguese–Brazilian case, the unidirectional character depicted here became more complicated. For voyages departing from Portugal, credit providers, merchants, ship outfitters, captains and ship owners were based both in Portugal and elsewhere in Europe – as there is evidence of credit and insurance for Portuguese–Brazilian slave trading voyages being secured in key European financial centres, such as Amsterdam, at least during the seventeenth century.[25]

However, unlike the English, French and Dutch, investors, merchants, outfitters and captains involved in slave voyages departing from Portugal did not necessarily invest in the whole venture. Many of them invested only in the trade of commodities between Europe and Atlantic Africa, whether products for barter in the African slave trade or products for local consumption. Additionally, they appear to have invested in the shipping business between

Table 4. Variations in net profit margins of freight prices in the Portuguese-Brazilian slave voyages over time and according to trade routes (some examples).

Year	Route	Average net profit margin from freights (%)*	Source
1749	Recife–Costa da Mina (present-day Bight of Benin)	14	(a)
1761–1769	Angola–Pernambuco (CGPP)	38	(b)
1761–1769	Pernambuco–Angola (CGPP)	30	(b)
1761–1769	Pernambuco–Lisbon (CGPP)	17	(b)
1761–1769	Lisbon–Angola (CGPP)	15	(b)

Sources: Table 3.
Notes: Table 3.
*It must be noted here that the freight prices of the Companhia Geral de Pernambuco and Paraiba and their respective profit margins very likely do not reflect entirely real transport costs and profits from the latter, as this company (as several others) benefited from privileges granted by the state. See: Leonor Freire Costa, 'Privateering and Insurance: Transaction Costs in Seventeenth-Century European Colonial Flows', in *Ricchezza del Mare, secc XIII–XVIII, Atti delle 'Settimane di Studi', Istituto Internazionale di Storia Economica 'F. Datini'*, eds. Simonetta Cavaciocchi (Prato, Firenza: Le Monnier, 2006), 703–26.

Atlantic Africa and the Americas, in particular Brazil, and to a less extent in the shipping business between Brazil and Portugal. A good example of these practices can be found in the accounting books of the General Company of Pernambuco and Paraíba (Companhia Geral de Pernambuco e Paraíba), which operated in the Portuguese–Brazilian slave trade business in the second half of the eighteenth century (see Tables 4 and 5). However, it must be noted that already in the early seventeenth century, insurers of Portuguese slave voyages organised by Sephardic merchants based in Amsterdam were insuring only one of the several legs of the slave journey.[26]

This situation has various implications. Unlike the British, French and Dutch cases, Portuguese–Brazilian slave voyages departing from Portugal and ending in the metropole seem to have been split into different legs, and each of these seems to have involved different actors (investors and merchants) with different goals and strategies. In these voyages, we can identify three main legs: Portugal–Africa; Africa–Brazil; and Brazil–Portugal. This has, of course, consequences for the calculations of net profit margins, as these vary on the different legs of the journey and for the different actors involved (as an example see Table 3). Portugal-based merchants appear to have invested mainly in commerce in the first leg, and in shipping in the second leg of the journey;

Table 5. Variations in net profit margins from sale of commodities and slaves in the Portuguese-Brazilian slave voyages over time and according to trade routes (some examples).

Year	Route	Average net profit margin from sale of slaves and commodities (%)	Source
1759–1775	Angola–Pernambuco: sale of mainly slaves	1	(b)
1759–1775	Lisbon–Angola: Sale of commodities	47	(b)
1759–1775	Pernambuco–Angola: sale of commodities	15	(b)
1759–1775	Portuguese Indiamen: sale of commodities	50	(b)
1759–1775	Angola–Rio: sale of mainly slaves	−44	(b)

Sources: Table 3.
Notes: Table 3.

whereas Angola-based merchants invested mainly in the second and Brazil-based and Europe-based merchants in the third. Thus, Portugal-based merchants seem to have invested mainly in commodity trade and in shipping in the South Atlantic, Angola slave merchants in the slave trade across the Middle Passage and Brazil-based and North-Western Europe-based merchants in the export of Brazilian slave-produced goods, the former mainly to Africa and the latter to Europe.[27]

This last point is directly tied to the bilateral trade routes connecting Brazil with West Central Africa and West Africa, in particular Angola and Bight of Benin, which developed from the late sixteenth and seventeenth centuries respectively. For these voyages, the investors, merchants, ship outfitters and captains could be based either in Brazil or in Portugal. Bilateral voyages between Brazil and Angola and between Brazil and the *Costa da Mina* could be organised by Brazil-based or Portugal-based merchants and/or ship captains – with the latter opting to sail from Portugal to Brazil and there engage in bilateral trade with Atlantic Africa, as has already been explained.

In the latter case, Portugal-based merchants appear to have invested mainly in the shipping of European and Asian products to Brazil, either for local consumption, including foodstuffs such as olive oil and dry salted cod, or other products, providing Asian and European textiles, European guns, varied metalware and so on. Additionally, Portugal-based merchants involved in these voyages would be busy shipping between Brazil and Africa and back. Brazil-based merchants and investors in these voyages appear mainly to have been involved in the export of locally produced goods, such as *jeribita*, sugar, gold, leather products and tobacco, all except the latter mainly produced with slave labour in the colony.

This situation has implications when it comes to attempting to estimate and/or calculate net profit margins obtained on these voyages. Given the different types of commodities traded and the types of services provided by these two groups of merchants, margin profits would also vary. Gustavo Acioli Lopes made these calculations for a voyage from Pernambuco to the Bight of Benin in 1749 and obtained different net margins for the different parties involved depending on the income they obtained from trade and shipping. Net profits from the slave trade and trade in slave-produced goods for Brazil-based merchants involved in the voyage seem to have been 3%, while for the owners of the ship (*senhorio do navio*) commerce generated a net profit of 4%; however, if the profits made from transport charges on goods are added, that value increases to 14%.[28]

Thus, in any attempt to calculate net profit margins in the Portuguese–Brazilian slave trade two key questions need to be kept in mind and carefully tackled: Whose net profit are we calculating? And on what products, commercial activity or services provided (such as shipping) are we calculating net profits? In order to address these two queries firstly we need to identify the main type of participant on each of the slave trade routes. Secondly, we need to identify their type of involvement in the trade, whether commodity trade, shipping or slave trading. Thirdly, we need to determine their investment in the different activities and the costs associated. Only then will it be possible to determine net profit margins for the different actors engaged in the Portuguese–Brazilian slave trade. Again, sources with data that allow these calculations are scarce, but the use of case studies for specific routes and periods can shed new light on the matter and allow us to gain a more comprehensive overview of the net profit margins for different participants in the trade.

In the Portuguese–Brazilian slave trade, this also implies trying to assess the profits of indirect participants in the trade, such as the Portuguese Crown, which leased out its monopoly rights over the different branches of the trade in Atlantic Africa (Cape Verde and Guinea Contract; the São Tomé contract, and the Angola Contract) to private merchants organised in consortia, the so-called *contratadores*, as well as tax farming over the transatlantic slave trade, often leased by the same businessmen. Equally important is to assess the net profits obtained by the mercantile consortia that leased the monopolies throughout the seventeenth and eighteenth centuries, derived from their four main activities: the collection of taxes from the slave trade and other trades in colonial products exported from Cape Verde, Guinea, São Tomé and Angola; the sale of trading licences (either in Lisbon or in Luanda) to private merchants to allow their engagement in slave voyages; direct participation in the trade through the organisation of voyages; and credit to Luanda-based merchants to allow them to carry out trade with the interior, and deliver enslaved Africans and elephant tusks to the ports of Luanda and Benguela for export to Brazil and Europe.[29]

Finally, it is paramount to estimate the net profit of the state chartered companies that controlled the Portuguese–Brazilian slave trade in the second half of the eighteenth century, the General Company of Grão-Pará and Maranhão (*Companhia Geral do Grão-Pará e Maranhão*) (1755–1778) and the General Company of Pernambuco and Paraíba (*Companhia Geral de Pernambuco e Paraíba*) (1756–1780), and in the period that followed the end of the monopoly in the late 1770s and 1780s until the abolition of the slave trade in the South Atlantic and its slow death in the first half of the nineteenth century. The implications of this trade for the Portuguese, the Brazilian and the Angolan economies of the time should also be considered.[30]

Profits from slave trading and slave-based produce, and the Portuguese metropolitan and colonial economies: a complex relationship

In the case of the British, French and Dutch, a considerable portion of the products loaded on board the ships involved in the slave trade, to outfit the voyage, guarantee the survival of the crew during the triangular voyage, cater for the needs of the trading stations in West Africa or to barter for enslaved Africans, was produced mainly in the metropole.[31] Another portion was produced in neighbouring countries or with raw materials imported from neighbouring countries, an example being weapons produced in Britain for the slave trade with metals imported from Sweden.[32] An important share was imported from India (mainly textiles) or produced locally by the developing textile industry in Britain, which tried to replicate the Asian clothing that was in demand in African markets.[33]

In the case of the Portuguese–Brazilian slave trade, like the slave voyages, the composition of ships' cargoes, either in terms of foodstuffs or in terms of bartering products for the trade, was not necessarily produced in the metropole. As early as the fifteenth and sixteenth centuries, European textiles imported from Antwerp, Castile (Spain) and England, as well as Asian textiles imported via the Portuguese Indiamen (*Carreira da Índia*) found their way to West Africa and later West Central Africa.[34] Additionally, and to cater specifically to the demands of African merchants, Portugal-based merchants also acquired textiles that were produced in different African regions. They tried to replicate African textile products through the development of a textile proto-industry in the Cape Verde Islands, whose production was used in the trade between the islands and the so-called *Rios da Guiné* (present-day Senegambia and Guinea Bissau region).[35] The volume of goods produced in Portugal and used to outfit slave voyages in this period appear to have been limited compared with the imported products.

With the development of bilateral routes between Brazilian, West Central and West African ports, goods produced in Brazil started to be used to feed the crew and enslaved Africans during slave ships' return voyages (with *mandioca*, or manioc, playing an important role in this respect), and they formed an important share of the cargo of bartering products that were used on the African coast for the slave trade. These cargos also included Asian textiles brought to Brazil by the Portuguese Indiamen, as the Portuguese run started to call at the territory regularly during the eighteenth century.

Acioli and Menz estimate that between 1699 and 1703 Brazilian *jeribita* paid for 13% of all slaves acquired in Angola.[36] In the *Costa da Mina*, the same authors estimate that Brazilian tobacco paid for the purchase of half to three-quarters of the slaves bought by Bahia- and Recife-based merchants. Brazilian gold was another important bartering product in the slave trade markets of this region. The same authors estimate that each year more than 10,000 *cruzados* (about 4 million *réis* or £1,122) were exported from Brazil to the Costa da Mina. Official figures do not exist as this was an illegal flow. Part of this gold ended up in the hands of the Dutch, the French and the English. More than 1 million gold *cruzados* per year were sold to the Dutch on the coast in exchange for enslaved Africans. English merchants sold slaves to Portuguese–Brazilian merchants in exchange for gold; whereas the French were paid in gold by Portuguese–Brazilian merchants in exchange for their European textiles.

Table 6. Origin of commodities imported by Luanda (%).

Years	Europe	Brazil	Asia
1785–1794	44	22	34
1795–1797	41	31	28
1798–1799	40	18	42
1802–1803	49	16	35
1808–1809	33	28	39

Source: Gustavo Acioli and Maximilian M. Menz, 'Resgate e Mercadorias: Uma análise comparada do tráfico Luso-Brasileiro de Escravos em Angola e na Costa da Mina (século XVIII)', *Afro-Ásia* 37 (2008), 43–73, 54.

In addition to these products, Brazil-based vessels and Portuguese vessels operating in the Brazil–Africa bilateral trade also exported Brazilian sugar, jaguar fur (*pele de onça*), ox tails, hammocks and aromatic herbs to the Bight of Benin. European and Asian textiles were an element of the bartering goods carried by these ships. Asian textiles were acquired in Brazil from Portugal-based merchants who imported them into Brazil or directly from the Portuguese Indiamen fleets, once these started to call regularly at Brazilian ports (mainly in the eighteenth century), as well as at the English, French and Dutch trading stations along the Grain, Gold, Ivory and Slave Coasts in West Africa. By the eighteenth century, Brazilian-produced goods represented 20%–35% (see Table 6) of products entering Angola for the slave trade, whereas in the *Costa da Mina* the Brazilian products used in the acquisition of enslaved Africans is likely to have reached 50%–75%.[37]

In view of this evidence some scholars, such as Jobson Arruda, argue that the Portuguese–Brazilian trade in enslaved Africans was more important for the development of the Brazilian colonial economy than for the Portuguese metropolitan economy. The volume and type of Brazilian products in demand at the African slave markets appear to have stimulated the development of agriculture and mining in the colony and the intensification of the use of slave labour, as most of the products mentioned here were produced or extracted mainly by enslaved Africans.

The agricultural and slave-based character of the Brazilian economy was further reinforced in the late eighteenth century and the first half of the nineteenth century with the development of coffee production for export. It has been estimated that this agricultural branch employed more than 1.5 million enslaved Africans imported to Brazil, either legally or illegally. According to Botelho and Terra, by 1808, slaves accounted for circa a quarter of Brazil's total population (24%) and more than 35% of the active population.[38]

This evidence does not mean that Portugal did not profit from colonial trade, the slave trade and the colonial economy at large. Brazilian sugar production in 1629, for instance, has been estimated at 1,211,000 *arrobas* (1 *arroba* = 15 kilograms). The bulk of this sugar was shipped to Portugal and from there re-exported elsewhere in Europe. In 1619, the revenue obtained by the Habsburg Crown from the *consulado* tax (a tax of 3% on imports) amounted to

972,186 *cruzados*. According to Christopher Ebert, 'the majority of this revenue was due to imports of Brazilian sugar'.[39] Another good example is tobacco. According to Miranda, between 1710 and 1737, the imports of Brazilian tobacco into Portugal amounted to 106,655,008 pounds.[40]

A third example is the Brazilian gold remittances sent to Portugal between 1720 and 1807. According to the available sources, their total value has been estimated at between 323,051 million *réis* and 270,803 million *réis*.[41] Additionally, Brazilian economic historian Johnson Arruda clearly demonstrated the weight of Portuguese exports in the various provinces of Brazil in the nineteenth century, arguing that a major role was played by certain Brazilian slave-based agricultural products in the development of Portuguese industries, in particular the use of Brazilian cotton in the Portuguese textile industry.[42] However, in a recent article, Costa, Palma and Reis have estimated that the contribution of the empire to Portuguese economic growth up to 1800 did not exceed 20%.[43]

The complex relationship between Brazilian colonial economic production and other countries

If the Portuguese–Brazilian participation in the transatlantic slave trade contributed mainly to the development of the Brazilian economy and only to a limited extent to the growth of the Portuguese metropolitan economy, it becomes clear that the Brazilian colonial economy enjoyed a degree of autonomy from the metropole that was different from the situation in the English, French and Dutch American colonies. This contributed to its development, and also to the intensification of slave-based agriculture and subsequent forms of exploitative labour extraction. From this evidence, one question arises. Who were the main consumers and beneficiaries of Brazilian slave-based agriculture and mining? Analysis of the commodity chains of sugar, gold and cotton over the early modern period can help us to shed new light on this matter.

For most of the sixteenth and seventeenth century, sugar was the main export from Brazil, together with Brazilian dyewood (*Paul-Brasil*). Brazilian sugar, although produced by small and medium land holders and processed in sugar mills (*engenhos de açúçar*), employed a considerable amount of slave labour in its cultivation, harvest, processing and refining, and was thus the main slave-based produce at the time. The bulk of Brazilian sugar was exported to Portugal, as the Crown held a monopoly over this commerce. However, the majority of the sugar shipped to Portugal did not stay in the kingdom, instead finding its way to North-Western European ports in the holds of ships heading to Antwerp, Hamburg and Amsterdam. There it was further refined and resold in retail markets all over North-Western Europe. Thus, the main importers, beneficiaries and final consumers of Brazilian slave-produced sugar for the period appear to have been the Dutch Republic and Hamburg.[44]

Table 7. Main European countries importing Brazilian cotton, 1796–1821 (thousands of réis).

Period	Country	Value of Cotton Imports
1796–1821	England	3,412,801,430
1796–1821	France	2,424,305,618
1796–1821	Castile	467,901,524
1796–1821	Hamburg	410,772,730
1796–1821	Italy	252,303,789
1796–1821	Holland	114,770,470

Source: Based on José Jobson de Andrade Arruda, 'O Algodão Brasileiro na época da Revolução Industrial', *America Latina en la Historia Economica* 23, no. 2 (2016): 167–203, 192–4, Table 7.

Similar trends can be found in Brazilian slave-based gold extraction in the eighteenth century. A substantial part of the gold shipped to Portugal, after being minted in Lisbon, found its way to England, as Portugal needed to use the gold coins to pay for the deficit of its trade balance with England: the value of British imports into Portugal considerably exceeded the value of Portuguese exports to England. In the period 1700 to 1790, it has been estimated that more than two-thirds of Brazilian slave-produced gold ended up in Britain, worth more than £45 million.[45] This was roughly the same amount as the English gross profit in the slave trade between 1761 and 1807. Another important share of the Brazilian gold also found its way to the Dutch Republic and to France, via the Portuguese–Brazilian slave trade in the Gulf of Benin in the eighteenth century, as already explained.

By the late eighteenth and early nineteenth centuries, the Brazilian colonial economy, of which more than 35% was based on slave labour, was exporting mainly to foreign countries. According to Jobson Arruda, the main countries consuming Brazilian products were England, Italy, France and Holland (the Netherlands), with clear percentage increases between 1796 and 1811.[46] During this period, cotton was one of the main Brazilian slave-produced products exported to these countries, with England and France being the larger importers, followed by Castile, Hamburg, Italy and the Netherlands (see Table 7).

This evidence suggests, therefore, that a significant part of the Brazilian slave-based agricultural produce and the products of mining ended up in North-Western European economies, contributing to their growth rather than to the development of the Portuguese economy.

Final remarks

This analysis of the Portuguese–Brazilian slave trade and of the relationship between the Portuguese metropolitan economy and the Brazilian colonial economy poses methodological problems for the dominant approach to the study of the impact and role of European participation in the transatlantic slave trade, the development of the Atlantic plantation economy and the industrial development and economic growth experienced in Europe during the eighteenth and nineteenth centuries. The Portuguese–Brazilian case challenges the idea that colonial economies produced only for the benefit of the metropole, as well as the idea that colonial economies were entirely dependent on the metropole.

This does not mean, however, that Brazilian slave-produced goods did not end up benefiting European economies, as clearly shown earlier. More importantly, the autonomy of the Brazilian economy did not result in its transformation and modernisation. Its deep involvement in the slave trade and the export of slave-produced goods contributed instead to an intensification of the institution of slavery in the course of the eighteenth and nineteenth centuries, and its replacement by other forms of abusive labour extraction after the legal and effective abolition of the slave trade in the mid-nineteenth century.

Therefore, the study of Portuguese–Brazilian participation in the transatlantic slave trade and assessment of its net profits as well as its impact on Portuguese and Brazilian economies requires a new methodological approach. This will entail moving beyond the one-way directional relationship between colonial and metropolitan economies as well as the idea that gains and gainers from the slave trade and slave-based products were only to be found in Europe, and that losses and losers were only to be accounted for in colonial spaces, either in Atlantic Africa or in the Americas. However, the potential and applicability of this methodological approach is not limited to the Portuguese Empire. The study of slave trading profitability in various imperial settings as well as across imperial spaces has a lot to gain from it.

Notes

1. Philip D. Curtin, *The Transatlantic Slave Trade: A Census* (Madison: University of Wisconsin Press, 1969). David Eltis, 'The Volume and Structure of the Transatlantic Slave Trade: A Reassessment', *The William and Mary Quarterly* 58, no. 1 (2001): 17–46. David Eltis, Stephen S. Behrendt, David Richardson and Herbet S. Klein, *The Trans-Atlantic Slave Trade*, CD-ROM (Cambridge: Cambridge University Press, 1999). David Eltis and David Richardson, *Routes to Slavery: Directions, Ethnicity, and Mortality in the Transatlantic Slave Trade* (London: Frank Cass, 1997). David Eltis and David Richardson, 'A New Assessment of the Transatlantic Slave Trade', in *Extending the Frontiers: Essays on the New Transatlantic Slave Trade Database*, eds. David Eltis and David Richardson (New Haven, CT: Yale University Press, 2008), 1–60.
2. Catia Antunes and Filipa Ribeiro da Silva, 'Amsterdam Merchants in the Slave Trade and African Commerce, 1580s–1670s', *Tijdschrift voor Economisch en Sociale Geschiedenis* 9, no. 4 (2012): 3–30. Ernest van den Boogaart and P.C. Emmer, 'The Dutch Participation in the Atlantic Slave Trade, 1596–1650', in *The Uncommon Market: Essays in the Economic History of the Atlantic Slave Trade*, eds. Henry A. Gemery and Jan S. Hogendorn (New York: Academic Press, 1979), 353–75. David Eltis, Stephen Behrendt and David Richardson, 'National Participation in the Transatlantic Slave Trade:

New Evidence', in *Africa and the Americas: Interconnections during the Slave Trade*, eds. José C. Curto and Renée Soulodre-La France (Trenton, NJ: Africa World Press Inc., 2005), 13–42.; P.C. Emmer, 'The West India Company, 1621–1791: Dutch or Atlantic', in *Companies and Trade: Essays on Overseas Trading Companies during the Ancien Regime*, eds. Leonard Blussé and Femme Gaastra (Leiden: Leiden University Press, 1981), 71–95. Henk den Heijer, *De geschiedenis van de WIC* (Zupten: Walburg Pers, 1994), chaps. 1–3. J.C. Miller, 'Capitalism and Slaving: The Financial and Commercial Organisation of the Angolan Slave Trade, according to the Accounts of Antonio Coelho Guerreiro (1684–1692)', *The International Journal of African Historical Studies* 17, no. 1 (1984): 1–56. Johannes Postma, *The Dutch in the Atlantic Slave Trade, 1600–1815* (Cambridge: Cambridge University Press, 1990), chap. 1. *Idem*, 'A Reassessment of the Dutch Atlantic Slave Trade', in *Riches from Atlantic Trade: Dutch Transatlantic Trade and Shipping, 1585–1817*, eds. Victor Enthoven and Johannes Postma (Leiden: Brill, 2003), 115–38. Alexandre Vieira Ribeiro, 'O comércio das almas e a obtenção de prestígio social: traficantes de escravos na Bahia ao longo do século XVIII', *Locus revista de história* 12, no. 2 (2006): 9–27. José Gonçalves Salvador, *Os cristãos-novos e o comércio no Atlântico meridional (com enfoque nas capitanias do Sul, 1530–1680)* (São Paulo: Livraria Pioneira, 1978). *Idem, Os magnatas do tráfico negreiro (séculos XVI e XVII)* (São Paulo: Livraria Pioneira, 1981). Filipa Ribeiro da Silva, 'Private Businessmen in the Angolan Slave Trade, 1590s to 1780s: Insurance, Commerce and Agency', in *Networks and Trans-Cultural Exchange: Slave Trading in the South Atlantic, 1590–1867*, eds. David Richardson and Filipa Ribeiro da Silva (Leiden: Brill, 2014), 71–100. Jelmer Vos, David Eltis and David Richardson, 'The Dutch in the Atlantic World: Perspective from the Slave Trade with particular Reference to the African Origins of the Traffic', in *Extending the Frontiers*, ed. Eltis and Richardson, 228–49.

3. Eric Williams, *Capitalism and Slavery* (London: André Deutsch, 1964). Robert Anstey, 'The Volume and Profitability of the British Slave Trade, 1761–1807', in *Race and Slavery in the Western Hemisphere*, eds. Stanley L. Engerman and Eugene D. Genovese (Princeton, NJ: Princeton University Press, 1975), 3–31. Herbert S. Klein, *The Middle Passage: Comparative Studies in the Atlantic Slave Trade* (Princeton, NJ: Princeton University Press, 1978). Gemery and Hogendorn, *The Uncommon Market*. Barbara L. Solow and Stanley L. Engerman, eds., *British Capitalism and Caribbean Slavery* (Cambridge: Cambridge University Press, 2004).
4. Karwan Fatah-Black and Matthias van Rossum, 'Beyond Profitability: The Dutch Transatlantic Slave Trade and its Economic Impact', *Slavery & Abolition* 31, no. 1 (2015): 63–83.
5. Throughout the article, we use two main expressions to refer to the merchants of Portuguese origin engaged in the transatlantic slave trade, namely 'Portuguese' and 'Portuguese-Brazilian'. The former expression is used mainly whenever referring to Portugal-based merchants involved in this business who operated mainly from Portugal for most of the sixteenth century. For the three following centuries we use the latter expression, because during this period there was a growing number of merchants operating in this business, with ships sailing under the Portuguese flag, who were either born and/or based in Brazil as well as in Africa. For an overview on the role of slavery in the Brazilian economy, see Gustavo Acioli Lopes, 'Brazil's Colonial Economy and the Atlantic Slave Trade: Supply and Demand', in *Networks and Trans-Cultural Exchange*, ed. Richardson and da Silva, 31–70. On the role of slavery in Portugal see, for instance: Jorge da Fonseca, *Escravos no Sul de Portugal, séculos XVI–XVII* (Lisbon: Editora Vulgata, 2002). *Idem, Escravos em Évora no século XVI*

(Évora: Câmara Municipal de Évora, 1997). *Idem, Escravos e senhores da Lisboa Quinhentista* (Lisbon: Edições Colibri, 2010). José Ramos Tinhorão, *Os Negros em Portugal: Uma presença silenciosa* (Lisbon: Caminho, 1988). A.C. de C.M. Saunders, *A Social History of Black Slaves and Freedmen in Portugal, 1441–1555* (Cambridge: Cambridge University Press, 1982).

6. Jaime Reis, *O Atraso Económico Português em Perspectiva Histórica: Estudos sobre a Economia Portuguesa na segunda metade do século XIX, 1850–1930* (Lisbon: Imprensa Nacional Casa da Moeda, 1993). Jorge Miguel Pedreira, 'Indústria e atraso económico em Portugal (1800–25). Uma perspective estrutural', *Análise Social* 23, no. 97 (1987): 563–96. Helder Adegar Fonseca, 'Agrarian Elites and Economic Growth in Nineteenth-Century Portugal: The Example of the Alentejo in the Liberal Era (1850–1910)', *Social History* 28, no. 2 (2003): 202–26.
7. Leonor Freire Costa, Nuno Palma and Jaime Reis, 'The Great Escape? The Contribution of the Empire to Portugal's Economic Growth, 1500–1800', *European Review of Economic History* 19 (2014): 1–22. Nuno Valério, 'Portuguese Economic Performance, 1250–2000', in *Homenage a Gabriel Tortella. Las Claves del Desarrollo Economico y Social*, eds. J.H. Andreu, J.H.G. Ruiz, J.M. Critz and J.M. Ortiz-Villajos (Madrid: Universidad de Alcalá, 2010), 431–44. António Maria Braga de Macedo de Castro Henriques, 'State Finance, War and Redistribution in Portugal, 1249–1527', unpublished PhD dissertation, University of York, 2008.
8. Jorge M. Pedreira, 'Costs and Financial Trends in the Portuguese Empire, 1415–1822', in *Portuguese Oceanic Expansion*, eds. Francisco Bethencourt and Diogo Ramada Curto (New York: Cambridge University Press, 2007), 49–87.
9. Joseph C. Miller, 'Slave Prices in the Portuguese Southern Atlantic, 1600–1830', in *Africans in Bondage: Studies in Slavery and the Slave Trade*, eds. Paul Lovejoy (Madison: University of Wisconsin Press, 1986), 43–78.
10. http://www.slavevoyages.org/. Portuguese National Archive (Arquivo Nacional Torre do Tombo, AN/TT), and the Portuguese Historical Overseas Archive (Arquivo Histórico Ultramarino, AHU). David Eltis, *The Rise of African Slavery in the Americas* (New York: Cambridge University Press, 2000), 293–7. David Richardson, 'Prices of Slaves in West and West-Central Africa: Toward an Annual Series, 1698–1807', *Bulletin of Economic Research* 43 (1991): 21–56. David Eltis, 'The Slave Trade & Commercial Agriculture in an African Context', in *Commercial Agriculture, the Slave Trade & Slavery in Atlantic Africa*, eds. Robin Law, Suzanne Schwarz and Silke Strickrodt (Woodbridge: James Currey, 2013), 28–53.
11. J. Bato'Ora Ballong-Wen-Mewuda, *São Jorge da Mina, 1482–1637: la vie d'un comptoir portugais en Afrique occidentale*, 2 vols. (Lisbon and Paris: Fondation Calouste Gulbenkian, 1993). Toby Green, *The Rise of the Trans-Atlantic Slave Trade in Western Africa, 1300–1589* (Cambridge: Cambridge University Press, 2012). António de Almeida Mendes, 'Slavery, Society, and the First Steps towards an Atlantic Revolution in Western Africa (Fifteenth–Sixteenth Centuries)', in *Brokers of Change: Atlantic Commerce and Cultures in Precolonial Western Africa*, eds. Toby Green (Oxford: Oxford University Press for the British Academy, 2012), 239–57. *Idem*, 'Les réseaux de la traite ibérique dans l'Atlantique nord (1440–1640)', *Annales. Historie, Sciences Sociales* 63, no. 4 (2008): 739–68. *Idem*, 'Portugal e o Tráfico de Escravos na primeira metade do século XVI', *Africana Studia* 7 (2004): 13–30. *Idem*, 'The Foundations of the System: A Reassessment of the Slave Trade to the Spanish Americas in the Sixteenth and Seventeenth Centuries', in *Extending the Frontiers*, eds Eltis and Richardson, 63–94. Maria Manuel Torrão, 'Actividade comercial externa de Cabo Verde: organização, funcionamento, evolução', in *História geral de Cabo Verde*, eds.

Luís de Albuquerque and Maria Emília Madeira Santos (Lisbon/Praia: Centro de Estudos de História e Cartografia Antiga, Instituto Nacional da Cultura de Cabo Verde, 1991), vol. 1, 249–55. *Idem*, 'Formas de participação dos portugueses no comércio de escravos com as Índias de Castela: abastecimento e transporte', in *II Reunião Internacional de História de África : A dimensão Atlântica da África, Rio de Janeiro, 30 de Outubro a 1 de Novembro de 1996* (São Paulo: University of São Paulo, 1997), 203–22. John L. Vogt, "The Early São Tomé-Príncipe Slave Trade with Mina, 1500–1540', *The International Journal of African Historical Studies* 6, no. 3 (1973): 453–67. *Idem, Portuguese Rule on the Gold Coast 1469–1682* (Athens: University of Georgia Press, 1979). *Idem*, 'Notes on the Portuguese Cloth Trade in West Africa, 1480–1540', *The International Journal of African Historical Studies* 8, no. 4 (1975): 623–51.

12. On the Portuguese slave trade in Angola, see among others: Arlindo Manuel Caldeira, *Escravos e Traficantes no Império Português: O Comércio Negreiro Português no Atlântico durante os séculos XV a XIX* (Lisbon: Esfera dos Livros, 2013). Joseph C. Miller, *Way of Death: Merchant Capitalism and the Angolan Slave Trade, 1730–1830* (Madison: University of Wisconsin Press, 1988). On the role of Luanda in the slave trade, see Arlindo Caldeira, 'Angola and the Seventeenth-Century South Atlantic Slave Trade', in *Networks and Trans-Cultural Exchange*, eds. Richardson and da Silva, 101–42. On the role of Benguela as an Atlantic slave port, see Mariana P. Candido, *An African Slaving Port and the Atlantic World: Benguela and its Hinterland* (New York: Cambridge University Press, 2013).
13. On the illegal slave trade in Angola, see Roquinaldo Amaral Ferreira, 'The Suppression of the Slave Trade and Slave Departures from Angola, 1830s–1860s', in *Extending the Frontiers*, eds. Eltis and Richardson, 313–34.
14. José Capela, 'Slave Trade Networks in Eighteenth-Century Mozambique', in *Networks and Trans-Cultural Exchange* eds. Richardson and da Silva, 165–94.
15. In the broader sense, the Costa da Mina corresponded to the stretch of the West African coast between Cape Mount and Cape Lopez. For the Portuguese-Brazilian merchants operating in the region, it referred to the ports located between the Volta and the Lagos Rivers. Gustavo Acioli Lopes, 'O Negócio da Costa da Mina e o Comércio Atlântico: Tabaco, Açúcar, Ouro e Tráfico de Escravos: Pernambuco (1654–1760)', unpublished PhD dissertation, University of São Paulo, Brazil, 2008, 176. Pierre Verger, *Fluxo e Refluxo do Tráfico de Escravos entre os Golfo de Benin e a Bahia de Todos os Santos: dos séculos XVII a XIX* (Salvador: Corrupio, 1997), 37.
16. José Capela, 'Slave Trade Networks'. *Idem*, O tráfico de escravos nos portos de Moçambique: 1733–1904 (Porto: Afrontamento, 2002). Gwyn Campbell, ed., *The Structure of Slavery in Indian Ocean Africa and Asia* (London: Frank Cass, 2004).
17. Mendes, 'The Foundations of the System', 63–94. Newson and Minchin, *From Capture to Sale: The Portuguese Slave Trade to Spanish South America in the early seventeenth century* (Leiden: Brill, 2007). Vila Vilar, *Hispanoamerica y el comercio de esclavos.*
18. Daniel Barros, Domingues da Silva and David Eltis, 'The Slave Trade to Pernambuco, 1561–1851', in *Extending the Frontiers*, eds. Eltis and Richardson, 95–129. Alexandre Vieira Ribeiro, 'The Transatlantic Slave Trade to Bahia, 1582–1851', in *Extending the Frontiers*, eds. Eltis and Richardson, 130–54. Manolo Florentino, *Em costas negras. Uma história do tráfico entre a África e o Rio de Janeiro* (São Paulo: Companhia das Letras, 1997). *Idem*, 'The Slave Trade, Colonial Markets, and Slave Families in Rio de Janeiro, Brazil, ca. 1790–ca. 1830', in *Extending the Frontiers*, eds. Eltis and Richardson, 275–312.

19. Lopes, 'O Negócio da Costa', 33–8. Biblioteca Nacional do Rio de Janeiro, Seção de Manuscritos, 11, 3, 1; 'Provisão do Conselho Ultramarino. Lisboa, 16 de Março de 1673', in *Cathalogo das Reaes Ordens existentes no arquivo da extinta provedoria de Pernambuco*, eds. Francisco Bezerra Cavalcanti de Albuquerque, 172–3.
20. Miller, 'Slave Prices'.
21. This data series has been selected because it has a considerable number of price references for the most important slave supplying market in West Central Africa – Angola. Eltis, *Rise of African Slavery*, 293–7. David Richardson, 'Prices of Slaves in West and West-Central Africa: Toward an Annual Series, 1698–1807', *Bulletin of Economic Research* 43 (1991): 21–56. Eltis, 'The Slave Trade', 28–53. Laird W. Bergad. *Slavery and the Demographic and Economic History of Minas Gerais, Brazil, 1720–1888* (New York: Cambridge University Press. 1999).
22. Lopes, 'O Negócio da Costa', 163–8.
23. To estimate minimum and maximum gross profit margins, we have used the total number of slaves embarking on and disembarked by vessels sailing under Portuguese-Brazilian flag. Figures provided in the TSTD. Similar methodology has been used by Fatah-Black and Van Rossum. For accuracy, we should have also used the highest and lowest known prices of slave purchase available for the Portuguese case. However, given the poor quality of the data series available, we have decided to use the data series built by David Richardson and David Eltis, and we have also decided to use an average price for each five-year period.
24. Conversion rate used: 11.5 guilders = 1 pound sterling. Extrapolated gross profit margins for the Dutch participation in the transatlantic slave trade 1595–1829 provided by Fatah-Black and Van Rossum, 'Beyond Profitability', 13, Table 4.
25. Filipa Ribeiro da Silva, *Dutch and Portuguese in Western Africa* (Leiden: Brill, 2011), chap. 5.
26. Ibid.
27. Christopher Ebert, *Between Empires: Brazilian Sugar in the Early Atlantic Economy, 1550–1630* (Leiden: Brill, 2008).
28. Lopes, 'O Negócio da Costa', 163–8.
29. In his recent PhD dissertation, Miguel Geraldes Rodrigues has attempted to calculate the profits of some *contractadores* of the Angolan slave trade. For details see Miguel Geraldes Rodrigues, 'Between West Africa and America: The Angolan Slave Trade in the Portuguese and Spanish Atlantic Empires (1560–1641)' (PhD dissertation, European University Institute, 2019), 94 and ss.
30. Leslie Bethell, *The Abolition of the Brazilian Slave Trade* (Cambridge: Cambridge University Press, 1970). Beatriz Mamigonian, *Africanos Livres: a abolição do tráfico de escravos no Brasil* (São Paulo: Companhia das Letras, 2017).
31. Angus Dalrymple-Smith and Ewout Frankema, 'Slave Ship Provisioning in the Long eighteenth Century. A Boost to West African Commercial Agriculture?' *European Review of Economic History* 21 (2017): 185–235.
32. Chris Evan and Goran Rydén, 'From Gammelbo Bruk to Calabar: Swedish Iron in an Expanding Atlantic Economy', in *Scandinavian Colonialism and the Rise of Modernity: Small Time Agents in a Global Arena*, eds. Magdalena Naum and Jonas M. Nordin (New York: Springer, 2013).
33. Kazuo Kobayashi, *Indian Cotton Textiles in West Africa: African Agency, Consumer Demands and the Making of the Global Economy, 1750–1850* (New York: Springer, 2019).
34. John Vogt, 'Notes on the Portuguese Cloth Trade in West Africa 1480–1540', *International Journal of African Historical Studies* 8 (1075): 623–51.

35. António Carreira, *Panaria cabo-verdiana*-guineense: Aspectos históricos e sócioeconómicos (Lisbon: Junta de Investigações do Ultramar, 1968).
36. Gustavo Acioli and Maximiliano M. Menz, 'Resgate e Mercadorias: Uma Análise Comparada do Tráfico Luso-Brasileiro de Escravos em Angola e na Costa da Mina (século XVIII)', *Afro-Ásia* 37 (2008): 43–73, 52.
37. Acioli and Menz, 'Resgate e Mercadorias', 64.
38. Tarcísio Botelho and Paulo Terra, 'Relações de Trabalho no Brasil, 1800–2000', in *Relações Laborais em Portugal e no Mundo Lusófono: História e Demografia*, eds. Marcelo Badaró Mattos, Filipa Ribeiro da Silva, Paulo Teodoro de Matos, Raquel Varela and Sónia Ferreira (Lisbon: Colibri, 2014), 133–55, 141, 144.
39. Ebert, *Between Empires*, 172.
40. Susana Münch Miranda, 'Risco e expectativas no monopólio do tabaco, 1722–1727', in *El Tabaco y La Esclavitud em la rearticulación imperial ibérica*, eds. Santiago de Luxán Meléndez, J. Figueirôa-Rêgo (Évora: CIDEHUS, 2018), 1–21.
41. Rita Martins de Sousa, 'Brazilian Gold and the Lisbon Mint House (1720–1807)', *e-JPH* 6, no. 1 (Summer 2008). See also Leonor Freire Costa, Maria Manuela Rocha and Rita Martins de Sousa, 'Brazilian Gold in the Eighteenth Century: A Reassessment', Working Papers GHES – Office of Economic and Social History 2010/42, ISEG – Lisbon School of Economics and Management, GHE – Social and Economic History Research Unit, University of Lisbon.
42. José Jobson de Andrade Arruda, 'O Algodão Brasileiro na época da Revolução Industrial', *America Latina en la Historia Economica* 23, no. 2 (2016): 167–203, 183–4.
43. Leonor Freire Costa, Nuno Palma and Jaime Reis, 'The Great Escape? The Contribution of the Empire to Portugal's Economic Growth, 1500–1800', *European Review of Economic History* 19, no. 1 (Feb. 2015): 1–22, 17.
44. Ebert, *Between Empires*, chap. 8.
45. Nuno Palma, 'Anglo-Portuguese Trade and Monetary Transmission during the Eighteenth Century', unpublished paper, 2012. Harold Edward Stephen Fisher, *The Portugal Trade: A Study of Anglo-Portuguese Commerce 1700–1770* (London: Methuen, 1971).
46. Arruda, 'O Algodão Brasileiro', 189.

Acknowledgements

I would like to thank the editors of this Special Issue, the anonymous reviewers and the participants in the Panel organised at the World Economic History Congress in July-August 2018 for reading earlier versions of this study and providing very useful feedback, comments and suggestions of revisions. Many thanks also to Gustavo Acioli Lopes and Maxilimiano Menz.

Disclosure statement

No potential conflict of interest was reported by the author(s).

Appendix 1: Estimated Gross Profits from slaves embarked in Portuguese-Brazilian ships, 1711–1835.

Periods/Gross Profits	Total slaves embarked	Average price of male slaves sold in Minas Gerais (Brazil) per five-year period (réis)	Average price of male slaves sold in Minas Gerais (Brazil) per five-year-period (sterling) (exchange rate 3565 réis = £1)	Average price of slaves bought in WCA per five-year-period (sterling)	Differential between WCA and Brazilian slave prices	Estimated gross profit of slaves embarked (réis)	Estimated gross profit of slaves embarked (sterling) (exchange rate 3565 réis = £1)	Comparison with British
1681–1685	4,890			3.7				
1686–1690	9,489			3.8				
1691–1695	16,554			4.3				
1696–1700	45,523			4.7				
1701–1705	29,593			4.8			112,201	
1706–1710	29,037			5.3				
1711–1715	45,745	184,000	51.6	5.8	8.9	8,417,080,000	2,361,032	
1716–1720	52,253	272,500	76.4	7.5	10.2	14,238,942,500	3,994,093	
1721–1725	87,482	190,700	53.5	10.7	5.0	16,682,817,400	4,679,612	
1726–1730	94,513	198,600	55.7	6.4	8.7	18,770,281,800	5,265,156	
1731–1735	75,473	207,800	58.3	4.6	12.7	15,683,289,400	4,399,239	
1736–1740	80,681	191,600	53.7	6.2	8.7	15,458,479,600	4,336,179	
1741–1745	90,258	183,200	51.4	7.4	6.9	16,535,265,600	4,638,223	
1746–1750	107,865	174,200	48.9	8.2	6.0	18,790,083,000	5,270,710	
1751–1755	74,221	128,400	36.0	7.6	4.7	9,529,976,400	2,673,205	
1756–1760	76,296	106,600	29.9	7.0	4.3	8,133,153,600	2,281,389	
1761–1765	73,753	102,400	28.7	10.9	2.6	7,552,307,200	2,118,459	2,118,45,9
1766–1770	83,011	88,200	24.7	13.9	1.8	7,321,570,200	2,053,736	2,053,736
1771–1775	70,692	78,800	22.1	16.8	1.3	5,570,529,600	1,562,560	1,562,560
1776–1780	67,301	75,400	21.2	13,3	1.6	5,074,495,400	1,423,420	1,423,420
1781–1785	99,533	80,600	22.6	19.5	1.2	8,022,359,800	2,250,311	2,250,311
1786–1790	72	81,600	22.9	23.4	1.0	5,894,131	1,653	1,653
1791–1795	118,705	79,800	22.4	18.5	1.2	9,472,659,000	2,657,127	2,657,127
1796–1800	127,491	92,400	25.9	23.4	1.1	11,780,168,400	3,304,395	3,304,395
1801–1805	16,866	96,000	26.9	23.0	1.2	1,619,136,000	454,175	454,175

(Continued)

Continued.

Periods/Gross Profits	Total slaves embarked	Average price of male slaves sold in Minas Gerais (Brazil) per five-year period (réis)	Average price of male slaves sold in Minas Gerais (Brazil) per five-year-period (sterling) (exchange rate 3565 réis = £1)	Average price of slaves bought in WCA per five-year-period (sterling)	Differential between WCA and Brazilian slave prices	Estimated gross profit of slaves embarked (réis)	Estimated gross profit of slaves embarked (sterling) (exchange rate 3565 réis = £1)	Comparison with British
1806–1810	185,256	101,000	28.3	22.6	1.3	18,710,856,000	5,248,486	5,248,486
1811–1815	229,812	105,200	29.5			24,176,222,400	6,781,549	
1816–1820	260,854	109,200	30.6			28,485,256,800	7,990,254	
1821–1825	237,142	137,200	38.5			32,535,882,400	9,126,474	
1826–1830	329,972	194,200	54.5			64,080,562,400	17,974,912	
1831–1835	30,733	282,000	79.1			8,666,706,000	2,431,053	
1836–1840	255,516							
1841–1845	84,982							
1846–1850	47,232							
1851–1855	3,754							
1856–1860								
1861–1863								
Total	3,637,072					375,313,975,031	105,277,412	21,074,326,99
Disembarked	3,307,382				Loss with Deaths (*c.* 10% rate)	37,531,397,503	10,527,741	2,107,433
Deaths	329,690				Final total	337,782,577,528	94,749,671	18,966,894,29
Mortality rate whole period	9.1							

Sources and Notes: see Figure 1.

OPEN ACCESS

Governance, value-added and rents in plantation slavery-based value-chains

Klas Rönnbäck

ABSTRACT

This article studies how the governance of a colonial value-chain impacted upon the value-added created. The article focuses on the value-chain of colonial sugar produced in the slave plantation complex in the Americas. Previous research has suggested that British planters in the Caribbean were able to reap high profits because of a protected market for sugar in Britain. In this paper, it is argued that it was mainly British refiners that were able to profit from these protectionist policies. Wholesale prices of muscovado sugar are shown to have been more or less on a par with those prevalent under free-market conditions, whereas the price of refined sugar was considerably higher in Britain than it presumably would have been in a free-market. Limited competition and active collusion between refiners seem to have increased the mark-up on the refined sugar relative to the price of muscovado in Britain. Focusing only on the profitability on certain links in value-chains associated with the slave plantation complex in the Americas (most importantly the slave trade) might detract attention from how the governance structure of the value-chains allowed profits to be reaped elsewhere in the same value-chains.

Introduction

Eric Williams' famous book *Capitalism and slavery* has spawned considerable discussion among scholars about the role that the transatlantic slave trade and American slavery played in the development of early modern Europe, not least for Britain. Most of this debate has been concerned with the profitability of the slave trade, as Williams himself claimed that it was the supposedly very high profits of the slave trade that enabled investment in the industrial revolution in Britain.[1] The slave trade was, however, not the only part of the value-chain connected to the slave plantation complex in the Americas that has been argued to have been highly profitable. Several scholars have, for example, argued that planters in particular were able to earn substantial profits from their exploitation of slave labour. However, these profits were not outcomes determined solely by the exploitation of the slaves but were also influenced by several other factors. One factor that has been said to have boosted the Caribbean planters' profit rates was Britain's protectionist policies in favour of its colonies in the Caribbean.

This article focuses specifically on the production of and trade in cane sugar. The aim is to analyse these activities through the prism of a value-chain analysis from a comparative perspective. By analyzing the slave plantation complex in this way, emphasis can be placed on how the governance of the value-chain of sugar – in the form of legislative and judicial governance as well as governance by the various actors involved in the trades – could influence the distribution of economic rents between different links in the value-chain. Governance policies affecting the value-chain allowed certain agents to capture substantial economic rents in particular links of the value-chain of slavery-based production.

Governance, value-added and rents in global value-chains

In the words of Raphael Kaplinsky and Mike Morris, a value-chain 'describes the full range of activities which are required to bring a product or service from conception, through the different phases of production [...] to final consumers'.[2] The actual production of a commodity is thus only one of several value-added links in this chain, and there are a number of activities involved in each link of the chain.

Value-chains are as a rule not the outcome solely of pure market relations but are coordinated relationships under the governance of several actors. On the one hand, if there are power asymmetries between the agents involved in a value-chain, more powerful agents can dominate the governance of the value-chain. Power asymmetries are explained in part by the level of competition at each link of the value-chain: while some value-chains might exhibit quite symmetrical competition throughout most or even all their links, others might be characterized by lead and captive firms with very asymmetrical power to influence the value-chain. A basic distinction has then been suggested between modern-day 'buyer-driven' and 'producer-driven' value-chains (where the former does not refer to the final consumers but to actors at the very end of the value-chain, such as retailers). There is, naturally, also legislative and judicial governance of the value-chain, including, for example, taxes or tariffs imposed at different links of the value-chain, and non-tariff trade barriers and regulations that also influence the operations of the value-chain.[3]

The value-added involved in each link of a value-chain is determined by a number of different factors. The factors of production (land, labour, capital) employed to produce, process or transport a good or a service naturally vary along a value-chain. One crucial aspect here is economic rents. Rents can arise at various links of a value-chain if there are barriers to entry to that particular link. Many of the theoreticians of value-chain analysis have suggested that the distribution of rents along a value-chain is a key determinant for who benefits from the chain.[4]

This article will focus on value-chains connected to the American slave plantation complex in the early modern era. That a value-chain is connected to the slave plantation complex is here taken to mean that the chain either deals with commodities produced in the slave plantation complex or provides necessary inputs into the complex. The most important input into the slave plantation complex was, naturally, the humans that had been coercively turned into commodities – the slaves themselves. This article will, however, focus on the value-chain of sugar produced in the American slave plantation complex.

The general character of these colonial value-chains is very well established in previous research.[5] Many of the commodities in growing demand in Europe during the early-modern period could not be cultivated in the Europe, as they required a tropical or sub-tropical climate. This became one of the drivers of the establishment of the American plantation complex. As these plantations required labour, which was a scarce resource in the Americas at the time, slaves were transported against their will across the Atlantic from Africa to be put to work on colonial plantations. Planters in the American colonies were operating under mercantilist regulations and as a rule, therefore, limited to only exporting raw materials to the markets in Europe. Only the most basic forms of processing needed for successful transatlantic transport of the commodities were allowed. Sugar cane juice, for example, had to be processed into raw sugar – often called *muscovado* – at the plantations since the unprocessed juice would have spoilt during transportation. In Europe, these raw materials were then processed into the final consumer products, such as refined sugar.

All these links in the value-chains entailed substantial amounts of value-added. In some recent research it has been shown that the value-added in the transatlantic slave trade and in the trade in goods from plantations in the Americas certainly was of a significant order of magnitude if compared, for example, with the value-added in the national or local economies in Europe.[6] The British involvement in the value-chains of slave-produced sugar, tobacco and cotton has, in this context, been found to have grown substantially over the eighteenth century, from a value equivalent to around 3% of British GDP in the early eighteenth century, to more than 10% by the end.[7] These estimates are shown in Figure 1, broken down by the different links of the value-chains involved.[8]

As can be seen in Figure 1, all four links of these value-chains grew economically over the eighteenth century, not only in absolute terms but also relative to British GDP. The slave trade, according to these estimates, accounted for the lowest share of value-added of the four links in the value-chains, followed by

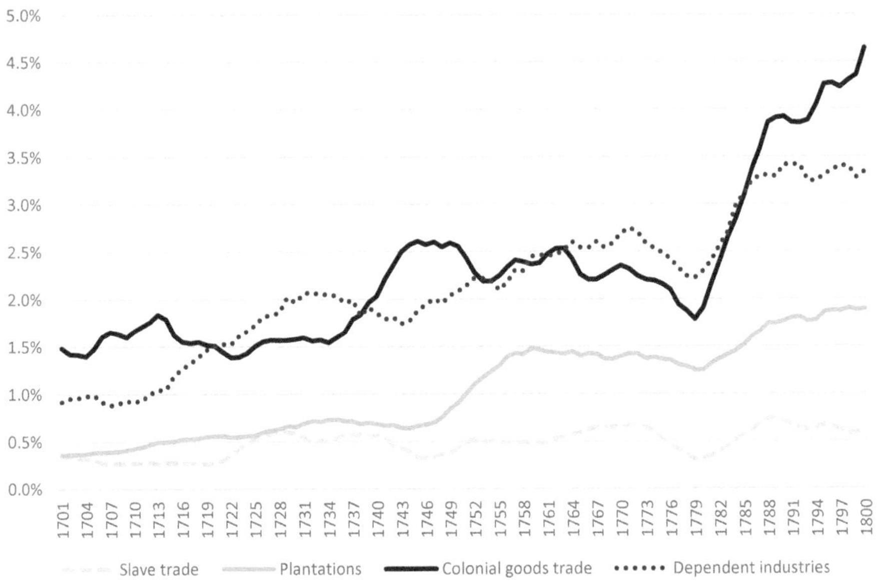

Figure 1. Value-added in British activities associated with the American slave plantation complex for sugar, tobacco and cotton, 1701–1800, relative to British GDP (per cent, nine-year moving averages).

Sources: elaboration on Rönnbäck, 'On the Economic Importance of the Slave Plantation Complex', figs. 1–6.

the value-added on the slave plantations. The subsequent links in the chain – the trade in and shipping of colonial commodities to Britain, and the industries in Britain dependent upon these inputs from the slave plantation complex (e.g. cotton textile mills or sugar refineries) – provided a somewhat larger value-added and also grew faster.

Profits in the value-chains of the slavery plantation complex

The value-added by different links of the value-chain was made up of different components, including costs of production, profits and rents that could be earned in the businesses involved. This brings us back to Williams' assertion that there were extraordinary profits to be made in the transatlantic slave trade. This statement has spawned a large amount of research, using a variety of methods and sources of data. The two most common methods to estimate the profitability of the slave trade have been to use examples of ships whose accounts books have been preserved and to use a cost–revenue analysis on an aggregate level. The results previous scholars have arrived at have varied considerably, ranging from a negative average return per voyage for some ships to a return exceeding 30% per voyage for some other ships.[9] For example, Guillaume Daudin has noted that estimates of profits per voyage cannot be compared directly with annual profits rates, as some voyages might have taken a more than one year to yield profits.[10] Estimates of the annual profit rates from the slave trade generally exhibit lower figures, in most cases in the range of 6–10% per year.[11]

Other scholars have instead focused on the profitability of the slave plantations. Estimates of the profitability of British Caribbean plantations vary, but often come to around 8–10% per year during most of the eighteenth century, though in some cases they approach as much as 20% per year.[12] Profits were similar on the sugar plantations on the French island of Saint-Domingue, where the returns have been estimated to at 8–12% per year.[13] Profits on Brazilian sugar plantations were of a similar magnitude.[14] The profitability of various slave plantations in the United States (primarily growing cotton as well as some commodities not grown extensively on Caribbean plantations) during the nineteenth century might have been somewhat lower: estimates suggest a return on investment of about 6–8% per year.[15]

The profits on the American plantations were an outcome not only of the productivity of the plantations, where the masters had found ways to exploit slaves to maximize their own profits, but also of the political-economic environment in which these plantations were operating. Past research has argued that British sugar planters in the Caribbean benefited greatly from Britain's protectionist trade policies. These policies have been claimed to amount to an effective 'monopoly' for British West Indian sugar producers, reducing the competition in the British sugar market. This allowed planters in the British colonies to increase the price of their output beyond what would have been possible in the competitive, 'free' markets of Continental Europe, such as the Netherlands. British policies thus allowed the planters to reap substantial rents, even though their plantations have been argued to have been generally less productive than others, such as those in the French Caribbean.[16] Some of the evidence in support of this theory stems from complaints by other parties against planters and organizations promoting planters' interests.[17] However, the main agents filing such complaints – British sugar refiners – were acting in their own self-interest as purchasers of the planters' raw sugar, so their statements cannot be taken on face value. The only previous scholar who has attempted to provide quantitative evidence on the topic is Philip Coelho.[18] Coelho's attempted to estimate a proxy for the wholesale price of muscovado sugar in England and compared that with the wholesale price of muscovado sugar in the Netherlands – with the assumption that the price in Amsterdam was representative of the 'free market' price of sugar in Europe. His estimates cover only 1768–72, but they suggest that the price of muscovado sugar was indeed substantially higher in England during this period.

The profitability of operations in later links of the value-chain of these colonial commodities have not been studied to the same extent. There is certainly a great amount of research into the social, political and economic history of Atlantic merchants in Britain, and into their connections to planters in the

Americas.[19] Only a few rare studies have looked at the profitability of this trade: Richard Grassby's study of British profits arrived at rates of profit from trading activities in the range of 6–12% per year and Daudin's study of the French West Indian trade found a similar annual rate of return.[20] Money lent to borrowers in the Caribbean yielded interest rates of around 7% per year.[21] The results from studies of the final stages of the value-chains – the industries dependent upon the inputs from the slave plantation complex – have been more varied. There is an enormous amount of research into the British textile industry, especially concerning the role it played in the British industrial revolution. Some of this research has also emphasized the connection to the slave plantation complex.[22] Studies of the sugar refining in Britain during the eighteenth century are, in contrast, scarce, and none of them has dealt with the issue of profitability.[23] The profitability of European sugar refining seems to have only been studied in the French case.[24]

Price levels in the colonial sugar trade compared

One central assertion, as mentioned above, was that British Caribbean planters' profits were driven to any significant extent by economic rents created by British protectionist trade policies. The controversy boils down to a critical empirical issue of how high British sugar prices actually were compared with prices elsewhere around the Atlantic. How well-founded is the idea that British prices of sugar were much higher than those on the European continent? As mentioned earlier, Coelho is the only scholar to have undertaken any systematic study of this question, but he covers only a very short period, and his does so indirectly through proxy estimates.

There is, however, much data that allows us to compare the prices on the markets in England and the Netherlands directly over the long run. Figure 2 shows the wholesale market price of muscovado sugar in London and Amsterdam from 1650 to 1820. Local prices and weights have here been converted into silver prices (based on the silver content of the coinage used) and metric weights in order to allow a direct comparison.

Comparisons such as this are certainly not without their problems: we cannot, for example, rule out the possibility that there were differences in the quality of the muscovado sugar sold on these two markets. The Dutch sources, however, contain data that enables us to distinguish between among varieties of sugar, potentially capturing any differences in quality. In Figure 2, data is reported on the two cheapest varieties of sugar sold in Amsterdam: sugar simply classified as muscovado in general, and sugar from the Dutch colony of Surinam. General muscovado sugar was somewhat more expensive during the late seventeenth century than the Surinam sugar, but from the middle of the eighteenth century, the Amsterdam prices were similar for the two (with the exception of some years during the Napoleonic

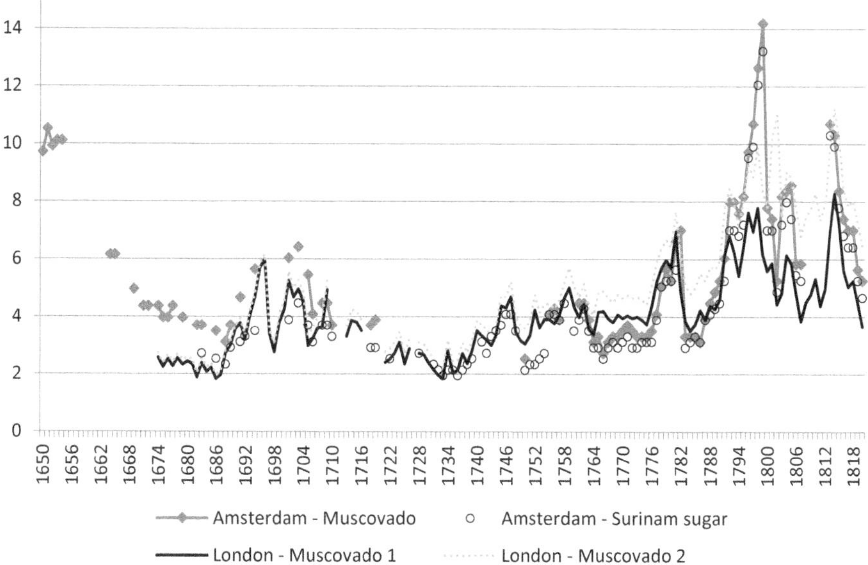

Figure 2. The price of muscovado sugar in Amsterdam and London, 1650–1820 (grams Ag/kg).
Sources: muscovado prices in London from Sheridan, *Sugar and Slavery*, appendix V; Deerr, *The History of Sugar*, 530–1. Prices in Amsterdam from Posthumus, *Nederlandsche Prijsgeschiedenis*, tables 57 and 59. Tariffs from Deerr, *The History of Sugar*, 430.

Wars), as is evident from the figure. Both these types of sugar were cheaper than sugar from the French colony of Saint-Domingue, but this might to some extent reflect a difference in quality of the sugar, as the French sugar most probably was clayed to improve the quality above that of the raw muscovado sugar.[25]

There is also the issue of the level and structure of tariffs. In the Netherlands, there were no tariff barriers on raw sugar during this period, but at the same time there were fairly high tariffs on the re-export of raw sugar, which was intended to stimulate refining in the country.[26] The Amsterdam prices for raw sugar can, from that perspective, be considered a proxy for a free market price. Britain, in contrast, levied substantial duties on sugar imports. It is unfortunately unclear whether the wholesale prices the sources report include these duties or whether they represent pre-tariff wholesale prices. For that reason, Figure 2 has two data series for London: Muscovado 1 shows the data as reported in the sources, while Muscovado 2 shows the price of muscovado with import duties added (assuming that the prices in the sources employed are pre-tariff wholesale prices).

One striking finding of the comparison is how similar the prices really were on these two markets for much of the period for which there is comparable data: the London prices (using the series for Muscovado 2) exhibit a correlation coefficient of 0.59 with the Amsterdam price for muscovado sugar, and a striking correlation coefficient of 0.87 with the Amsterdam prices for Surinam sugar.

More importantly, until the 1750s, the price of muscovado sugar in London (regardless of which of the two data series we focus upon) was more or less on par with the price of the general muscovado sugar sold in Amsterdam and only had a marginally higher price than Surinam sugar.

This only started to change by the second half of the eighteenth century. From this time onwards, the two price series for London started to diverge as tariff levels were raised several times in the second half of the eighteenth century. The assumption made as to whether the prices reported in the sources incorporate the duties therefore has a large impact upon the estimates from this time onwards. If one assumes that the London prices reported in the sources already incorporate duties that had to be paid (Muscovado 1), the price of muscovado in London was higher only for a short period of time in the 1760s and 1770s – which happens to be the short period studied by Coelho – but later returned to being on par with prices in Amsterdam for much of the remaining period. If one instead assumes that the London prices reported in the sources represent pre-tariff prices (Muscovado 2), the data suggest that prices (including the duties) remained somewhat higher in London than in Amsterdam from this time onwards, with the exception of some years during the Napoleonic Wars.

This data does certainly not disprove the claim that French planters were more productive than British ones. On the contrary, the prices in both the Dutch and British markets were substantially higher than the price of muscovado sugar in France.[27] What the figures do show is that, if we compare the wholesale prices in London to the presumed free market price in Amsterdam, the protection from the British tariffs and trade policies actually does not seem to have led to systematically higher wholesale prices in Britain for a large part of the period under study, with any impact coming only during the second half of the eighteenth century.

We will discuss potential explanations for this below. First, however, there is another important thread to this story: the final consumer prices of sugar. Figure 3 shows the final consumer price of refined sugar in England and the Netherlands (again in grams of silver per kilogram of sugar), based on the prices paid by the Lord Steward in London, and the prices on the Amsterdam Bourse.

With the exception of the years of the French Revolutionary and Napoleonic Wars, the price of refined sugar was consistently much higher in England than in the Netherlands, on average approximately 1.5 shillings per pound of sugar, the equivalent of the difference of about 3 grams of silver per kilogram of sugar (as shown in the figure).

Combining the information from these two links in the value-chain reveals major differences between the Dutch and the English markets in the mark-up in price between muscovado and refined sugar. This is shown in Figure 4, which uses moving average figures in order to show the long-term trends rather than the fluctuations specific years. As it is the mark-up after tariffs had been paid

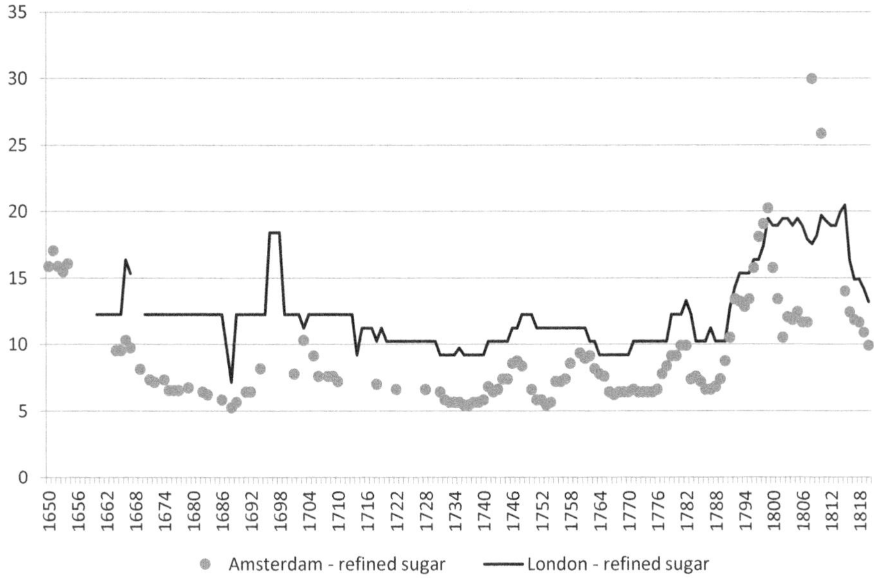

Figure 3. The price of refined sugar in Amsterdam and London, 1650–1820 (grams Ag/kg sugar).

Sources: underlying data for sugar prices in London from Gregory Clark's dataset, 'England, Prices and Wages since 13th Century' (Davis: University of California, 2006), http://gpih.ucdavis.edu/, data series for Lord Steward's Account. Prices in Amsterdam from Posthumus, *Nederlandsche Prijsgeschiedenis. D. 1, Goederenprijzen Opde Beurs van Amsterdam 1585–1914, Wisselk Oersen Te Amsterdam 1609–1914*, table 63.

Figure 4. Mark-up on price of refined sugar relative to price of muscovado sugar in Amsterdam and London, 1650–1820 (%, nine-year moving average).

Sources: muscovado prices in London from Sheridan, *Sugar and Slavery*, appendix V; Deerr, *The History of Sugar*, 530–1; in Amsterdam from Posthumus, *Nederlandsche Prijsgeschiedenis*, tables 57 and 59. Refined sugar prices in England from Gregory Clark's dataset, 'England, Prices and Wages since 13th Century', data series for Lord Steward's Account; in Amsterdam from Posthumus, *Nederlandsche Prijsgeschiedenis*, table 63.
Note: mark-up in England calculated using the Muscovado 2 price series.

that we are interested in here, the London Muscovado 2-series (see explanation of Figure 2) is used for these calculations.[28]

In Amsterdam, refined sugar normally sold for prices 50–100% higher than the price of muscovado sugar (and around 100–150% higher than the price of Surinam sugar, which is not shown in the figure), and only in exceptional years did it increase to higher levels. In London, however, the mark-up on refined sugar was 400–500% in some years of the late seventeenth century, decreasing to 200–300% during the first half of the eighteenth century and further to around 100–150% in the decades just preceding the French Revolution and Napoleonic Wars before increasing again to around 200%.

The flipside of this high mark-up in Britain was, naturally, that sugar refined in Britain was unable to compete on foreign markets. The amount of refined sugar exported from Britain was negligible given the vast amount of raw sugar imported during the first half of the century. Only by the 1760s, when the mark-up in the British market had dropped to close to the mark-up in the Netherlands, did the export of refined sugar from Britain account for more than a few percentage points of the sugar refined in the country.

Governance, competition and rents of the colonial sugar trade

While previous scholars are correct that sugar prices were higher in London than in Amsterdam during the period under study, the major difference throughout much of the period under study here was not at the wholesale level, but in the price for the final consumer. The mark-up between the price of refined sugar and the wholesale price of muscovado differed vastly between the two markets. There are a number of factors that could have influenced the price of refined sugar in the two countries.

First, it is theoretically possible that local transportation costs were higher in London than in Amsterdam. But as both price series refer to transactions in major cities – the Lord Steward being the representative of the English Royal Household in London – it does not seem plausible that the differences in price are attributable to differences in local transport costs given the fairly short distances from the refineries to the consumers.

The second factor is the representativity of the data. It is possible that prices are not equally representative of final consumer market prices in England and the Netherlands, respectively. For example, it is possible that there were discounts when the sugar was traded in bulk, as was done on the Amsterdam Bourse. The prices for refined sugar on the Amsterdam Bourse were, however, generally similar to the prices paid by institutional consumers in the Netherlands, such as St Bartholomew's Hospital in Utrecht or the Holy Ghost Hospital in Leiden.[29] The prices in London are based on the purchases by the Lord Steward, presumably the single most important consumer of sugar in England – a comparable institutional consumer. Thus, representativity does not seem to be a significant factor.

Third, there might have been differences in the quality of what was labelled refined sugar in the primary sources from the two countries. Previous research has shown that contemporary agents distinguished between a quite large number of different types of sugar.[30] In this case, there are several series of data from London, allowing for a comparison of qualities on that market. The price that Westminster Abbey paid for what in their accounts was classified as 'fine' sugar was systematically lower than the price that the Lord Steward paid for refined sugar and much closer to the prices of refined sugar in Amsterdam. Further substantial differences in the price of the refined sugar could also be found based on the number of times the sugar had gone through refining. One can therefore find prices not only for refined sugar on the market, but also 'double refined' and even 'treble refined' sugar (the Lord Steward in general seems to have paid a premium of around 50% more for sugar that was 'treble refined', relative to the price of refined sugar). Even when we take this into account, however, the price difference between the cheaper 'fine' sugar in London and the refined sugar in Amsterdam is substantial for most of the years in the sample.

Fourth, there might have been differences in the when and how sugar was taxed in the two countries. Customs duties levied on British imports of sugar have already been discussed and analysed. There is still the possibility of additional taxation in later stages of the value-chain, explaining the higher price of refined sugar in London. During the seventeenth century, temporary excise taxes had at times been levied on sugar in England, in addition to the import duties. The last such excise expired in 1693.[31] Later attempts to tax sugar seem to have come exclusively in the form of raising duties on sugar imports, as there is no mention in the literature of any other taxes on sugar in England at the time.[32]

All these factors thus find little empirical support or seem insufficient to explain the major differences between the two markets. A fifth potential explanation is economic rents, created by the barriers to entry into this particular link of the value-chain. The legislative governance of the value-chain – British trade policies – was undoubtedly of great importance. This is shown in Table 1. The table reports the absolute price gaps between the markets, that is the price in the Amsterdam subtracted from the price in the London market, using the Muscovado 1 price series (which likely represent pre-tariff prices), as these show the difference in gross earnings for merchants or planters selling sugar on the English and Dutch markets, respectively.[33] The data is reported for a number of benchmark years. The years were selected as the first years with matching price data in both London and Amsterdam after British tariff schedules for sugar were revised, which occurred in 1698, 1705, 1747, 1759 and 1782, followed by several minor revisions in the

Table 1. Price gap and tariffs for sugar, selected years 1701–1800 (£/cwt).

	Muscovado			Refined sugar	
	Price gap London-Amsterdam (£/cwt)	Tariff foreign muscovado (£/cwt)	Tariff home muscovado (£/cwt)	Price gap London-Amsterdam (£/cwt)	Tariff foreign sugar (£/cwt)
1701	−0.35	0.38	0.14	2.05	1.62
1705	−1.12	0.57	0.17	1.43	2.42
1747	.	0.77	0.24	1.14	3.27
1761	−0.22	0.97	0.32	1.05	4.12
1782	−0.97	1.30	0.59	1.54	4.71
1800	−1.00	1.70	1.00	1.45	5.18

Source: tariffs from Deerr, *The History of Sugar*, 430. Price gaps see Figures 2–3.
Note: cwt = hundredweight. 1 cwt = 112 lb.

1787–1805 period. The table also reports the British tariff levels for these benchmark years.

Much of the sugar traded on the Dutch market was imported from French harbours, as Tamira Combrink has shown.[34] British merchants could presumably have purchased French sugar for a similar price if British trade policies had allowed it, yet French exports to Britain were negligible.[35] This is hardly surprising given the data presented in this article: the wholesale prices that the sellers received for their muscovado, after tariffs, were actually lower in London than in Amsterdam for these particular benchmark years, as well as for most other years during the period, as shown in Figure 2. Regardless of tariffs, a planter or merchant earned more from selling their muscovado sugar on the Dutch market than on the English market.

The situation was quite different in the case of refined sugar. Here, there were sizeable price gaps between the London and Amsterdam markets, in the range of £1–2 more per hundredweight in London. Had there been no tariffs on the refined sugar, merchants could likely have exported refined sugar from Amsterdam to London at a profit, depending on the transport costs. British tariffs were – at least from 1705 onwards – set at a clearly prohibitive level, so as to effectively hinder any imports of refined sugar from the continent. At the same time, the Netherlands also imposed protectionist tariffs on the imports of refined sugar.[36] So even though there was a quite significant price gap between the London and Amsterdam markets for refined sugar throughout most of the period (Figure 3), prohibitive tariff policies stopped the prices from converging.

But why were British planters then not able to benefit more from the high British tariff protection against foreign muscovado sugar by charging higher prices for the muscovado sugar? This can potentially be explained by the level of domestic competition within the British Empire in the different links of the colonial sugar value-chain.

In the plantation link, the British West Indies as a whole had a 'monopoly', as some scholars have put it, on the production and sale of raw sugar in Britain. But the term 'monopoly' in this context obfuscates the issue, as there was no single agent with a monopoly position on the market. In reality, there existed a quite large number of British planters operating in the British Caribbean, to a greater or lesser extent competing with each other for a share of the British sugar market. In Barbados, for a long time the leading sugar-producing British island, there were more than 1,000 planters established by the late seventeenth century, a majority of whom were involved in sugar production. On other British Caribbean islands, there were hundreds of planters more. The number of planters running plantations on different islands would certainly fluctuate considerably over time and the crops they cultivated also varied, but in all there might have been hundreds, if not thousands, of planters operating sugar plantations in the British Caribbean at any point in time during the eighteenth century.[37] Several of the most influential planters, organized in the form of the so-called 'West India Interest' were certainly highly active in trying to influence the British Parliament to enact legislation favouring the planters, such as keeping foreign competitors out of the British market.[38] In contrast, they do not seem to have organized collectively to control the market for their own product. Richard Sheridan claims that British sugar planters did not organize cartels among themselves in order to control the prices of their output and other scholars writing about the West India Interest do not mention this issue.[39] Of course, it is possible that the issue has been neglected by previous researchers or that planters attempted to form cartels informally or even in secret, so that their attempts left no traces in surviving documents. What we can say, however, is that there is no suggestion in the literature that they ever tried to do so.

The link at the other end of the sugar value-chain, the refiners, exhibited a very different market structure. Surprisingly, this sector of the European economies has received little attention in previous research. From what we know, there were several hundred sugar refineries on the Continent. In Amsterdam alone, there were around 95 sugar refineries by the middle of the eighteenth century, increasing to around 150 by 1770.[40] There were also sugar refineries established in other Dutch cities, such as Rotterdam.[41] In Britain, by contrast, the competition among sugar refiners was much more limited. By 1660, some 50 refineries had been established, almost all in London. The late seventeenth and early eighteenth centuries saw a growing number of sugar refineries in Britain, primarily in London and Bristol, but also some in Scotland.[42] But by the middle of the eighteenth century, after several new refineries had been established, the total number of sugar refineries in Britain was still only around 120.[43] Dutch sugar refiners might thus have faced much more competition in absolute terms than their British counterparts. The difference is even more striking when we also take into account the fact that Britain in general, and British cities in particular, were much more populous than the Netherlands, so the potential domestic market for refined sugar would have been larger in Britain.[44]

That Britain only had a limited number of refineries is an intriguing fact. It would suggest significant barriers to entry into this link of the value-chain. The capital requirements for investing in a sugar refinery at the time were not enormous, at least not compared with the capital required to establish a plantation. The cost of establishing or acquiring a sugar refinery might have been around £3,000–5,000 in the early eighteenth century, potentially increasing to around £10,000–15,000 by the second half of the century.[45] The cost of establishing or acquiring a sugar plantation in the Caribbean was twice as high: perhaps £5,000–10,000 in the early eighteenth century, rising to £20,000–30,000 later in the century.[46] Capital requirements therefore were less of a barrier to entry into the refining link of the value-chain than they were for establishing or acquiring a plantation. Nonetheless, sugar refining seems to have been much more concentrated with a smaller number of competitors in Britain than it was at least in the Netherlands.

Economies of scale might have created a potential barrier to entrance into sugar refining. This is, however, hard to test as we only have anecdotal data on the sizes of particular refineries in Britain, such as how many workers they employed or how many pans they had, and very little comparable data from Dutch refineries.[47] What available anecdotal evidence there is does not suggest that the British refineries were of a size significantly different from the Dutch ones. The mere fact that so few refineries were able to process all the raw sugar in Britain also suggests that several of the British refineries must have been large. Therefore, if there were any economies of scale in sugar refining at the time, they would not have favoured the Dutch. Furthermore, the techniques employed in sugar refining seem to have been quite similar across the continent and did not change much over the century.[48] Entrepreneurs wanting to establish a new refinery in England might, however, have experienced a barrier when trying to recruit sufficient numbers of skilled workers to operate the refineries. Several of the skilled sugar refiners in England had to be recruited from the continent, in particular from the Netherlands or Germany.[49] This was similar to how many French refineries had to operate during the eighteenth century, a factor that might explain why French refineries had a hard time competing with Dutch ones.[50]

Significantly, there were also deliberate attempts to limit the competition in the market. English sugar refiners actually seem to have banded together into one or more cartels. Unfortunately, very little is yet known about the details of these cartels. Sheridan has noted that some sources refer to how the sugar refineries were aligned into 'combinations' and how those attempted to push down the wholesale price of muscovado in Britain.[51] Walter Stern has also found evidence of a Sugar Refiners' Club in London by the late eighteenth century, which seems to have organized most or even all of the city's sugar refiners. From the little evidence available on this club, the purchasing price of raw sugar seems to have been a key concern. The fragmentary evidence also shows that the club organized temporary sugar boycotts in 1771–72, and again in 1781, in order to reduce the price of the raw sugar.[52] Evidence from

Bristol suggests that there were similar attempts by sugar refiners to organize collectively there.[53] Whether these combinations also attempted, and managed, to create further barriers to entry into this link of the value-chain is not known.

The more concentrated link of sugar refiners, and their collective organization, might thus have helped the latter to promote their interests more effectively than the Caribbean planters. While the planters certainly might have tried to utilize the opportunities that the protectionist policies created, the fact that the sugar refiners and their combinations at the other end of the value-chain had a different interest (in keeping their input prices down), and possibly better ability to further that interest, could go a long way in explaining why the protectionist policies seem to have had little or no discernible effect upon the wholesale price of muscovado sugar. The evidence does, at the same time, also point to another hypothesis: that the sugar refiners and their combinations might have been successful not only in keeping the price of raw sugar down, but also in increasing the price of their refined sugar. This would be in line with what Philip Curtin once noted briefly but never elaborated upon: British sugar refineries, rather than planters, might have been the main beneficiaries of the protectionist trade policies.[54] Put in the terminology of value-chain analysis, they were potentially able to gain considerable economic rents from the governance of a buyer-driven value-chain. If that indeed was the case, this ought to show up in the return on investments in this sector. This could be a fruitful venue for future research.

Conclusion

Many scholars have noted how the protection against foreign muscovado sugar created a safe market for British colonial planters in the Caribbean during the eighteenth century and have asserted that this political-economic context was an important factor driving the planters' profits – in addition, of course, to the exploitation of slaves on the plantations. This article has shown that, for the final consumers, it was primarily the prohibitive tariffs on refined sugar that mattered. The wholesale price of muscovado sugar has been shown to have not been significantly higher on the protected London market than it was on the supposedly free Amsterdam market throughout most of the period under study; for long periods it was actually somewhat lower. By contrast, the price of refined sugar was found to be consistently higher in London than in Amsterdam.

This article argues that a value-chain analysis can help us understand this evidence better. What the analysis shows is that, even though the British tariff structure erected high barriers against competition from foreign planters on the British market, there appears to have been quite a high level of internal competition in the plantation link of the value-chain of British colonial sugar.

Hundreds, if not thousands, of British Caribbean sugar planters competed on the British market. There was, in contrast, much less competition in the later link of sugar refining, both because there was a more concentrated market structure, with a limited number of competitors, in the first place and because these competitors organized collectively into cartels to push down the price of their input: the muscovado sugar sold by the Caribbean planters. The British legislative governance of this value-chain also erected barriers to entry into this link of the value-chain in the form of prohibitive tariffs against foreign imports of refined sugar, thereby stopping foreign sugar refiners from competing with the domestic ones.

This evidence should in no way be interpreted to mean that British planters in the Caribbean were unable to reap economic rents from their exploitation of slave labour. What the evidence suggests is that the planters might not have been more successful at reaping such rents than European planters elsewhere in the Caribbean were, despite the protectionist policies often emphasized in the literature. The beneficiaries of the protectionist policies were instead agents in later links in the value-chain. In this article, it has been suggested that the sugar refiners in Britain might have been the main beneficiaries of such policies. Focusing solely on the magnitude of the profits from the transatlantic slave trade (or from plantations in the Caribbean), as Williams and many scholars following his lead have done, detracts attention from profits or rents made in other parts of same value-chain. Most importantly, it can easily lead to overlooking the interactions between the links in a value-chain: how processes within the value-chain and policies governing the value-chain might have shifted profits from one link of the chain to another.

Notes

1. Eric Eustace Williams, *Capitalism & Slavery* (London: Deutsch, 1964).
2. Raphael Kaplinsky and Mike Morris, *A Handbook for Value-chain Research* (Ottawa: IDRC, 2001), 4.
3. Raphael Kaplinsky, 'Globalisation and Unequalisation: What Can Be Learned from Value-chain Analysis?', *Journal of Development Studies* 37, no. 2 (2000): 124–5; Kaplinsky and Morris, *Value-chain Research*, 29–31; Gary Gereffi and Joonkoo Lee, 'Why the World Suddenly Cares about Global Supply Chains', *Journal of Supply Chain Management* 48, no. 3 (2012): 25–6.
4. Kaplinsky, 'Globalisation and Unequalisation', 122–3, 127–8; Kaplinsky and Morris, *Value-Chain Research*, 25.
5. See e.g. Philip D. Curtin, *The Rise and Fall of the Plantation Complex: Essays in Atlantic History* (Cambridge: Cambridge University Press, 1998); Victor Bulmer-Thomas, *The Economic History of the Caribbean Since the Napoleonic Wars* (Cambridge: Cambridge University Press, 2012), 36.
6. Matthias van Rossum and Karwan Fatah-Black, 'Wat Is Winst? De Economische Impact van de Nederlandse Trans-Atlantische Slavenhande', *Tijdschrift Voor Sociale En Economische Geschiedenis/The Low Countries Journal of Social and*

Economic History 9, no. 1 (2012); Klas Rönnbäck, 'Sweet Business: Quantifying the Value Added in the British Colonial Sugar Trade in the 18th Century', *Revista de Historia Económica/Journal of Iberian and Latin American Economic History (New Series)* 32, no. 2 (2014): 223–45; Karwan Fatah-Black and Matthias Van Rossum, 'Beyond Profitability: The Dutch Transatlantic Slave Trade and Its Economic Impact', *Slavery & Abolition* 36, no. 1 (2015): 63–83; Gerhard de Kok, 'Cursed Capital: The Economic Impact of the Transatlantic Slave Trade on Walcheren around 1770', *Tijdschrift Voor Sociale En Economische Geschiedenis/The Low Countries Journal of Social and Economic History* 13, no. 3 (2016). See also a critique in David Eltis, Pieter C. Emmer, and Frank D. Lewis, 'More than Profits? The Contribution of the Slave Trade to the Dutch Economy: Assessing Fatah-Black and Van Rossum', *Slavery & Abolition* 37, no. 4 (2016): 724–35; and a response in Karwan Fatah-Black and Matthias van Rossum, 'A Profitable Debate?', *Slavery & Abolition* 37, no. 4 (2016): 736–43.

7. Klas Rönnbäck, 'On the Economic Importance of the Slave Plantation Complex to the British Economy during the Eighteenth Century: A Value-Added Approach', *Journal of Global History* 13, no. 3 (November 2018), fig. 6, https://doi.org/10.1017/S1740022818000177.
8. These estimates are certainly crude, based on a number of different sources (which all have different problems of reliability), and a set of assumptions in cases where empirical data was missing. As new research is produced, such estimates can be refined. One example is the new estimates on the value of the output of slaves on Caribbean plantations in Trevor Burnard, Laura Panza and Jeffrey Williamson, 'Living Costs, Real Incomes and Inequality in Colonial Jamaica', *Explorations in Economic History* 71 (January 1, 2019), 55–71, appendix B, https://doi.org/10.1016/j.eeh.2018.09.002. Using data on the output, together with data on the price of slaves in the Caribbean, it has been shown that previous assumptions by David Eltis and Stanley Engerman (also used by Rönnbäck in his estimates) for the value-added on plantations might be reasonable for most of the eighteenth century, but that when the prices of slaves started to increase in the Caribbean – particularly towards the end of the century – the assumptions used in the previous calculations yield too low a value for the inputs at this stage of the value-chain, and therefore inflate the value-added on the plantations slightly (at a level of perhaps 0.3–0.4%). There were, on the other hand, important by-products on many plantations, such as the production of molasses and rum on sugar plantations, which accounted for a most substantial additional value-added to the production on the plantations or further refining in Europe, which are not captured in these estimates – see Richard B. Sheridan, *Sugar and Slavery: An Economic History of the British West Indies 1623–1775* (Baltimore, MD: Johns Hopkins University Press, 1974), 339–42; Frederick Harold Smith, *Caribbean Rum: A Social and Economic History* (Gainesville: University Press of Florida, 2005), fig. 3.8.
9. For some key contributions, see Joseph Inikori, 'English Trade to Guinea' (PhD diss., University of Ibadan, 1973), 424; Roger Anstey, *The Atlantic Slave Trade and British Abolition, 1760–1810* (London: Macmillan, 1975), table 2; Robert Stein, 'The Profitability of the Nantes Slave Trade, 1783–1792', *The Journal of Economic History* 35, no. 4 (1975): 779–93; Robert Stein, *The French Slave Trade in the Eighteenth Century: An Old Regime Business* (Madison: University of Wisconsin Press, 1979), table 10.3; David Richardson, 'Profitability in the Bristol–Liverpool Slave Trade', *Revue Française d'histoire d'outre-Mer* 62, no. 226 (1975): 301–8, https://doi.org/10.3406/outre.1975.1834; David Richardson, 'Profits in the Liverpool Slave Trade: The Accounts of William Davenport, 1757–84', in *Liverpool, the African Slave Trade,*

and Abolition, eds. Roger Anstey and P.E.H. Hair (Liverpool: Historical Society of Lancashire and Cheshire, 1976), 60–90; Joseph Inikori, 'Market Structure and the Profits of the British African Trade in the Late Eighteenth Century', *The Journal of Economic History* 41, no. 4 (1981): 772; Johannes Postma, *The Dutch in the Atlantic Slave Trade, 1600–1815* (Cambridge: Cambridge University Press, 1990), appendix table 25; David Hancock, *Citizens of the World: London Merchants and the Integration of the British Atlantic Community, 1735–1785* (Cambridge: Cambridge University Press, 1995), table AIV.3; Guillaume Daudin, 'Profitability of Slave and Long-Distance Trading in Context: The Case of Eighteenth-Century France', *The Journal of Economic History* 64:1 (2004): 144–71, table 2; Guillaume Daudin, *Commerce et Prospérité: La France au XVIII*[e] *Siècle*, Collection Roland Mousnier, 1621–4129, 19 (Paris: Presses de l'Université Paris-Sorbonne, 2005), tables 25 and 44.

10. Daudin, 'Profitability of Slave and Long-Distance Trading', 147–9.
11. Anstey, *Atlantic Slave Trade*, table 1; Roger Anstey, 'The Volume and Profitability of the British Slave Trade, 1761–1807', in *Race and Slavery in the Western Hemisphere: Quantitative Studies*, eds. Stanley Engerman and Eugene Genovese (Princeton, NJ: Princeton University Press, 1975), 3–32, table 6; Richardson, 'Bristol–Liverpool Slave Trade'; Richardson, 'Profits in the Liverpool Slave Trade'; William Darity, 'The Numbers Game and the Profitability of the British Trade in Slaves', *The Journal of Economic History* 45, no. 3 (1985): 693–703, table 3; Stephen D. Behrendt, *The British Slave Trade, 1785–1807: Volume, Profitability and Mortality* (Madison: University of Wisconsin, 1993), 108; Daudin, 'Profitability of Slave and Long-Distance Trading', 150; Daudin, *Commerce et Prospérité*, table 24; Cheryl S. McWatters, 'Investment Returns and La Traite Négrière: Evidence from Eighteenth-Century France', *Accounting, Business & Financial History* 18, no. 2 (2008): 161–85.
12. R. Keith Aufhauser, 'Profitability of Slavery in the British Caribbean', *The Journal of Interdisciplinary History* 5, no. 1 (1974): 45–67; John R. Ward, 'The Profitability of Sugar Planting in the British West Indies, 1650–1834', *The Economic History Review* 31, no. 2 (1978): 197–213, table 9; Seymour Drescher, *Econocide: British Slavery in the Era of Abolition*, 2nd ed. (Chapel Hill: University of North Carolina Press, 2010), 44; Trevor Burnard, *Planters, Merchants, and Slaves: Plantation Societies in British America, 1650–1820* (Chicago: University of Chicago Press, 2015), 16, 126, 131, 141.
13. Alex Dupuy, 'French Merchant Capital and Slavery in Saint-Domingue', *Latin American Perspectives* 12, no. 3 (1985): 92; J.H. Galloway, *The Sugar Cane Industry: An Historical Geography from Its Origins to 1914* (Cambridge: Cambridge University Press, 1989), 89–90.
14. Stuart Schwartz, *Sugar Plantations in the Formation of Brazilian Society: Bahia, 1550–1835* (Cambridge: Cambridge University Press, 1985), 226.
15. Richard Sutch, 'The Economics of African American Slavery: The Cliometrics Debate', in *Handbook of Cliometrics*, 2nd edn, eds. Claude Diebolt and Michael Haupert (Cham, Switzerland: Springer, 2019), table 1.
16. Richard B. Sheridan, 'The Molasses Act and the Market Strategy of the British Sugar Planters', *The Journal of Economic History* 17, no. 1 (1957): 64; Richard Pares, *Merchants and Planters* (Cambridge: Cambridge University Press, 1960), 26; Philip R.P. Coelho, 'The Profitability of Imperialism: The British Experience in the West Indies 1768–1772', *Explorations in Economic History* 10, no. 3 (1973): 279; Sheridan, *Sugar and Slavery*, 54; Ward, 'The Profitability of Sugar Planting', 197; Kenneth Morgan, *Slavery, Atlantic Trade and the British Economy, 1660–1800* (Cambridge:

Cambridge University Press, 2000), 56; Knick Harley, 'Slavery, the British Atlantic Economy, and the Industrial Revolution', in *The Caribbean and the Atlantic World Economy: Circuits of Trade, Money and Knowledge, 1650–1914*, eds. Adrian Leonard and David Pretel (Basingstoke: Palgrave Macmillan, 2015), 161.

17. See e.g. Walter Stern, 'The London Sugar Refiners Around 1800', *Guildhall Miscellany* 1, no. 3 (1954): 32–3; Sheridan, 'The Molasses Act', 81; Pares, *Merchants and Planters*, 26; Sheridan, *Sugar and Slavery*, 71–3.
18. Coelho, 'The Profitability of Imperialism', 260–6.
19. See for example Pares, *Merchants and Planters*; Richard Grassby, 'English Merchant Capitalism in the Late Seventeenth Century: The Composition of Business Fortunes', *Past & Present* 46 (1970): 87–107; Sheridan, *Sugar and Slavery*, 306–338; Jacob M. Price, 'What Did Merchants Do? Reflections on British Overseas Trade, 1660–1790', *The Journal of Economic History* 49, no. 2 (1989): 267–84; Kenneth Morgan, *Bristol and the Atlantic Trade in the Eighteenth Century* (Cambridge: Cambridge University Press, 1993); Hancock, *Citizens of the World*; Peter A. Coclanis, *The Atlantic Economy during the Seventeenth and Eighteenth Centuries: Organization, Operation, Practice, and Personnel* (Columbia: University of South Carolina Press, 2005); Simon D. Smith, *Slavery, Family and Gentry Capitalism in the British Atlantic: The World of the Lascelles, 1648–1834* (Cambridge: Cambridge University Press, 2006); Nuala Zahedieh, *The Capital and the Colonies: London and the Atlantic Economy 1660–1700* (Cambridge: Cambridge University Press, 2010); Klas Rönnbäck, *Commerce and Colonisation: Studies of Early Modern Merchant Capitalism in the Atlantic Economy* (Gothenburg: University of Gothenburg, 2010).
20. Richard Grassby, 'The Rate of Profit in Seventeenth-Century England', *The English Historical Review* 84, no. 333 (1969): 733; Daudin, 'Profitability of Slave and Long-Distance Trading', 149–50, table 2.
21. Simon D. Smith, 'Merchants and Planters Revisited', *The Economic History Review* 55, no. 3 (2002): 434–65, table 5.
22. See e.g. Joseph Inikori, 'Slavery and the Revolution in Cotton Textile Production in England', *Social Science History* 13, no. 4 (January 1989): 343–79, https://doi.org/10.1017/S0145553200020514; Ronald Bailey, 'The Other Side of Slavery: Black Labor, Cotton, and Textile Industrialization in Great Britain and the United States', *Agricultural History* 68, no. 2 (1994): 35–50; David Eltis and Stanley L. Engerman, 'The Importance of Slavery and the Slave Trade to Industrializing Britain', *The Journal of Economic History* 60, no. 1 (2000): 123–44; Joseph Inikori, *Africans and the Industrial Revolution in England: A Study in International Trade and Economic Development* (New York: Cambridge University Press, 2002); Giorgio Riello, *Cotton: The Fabric That Made the Modern World* (Cambridge: Cambridge University Press, 2013); Harley, 'Slavery, the British Atlantic Economy, and the Industrial Revolution'.
23. For some rare examples, see e.g. Stern, 'The London Sugar Refiners'; Richard Pares, 'The London Sugar Market, 1740–1769', *The Economic History Review* 9, no. 2 (1956): 254–70; Thomas C. Smout, 'The Early Scottish Sugar Houses, 1660–1720', *The Economic History Review* 14, no. 2 (1961): 240–53; Kenneth Morgan, 'Sugar Refining in Bristol', in *From Family Firms to Corporate Capitalism: Essays in Business and Industrial History in Honour of Peter Mathias*, eds. Kristine Bruland and Patrick O'Brien (Oxford, UK: Clarendon Press, 1998), 139–69; Zahedieh, *The Capital and the Colonies*, 218–20.
24. Maud Villeret, *Le Goût de l'or Blanc: Le Sucre en France au XVIIIe siècle* (Rennes: Presses Universitaires de Rennes, 2017), 225.

25. Nicolaas Wilhelmus Posthumus, *Nederlandsche Prijsgeschiedenis. D. 1, Goederenprijzen Opde Beurs van Amsterdam 1585–1914, Wisselk Oersen Te Amsterdam 1609–1914* (Leiden: Brill, 1943), table 60; Tamira Combrink, 'From French Harbours to German Rivers: European Distribution of Sugar by the Dutch in the Eighteenth Century', in *La Diffusion des Produits Ultramarins en Europe, XVIe-XVIIIe siècle*, eds. Marguerite Martin and Maud Villeret (Rennes, France: Presses Universitaires de Rennes, 2017), 48–50.
26. Combrink, 'From French Harbours', 45, 48.
27. Villeret, *Le Goût de l'or Blanc*, fig. 3.
28. If the London prices reported in the sources represent wholesale prices already including tariffs, the mark-up on the London market would be even larger than estimated in Figure 4. The differences between the two markets would consequently also be larger.
29. Nicolaas Wilhelmus Posthumus, *Inquiry into the History of Prices in Holland*, vol. 2 (Leiden: Brill, 1964), tables 117 and 263.
30. Zahedieh, *The Capital and the Colonies*, 220; Villeret, *Le Goût de l'or Blanc*, 113–14.
31. Stephen Dowell, *A History of Taxation and Taxes in England from the Earliest Times to the Year 1885*, vol. 4 (London: Longmans, 1888), 19.
32. Dowell, *A History of Taxation*, 20–3. See also, Peter Mathias and Patrick O'Brien, 'Taxation in Britain and France, 1715–1810: A Comparison of the Social and Economic Incidence of Taxes Collected for the Central Governments', *Journal of European Economic History* 5, no. 3 (1976): 617–20; Patrick K. O'Brien, 'The Political Economy of British Taxation, 1660–1815', *The Economic History Review* 41, no. 1 (1988): 1–32, table 5; John V. Beckett and Michael Turner, 'Taxation and Economic Growth in Eighteenth-Century England', *The Economic History Review* 43, no. 3 (1990): 391–5.
33. If the data reported in the sources represents prices that include tariffs, the prices that sellers on the British market received would be lower – and consequently the price gap between the two markets would also be lower than is indicated in Table 1.
34. Combrink, 'From French Harbours'.
35. Villeret, *Le Goût de l'or Blanc*, 72.
36. Combrink, 'From French Harbours', 45.
37. Richard Dunn, *Sugar and Slaves: The Rise of the Planter Class in the English West Indies, 1624–1713* (New York: W.W. Norton, 1972), table 6; David Watts, *The West Indies: Patterns of Development, Culture and Environmental Change since 1492* (Cambridge: Cambridge University Press, 1987), 328–47; Burnard, *Planters, Merchants, and Slaves*, 164.
38. Lillian M. Penson, 'The London West India Interest in the Eighteenth Century', *The English Historical Review* 36, no. 143 (1921): 373–92; Sheridan, *Sugar and Slavery*, 54–74; Andrew O'Shaughnessy, 'The Formation of a Commercial Lobby: The West India Interest, British Colonial Policy and the American Revolution', *The Historical Journal* 40, no. 1 (1997): 71–95; David Beck Ryden, *West Indian Slavery and British Abolition 1783–1807* (Cambridge: Cambridge University Press, 2009), 40–82.
39. Sheridan, *Sugar and Slavery*, 69, 220.
40. Deerr, *The History of Sugar*, 453–4.
41. Marjolein't Hart and Hilde Greefs, 'Sweet and Sour: Economic Turmoil and Resilience of the Sugar Sector in Antwerp and Rotterdam, 1795–1815', *BMGN – The Low Countries Historical Review* 133, no. 2 (2018), 18.
42. Morgan, 'Sugar Refining in Bristol', 144; Smout, 'The Early Scottish Sugar Houses'.
43. Deerr, *The History of Sugar*, 458–9; Pares, 'The London Sugar Market', 256; Sheridan, *Sugar and Slavery*, 29–30.

44. Jonathan Fink-Jensen, 'Total Population' (Clio Infra, 2015), http://hdl.handle.net/10622/SNETZV; Jonathan Fink-Jensen, 'Total Urban Population' (Clio Infra, 2015), http://hdl.handle.net/10622/KICLW5.
45. Smout, 'The Early Scottish Sugar Houses', 248; Morgan, 'Sugar Refining in Bristol', 149.
46. Russell Menard, *Sweet Negotiations: Sugar, Slavery, and Plantation Agriculture in Early Barbados* (Charlottesville: University of Virginia Press, 2006), 129–36.
47. Smout, 'The Early Scottish Sugar Houses' 248; Morgan, 'Sugar Refining in Bristol', 144, 149; Hart and Greefs, 'Sweet and Sour', 13, 18.
48. Villeret, *Le Goût de l'or Blanc*, 172–3.
49. See e.g. Smout, 'The Early Scottish Sugar Houses', 248–9; Morgan, 'Sugar Refining in Bristol', 152.
50. Villeret, *Le Goût de l'or Blanc*, 131–2; Maud Villeret, 'L'art Délicat Du Raffinage Du Sucre: La Discrète Évolution Des Techniques (France, Fin XVIIe-Fin XVIIIe Siècle)', *Artefact* 6 (2018).
51. Sheridan, 'The Molasses Act', 66, 73–4; Richard B. Sheridan, 'Planters and Merchants: The Oliver Family of Antigua and London 1716–1784', *Business History* 13:2 (1971), 108; Sheridan, *Sugar and Slavery*, 71–3.
52. Stern, 'The London Sugar Refiners', 31–4.
53. Morgan, 'Sugar Refining in Bristol', 150.
54. Philip D. Curtin, 'The British Sugar Duties and West Indian Prosperity', *The Journal of Economic History* 14, no. 2 (1954): 158, https://doi.org/10.1017/S002205070006544X.

Acknowledgements

The author would like to thank the participants and the audience at the session 'Europe and Slavery: Estimating the Share of Slave-Based Activities in European Economies, 1500–1850' at the World Economic History Congress, Boston, 2018 for comments on the research underlying this article. The author would also like to thank Matthias van Rossum and Tamira Combrink and an anonymous reviewer for most helpful feedback on a draft version of this article.

Disclosure statement

No potential conflict of interest was reported by the author(s).

OPEN ACCESS

Slavery and the Dutch economy, 1750–1800

Pepijn Brandon and Ulbe Bosma

ABSTRACT
This article presents the first methodologically grounded calculation of the weight of Atlantic slave-based activities in the Dutch economy of the second half of the eighteenth century. In this period, the Dutch Republic was one of the most developed commercial societies in Europe. The import, processing and export of slave-produced goods such as sugar, coffee and tobacco played an important role in this economy. In 1770, 5.2% of the GDP of the Dutch Republic and 10.36% of the GDP of its richest province Holland was based on Atlantic slavery. In this year, 19% of Dutch imports and (re-) exports consisted of goods produced by the enslaved in the Atlantic. These high percentages were dependent on the prominent role that the Dutch Republic and the province of Holland in particular played in Atlantic slavery-based commodity chains. These chains ran from the provisioning of slave ships in the Dutch Republic, through the slave trade, to the plantations, the transport of tropical products to Europe, their processing in the Dutch Republic, to their final export to the European hinterland. As much as 40% of all the growth of the economy of Holland in the decades around 1770 can be traced back to slavery.

Introduction

In this article, we assess for the first time the importance of late eighteenth-century Atlantic slave-based activities to the Dutch Republic's gross domestic product.[1] The question of how much European societies gained from their involvement in various aspects of Atlantic slavery has long been contentious, both in academic journals and in society more broadly, in the Netherlands and internationally. Some of the issues relating to the Dutch Republic are common to the debates that followed the publication of Eric Williams' seminal *Capitalism and Slavery*.[2] These centred on how slavery contributed to capitalism in general and whether the gains from the slave trade were so great that they could be identified as the necessary condition for Britain's ascendancy as the world's earliest industrialising nation. The debates spilled over to the Netherlands even though the Dutch Republic, like its successor the Kingdom of the Netherlands, was not an early industrialiser. Yet the discussion of capitalism and slavery is relevant for the Dutch Republic, which left a large imprint on the history of pre-industrial capitalism, and throughout the early modern period had an advanced maritime and (financial) service sector. Moreover, Dutch involvement in Atlantic slavery stretched over two and a half centuries.[3] It encompassed the slave trade and plantation production in Atlantic colonies, and in the course of the eighteenth century went through successive bouts of rapid growth.[4]

The debate on the importance of slavery in the Dutch Republic's economy stands out for the almost complete absence of discussion about which analytical framework should be applied and which data examined.[5] This is in marked contrast to the level of sophistication with which economic historians have addressed the question of slavery's significance in the British economy. The only partial exception to this has been the debate on the profitability and potential impact of the slave trade on the Dutch economy, which has recently been revived in an influential article by Karwan Fatah-Black and Matthias van Rossum.[6] However, as we will show, while it was obviously of crucial importance to the existence of the Atlantic slavery system, the slave trade played only a minor role in the Dutch metropolitan economy. David Eltis, Pieter C. Emmer and Frank D. Lewis have estimated that its contribution to Dutch national income was as small as 0.5%.[7] We will show why the slave trade is neither a good indicator of the total contribution of slave-based activities to the Dutch economy, nor a reliable proxy for the change in this share over time. General conclusions about the importance of slavery for the economy based on the profitability or even the overall size of the slave trade are partial at best and misleading at worst. A much more comprehensive approach is needed to make meaningful estimates of the contribution of slave-based activities to the Dutch economy.

Interestingly, an attempt to comprehensively estimate the total income from slave-based activities was undertaken in the 1730s, although it only examined the city of Amsterdam. In an anonymous memorandum, which can now be found in the archive of the mayors of Amsterdam, the author estimated that Suriname, the Netherlands' most important Atlantic plantation colony, contributed fl.2,238,755 per year to the city's income. This figure was based on calculations that included income from the trade in sugar, coffee and cacao, the domestic processing industry and a wide range of provisioning industries for the overseas colony and for the merchant fleet serving the trade.[8] Of course, the document only pertains to a single colony and a single city, and the estimates made by this eighteenth-century observer should be approached with caution, since his explicit aim was to solicit municipal support for those involved in the Suriname trade. Nevertheless, the document shows that contemporaries were well aware that the economic importance of slave-based activities went well beyond the slave trade, and even the slave trade together with the trade in commodities that were produced on the plantations. The author's conclusion was that 'no working man can be found in Amsterdam … who does not earn a piece of bread from this colony'.[9] This bold hypothesis has important repercussions. While a large section of the Dutch population never came into direct contact with plantation slavery, many branches of the economy as a whole or in part revolved around commodities that were produced by slaves in the Atlantic world or were produced for the upkeep of plantations or the slave trade. Carefully estimating the scope of all the activities involved in moving, processing and retailing the goods derived from the forced labour performed by the enslaved in the Atlantic world will allow us to see much more clearly in what ways the gains from slavery percolated through the Dutch economy. By linking this to known estimates of Dutch GDP in this period, we will gain a better sense of the economic weight of Atlantic slave-based activities and also improve our understanding of the distribution of slave-based revenues in different sectors of the Dutch economy. For a substantial number of wage labourers, earning the 'piece of bread' mentioned by the anonymous author might have connected them knowingly or unknowingly to the enslaved in Suriname and other Dutch colonies, as well as in non-Dutch colonies such as Saint Domingue, which was one of the main suppliers of slave-produced goods to the Dutch economy until the enslaved revolted in 1791 and brought an end to the trade. For a far smaller segment of the population, Atlantic slavery was not just the source of a piece of bread, but of great fortune. A significant part of the eighteenth-century Dutch elite was actively engaged in financing, insuring, organising and enabling the slave system, and drew much wealth from it.

This article presents a calculation of the proportion of slave-based activities in Dutch GDP for 1770. In order to do this, we have related our data to the per-sector estimates of the GDP of Holland in the early modern period that were published in 2011 by Jan Luiten van Zanden and Bas van Leeuwen.[10] The result is a verifiable assessment of the economic weight of Atlantic slave-based activities in the Dutch economy. We conclude that slave-based activities contributed as much as 5.2% to Dutch GDP in 1770, and as much as 10.36% in its richest province of Holland. Such amounts are in no sense marginal or small. A recent research report from economists at the Erasmus University in Rotterdam concluded that Rotterdam Harbour, including all dependent logistics, industry and financial services, represented 6.2% of Dutch GDP in 2017.[11] Economists of the US Bureau of Economic Analysis have estimated that the digital economy contributed 6.5% to American GDP in 2016, concluding that this made the sector a 'notable contributor to the overall economy'.[12] The large contribution of slave-based activities to Dutch GDP becomes less surprising when we consider that a staggering 19% (expressed in value) of the Dutch

Republic's trade in 1770 consisted of Atlantic slave-produced goods such as sugar, coffee, or indigo, either as raw products or re-exported after undergoing domestic processing. An extensive annex accompanying this article, published on the *Slavery & Abolition* website, provides the underlying data, such as the trade estimates just mentioned, as well as the methodological basis for calculating contributions to GDP. In the article, we will situate our approach in international debates, show the flaws in earlier speculations about the role of slavery in the Dutch economy, give a broad overview of our methods and a sectoral breakdown of the outcomes, and finally examine what our calculations for the single year 1770 can tell us in qualitative terms about the potential impact of slave-based activities on the development of the Dutch economy in the second half of the eighteenth century.

The international debate

There is in fact not a single debate about the economic impact of Atlantic slavery. Under the umbrella of this large problem, historians have crossed swords over a wide variety of issues, such as the significance of the trade in colonial goods for domestic economic growth; the relationship between investments in the plantation system and European industrial capital formation and capital accumulation; slavery's impact on technology, institutions, geopolitics, international finance and systems of accounting; and how slavery in the long run affected the development of the modern world system.[13] Each of these debates has been driven at least in part by public concerns, related to major questions about how contemporary societies are influenced by and account for their historic involvement in Atlantic slavery.[14] To address these questions meaningfully, it is necessary to establish a base line for the economic weight of slave-based activities within the economy as a whole. For this reason, we focus here on a single question: the contribution of Atlantic slavery to Dutch GDP. We do not intend to suggest that calculating this contribution is sufficient to answer any of the major questions raised here, but merely offer the calculation as a crucial piece in a larger puzzle.

The debate on the importance of the slave trade and the plantation sector for the domestic economy of European nations is in itself wide-ranging. Slave-based activities created commodity chains that stretched across the globe and had a lasting social and economic impact on societies in Africa, the Americas, Europe and Asia. A substantial part of the revenues from these chains ended up in European societies. After all, the entire gigantic edifice of the transatlantic slave trade and American slave-societies was set up primarily to serve the economic interest of merchants and investors in the leading imperial states. Almost 250 years ago, in the 1770s, Edward Long applied his embryonic understanding of commodity chains when he assessed the benefits of the West Indies for the British economy. He made some rough reconstructions of the income drawn from capital transfers and from different segments of the commodity chain, including the slave trade, freighting of goods produced by the enslaved, the insurance sector and brokerage. On this basis, he arrived at the conclusion that in 1773 the net revenue reaped by Britain from the Jamaican plantation economy was £1,249,164.[15] Almost two centuries later, Long's calculations were considered by Richard Sheridan in his article 'The Wealth of Jamaica in the Eighteenth Century', resulting in a debate with Robert Paul Thomas – who disputed the claim that Britain had made substantial gains from its West Indies possessions.[16]

This debate ended in confusion, partly because of questions about whether or not the impressive tax revenues, duties, bounties and military expenditure in defending the precious West Indies had to be included in the equation. The answers of course depend on how national income is defined. Before Sheridan, Ralph Davis had already argued that the rise in manufacturing output in Britain was undergirded by the country's imperial expansion. He pointed out that while the exports to the European continent stagnated, the share of exports to Africa and the Americas in Britain's total exports more than doubled in the first seventy years of the eighteenth century.[17] Sheridan further submitted that 'the redirection of trade from continental Europe to the American Colonies … gave access to new sources of primary products, new markets, new fields of investment – in sum, the innovations … were both cause and effect of the fundamental locational shift in the world's economy'.[18]

The debate between Sheridan and Thomas demonstrated how difficult it is to reach consensus on what should be included when comparing incomes derived from slavery with the size of the national economy. Obviously, the very attempt also raised a question about the extent to which the nation is the proper framework within which to capture the economic significance of a phenomenon that always transcended national and imperial borders. Stanley Engerman chose a rather modest approach by limiting himself to the profitability of the slave trade. Instead of looking at the British economy as a whole, he singled out British capital formation as the crucial factor. While he intended to 'comment on the Williams thesis', he had to admit that Williams himself had adopted a broader perspective in which the slave trade was just one indispensable element of the broader slave-based Atlantic economic complex.[19] Engerman concluded that the contribution of the profits of the slave trade to British national income did not exceed 0.5%, although at their peak they represented 10.8% of annual savings.[20] As William Darity observed in 1990, the way in which Engerman narrowed the debate over the impact of slavery to the slave trade would have a lasting effect.[21] It not only informed the way economic historians in the following decades would approach the British Atlantic but also found many followers among historians of other Atlantic empires, including the Dutch.[22]

In 1983, Barbara Solow published a critical appraisal of both Engerman's and Thomas' downplaying of Britain's gains from its Caribbean colonies. While Engerman had claimed that even if the slave trade had contributed 1% to

British national income, which he emphasised was an extremely generous assumption, it was still economically insignificant. Solow replied that this 1% of national income equalled 39% of total commercial and industrial investment.[23] She also discarded Thomas' insistence on opportunity costs by showing that the £30–37 million invested in the West Indies would only have produced 15% of the profits generated in the Atlantic slave complex had they been invested in England.[24] According to Solow, the real issue at stake was a much wider one, namely that 'Slavery made more profits for investment, a larger national income for the Empire, and a pattern of trade which strengthened the comparative advantage of the home country in industrial commodities.'[25] Following up on this suggestion, Joseph Inikori showed that in the crucial period from the 1750s to 1776, the entire growth of Britain's exports could be attributed to Atlantic exports and even compensated for declining exports to European markets.[26] Inikori also hinted at the obvious fact that the relationship between Atlantic slavery and Britain's socio-economic development was multidirectional. The tripling of West Indies imports into Britain between the 1740s and 1776 coincided with rapid change within British society itself. The growing West Indies economy, argued Richardson in an article that appeared side by side with Inikori's, may have been responsible for almost half of the growth of Britain's domestically produced exports, and industrially produced goods in particular, in this period.[27]

The points made by Inikori and Richardson prefigured a new turn in this debate, which resulted from a revaluation of the old question about whether trade with the 'periphery' mattered to the development of the British domestic economy in the first place. In a seminal article from 1982, Patrick O'Brien denied this, on the basis of the allegedly small size of oceanic trade as a proportion of total economic activities in Britain.[28] However, O'Brien explicitly reconsidered this conclusion in his later work, admitting that imperialism and mercantilism might have contributed significantly to the British economy. He now emphasised that the exploitation of the Americas 'should not be designated as "peripheral"'.[29] This conclusion has been shared more recently by historians who point out the spectacular growth of Atlantic trade during the early modern period, and the uneven distribution of the benefits of this growth (in terms of both direct revenues and institutional effects) for different societies in Europe. Thus, Acemoglu, Johnson and Robinson argued that:

> between 1500 and 1850, the growth of nations with access to the Atlantic, and the growth of Atlantic ports, account for most of the differential growth of Western Europe relative to Eastern Europe. It therefore appears that the rise of Europe between 1500 and 1850 was largely the rise of Atlantic Europe and the rise of Atlantic ports.[30]

Nuala Zahedieh gave a very different spin on the institutional impact of the Atlantic economy, but came to similar conclusions for the long-term economic effects.[31] Others, such as Klas Rönnbäck, have reopened the debate on the contribution of slavery to British GDP in ways that are quite similar to the one explored in this article, examining the different links in the commodity chain.[32] One positive side effect of their approach is that it turns the debate outward from myopic discussions on the relationship between Britain and its Atlantic complex towards other European countries that profited from Atlantic slave-based activities. A narrowing of the debate on slavery's relationship to capitalism to the question of its relationship to the Industrial Revolution in Britain easily obscures the many other forms in which European nations, and in a wider sense the development of capitalism as not only a system of production but also of trade, finance and societal organisation, potentially benefited from Atlantic slavery.[33] The Dutch example, in which Atlantic trade did not stimulate an Industrial Revolution but, as we will argue, was pivotal to the prevention of economic collapse in the late eighteenth century and to reorienting the Netherlands' traditionally strong commercial sector to gain from new international opportunities, not only builds upon but also helps to further internationalize these debates.

Slavery and the Dutch economy: slave trade or Atlantic trade?

Several Dutch authors have reflected on the importance for the Dutch economy in the late eighteenth century of either the slave trade alone or the Atlantic trade in its entirety.[34] However, so far no one has attempted to clearly delineate what economic activities should be considered to be slave-based and how these activities should be weighed against each other. Furthermore, the debate so far has lacked explicit methodological parameters that allow for clear judgements on what to compare, how to compare it and the conclusions to draw from this. Finally, the framing of the Dutch debate in terms directly derived from the British debate has allowed some authors to shortcut any meaningful discussion. These authors content themselves with the simplistic argument that since no Industrial Revolution occurred in the Netherlands and since the slave sector did not continue to grow unabatedly throughout the period of its existence, slavery could not have contributed to the development of Dutch capitalism.[35]

While discarding the industrialisation nexus that plays such a prominent role in the British debate, Dutch authors copied without further scrutiny the methodologically flawed exclusive focus on the slave trade popular among some writers on the British case. This is hard to understand, because despite the indispensable role of the slave trade in maintaining a particular system of exploitation of forced labour in the plantation colonies, the revenues drawn from the slave trade, especially in the Dutch case, formed neither a large component of the totality of slave-based economic activities nor a good indication of their development. The economic significance of the slave trade can only be appraised properly by situating it within a much larger economic complex, which ultimately revolved around the production of tropical commodities.[36] It is therefore not surprising that the main revenues from slave-based activities were actually drawn from the forced labour that was performed year in, year out by the enslaved, not from the initial act of their enslavement and transportation to the New World. The human misery on the plantations for many Europeans remained hidden behind the impersonal fluctuations in commodity prices and the technicalities of financial constructions, as the plantations were clearly situated far away in overseas colonies. Nevertheless, the figures presented in the next sections demonstrate that the trade in slave-produced sugar, coffee and other commodities constituted the main route through which slavery contributed to the Dutch economy.

The implication is that the development of slave trade profits, revenues based on the gross margin obtained on the sale of slaves, or even the total turnover in the slave trade and its subsidiaries, cannot reliably indicate the proportion of slave-based activities in the economy as a whole. This was demonstrably the case in the Netherlands, where during the eighteenth century the size of the slave trade remained relatively stable, while the total value of the trade in slave-produced commodities grew rapidly (see Figure 1). Any attempt to

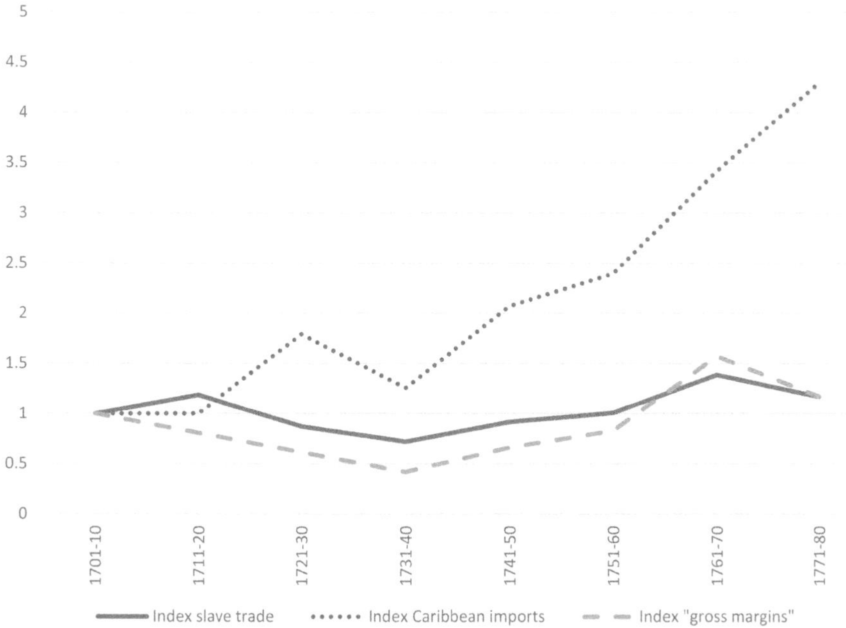

Figure 1. Development Dutch slave trade, revenues of the slave trade, and value Dutch West Indian imports compared (index figures, 1701–10 = 100).

Sources: slave trade index based on http://www.slavevoyages.org/ (accessed February 21, 2019), revenues from the slave trade based on 'gross margin' as calculated in Karwan Fatah-Black and Matthias van Rossum, 'Beyond Profitability. The Dutch Transatlantic Slave Trade and its Economic Impact', Slavery & Abolition 36, no. 1 (2015): 63–83; value Dutch Caribbean imports per decade Wim Klooster, *Illicit riches. Dutch trade in the Caribbean, 1648–1795* (Leiden: KITLV Press, 1998), 176.

estimate the economic contribution of slavery by generalising from slave trade data therefore inevitably produces partial results at best. Fatah-Black and Van Rossum provided a welcome reprise of the debate on the significance of slave trade revenues for the Dutch economy by using gross margins in slave sales rather than the net profits of slave-trading companies. Despite using this wider lens, the authors showed that the revenue obtained from the slave trade accrued to no more than fl.63–79 million over the entire period 1595–1829.[37] In their response to the article, Eltis, Emmer and Lewis alleged that this figure confirmed their view of slavery's significance for the Dutch economy as marginal. However, they too easily assumed that since the revenues from the slave trade were relatively small, the overall contribution of slavery must have been rather limited as well.[38] Indeed, no correlation exists between the gross revenue harvested from the slave trade, calculated according to Fatah-Black and Van Rossum's method, and the import of slave-produced commodities from the Dutch West Indies (see Table 1), the major area from which slave-based income was derived. Nevertheless, Fatah-Black and Van Rossum were completely right in assigning to the slave trade an economically strategic role in the entirety of the Atlantic system, an argument that is brushed aside by Eltis, Emmer and Lewis. This is plainly shown by the correlation between the numbers of slaves who disembarked in the Dutch Guianas and the value of imports from the Dutch West Indies, especially when a time lag is factored in to account for the fact that an increase in the volume of labour power wrung out of the enslaved population in the Caribbean only fully translated into more produce after several years (see Figure 2 and Table 1). Furthermore, Fatah-Black and Van Rossum's critics considerably undermined their own case by providing a series of seemingly random speculations, which led to the conclusion that 'neither the slave trade nor the whole Atlantic slave system' could possibly have been of importance to the Dutch economy.[39]

Quite separate from these attempts to derive conclusions about the impact of slavery on the Dutch economy from slave trade data, there is a growing literature on the increased importance of the Atlantic sector as a whole for the Dutch economy in the second half of the eighteenth century. Unsurprisingly, the conclusions from this literature come much closer to ours, since it includes not

Table 1. Correlation between slave trade and value of West Indian trade.

		95% critical values, Pearson test
Slave trade and value West Indian trade, 1701–1780 (decades)	0.54	N-2=6; 0.707 No significant correlation
'Gross margin' in the slave trade and value West Indian trade, 1701–1780 (decades)	0.65	N-2=6; 0.707 No significant correlation
Number of slaves entering Dutch Guyana and value West Indian trade, 1701–1780 (decades)	0.80	N-2=6; 0.707 Significant correlation
Number of slaves entering Dutch Guyana and value West Indian trade, 1711–1780, factoring in 10 years' time lag	0.94	N-2=5; 0.754 Strong and significant correlation

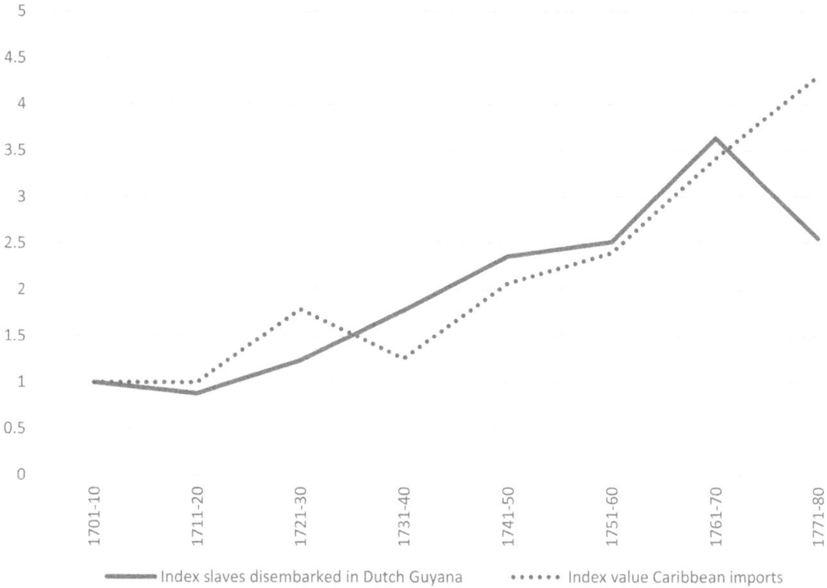

Figure 2. Numbers of slaves disembarked in Dutch Guyanas and value Dutch West Indian imports compared (Index figures, 1701–10 = 100).

Sources: slave trade index based on http://www.slavevoyages.org/ (accessed February 21, 2019), value Dutch Caribbean imports Wim Klooster, *Illicit riches. Dutch trade in the Caribbean, 1648–1795* (Leiden: KITLV Press, 1998), 176.

only the slave trade, but also all trade in slave-produced commodities arriving in Dutch ports, and often slave-produced commodities re-exported to the European hinterland. Despite being incomplete and problematic, the availability of custom records, as well as the contemporary estimates of Dutch foreign trade by Cornelis van der Oudermeulen, make it possible to gauge the great importance that Atlantic trade routes had for the Dutch Republic by the second half of the eighteenth century.[40] Table 2 summarises the available estimates of the value of imports and exports on the different sea routes at different moments between 1770 and the mid-1780s.[41] Van der Oudermeulen and De Vries and Van der Woude took direct Atlantic trade to have constituted around 10% of the total value of Dutch trade at the time. De Vries and Van der Woude concluded that by the end of the eighteenth century direct trade with the Atlantic slightly exceeded that of the Dutch East India Company, at fl.24 million, a figure that De Vries later corrected upward to fl.28.4 million.[42] Welling's reconstruction based on the tax on ships docking in Amsterdam's harbour (the *paalgeld*) showed that the Atlantic played an even greater role for that city. In Amsterdam, almost a quarter of all imports in 1771 were direct imports from Africa and the Americas.[43]

One point that deserves considerable emphasis is that the growing importance of Atlantic trade within the overall trade of the Dutch Republic did not just depend on the increasing output of the Dutch Atlantic slave colonies. By

Table 2. Different estimates for the total size of Dutch trade, ca. 1770.

	VDO		dV&vdW		ENT	
	c.1780 Neth.		1770s Neth.		c.1780 Neth.	
Region	Value (*f* mln)	%	Value (*f* mln)	%	Value (*f* mln)	%
Europe: Sont						
Import	27		22			
Export	17		17			
Total	44	15.4	39	15.7		
Europe: Rest						
Import			73			
Export			55			
Total	143.3	50.1	128	51.7	135.0[b]	44.2
River trade						
Import			10			
Export			20			
Total	34	11.9	30	12.1	62.7[c]	20.5
East Indies						
Import	20.5		20			
Export	14.5		2			
Total	35	12.2	22	8.9	37.9	12.4
Atlantic						
Import	22		22.4			
Export	7.5		6			
Total	29.5	10.3	28.4[a]	11.4	70[d]	22.9
Total	285.8	100	247.4[a]	100	305.6	100

[a]De Vries made an upward readjustment of the earlier estimates for Atlantic trade made by him and Van der Woude, which is included here.
[b]Includes the Sound trade.
[c]Marked as 'not specified'.
[d]The reason why Victor Enthoven's figures for colonial trade are such outliers, is that he counts European imports and re-exports of colonial goods as part of the totals of Asiatic and Atlantic trade.
Sources: Cornelis van der Oudermeulen, *'Iets dat tot voordeel der deelgenooten van de Oost-Indische Compagnie en tot nut van ieder ingezeten van dit gemeenebest kan strekken', included in G.K. van Hogendorp, Stukken raakende den tegenwoordigen toestand der Bataafsche bezittingen in Oost-Indië* (The Hague / Delft 1801) (excluding his figures for gold and coin exported to settle trade imbalances); George M. Welling, *The prize of neutrality. Trade relations between Amsterdam and North America 1771-1817. A study in computational history* (Amsterdam: AUP, 1998); Jan de Vries and Ad van der Woude, *The First Modern Economy. Success, Failure, and Perseverance of the Dutch Economy, 1500–1815* (Cambridge: Cambridge University Press, 1997), 499; Jan de Vries, 'The Dutch Atlantic Economies', in *The Atlantic Economy during the Seventeenth and Eighteenth Centuries. Organization, Operation, Practice, and Personnel*, ed. Peter A. Coclanis (Columbia: University of South Carolina Press, 2005), 1–29, 28n63; Victor Enthoven, 'An Assessment of Dutch Transatlantic Commerce, 1585–1817', in *Riches from Atlantic Commerce. Dutch Transatlantic Trade and Shipping, 1585–1817*, ed. Johannes Postma and Victor Enthoven (Leiden / Boston: Brill, 2003), 385–445, 444.

1770, the Dutch imported over fl.8 million worth of sugar and coffee from French ports. In addition, large amounts of French plantation products reached the Dutch Republic through its Caribbean entrepôts St Eustatius and Curaçao. Combined, these two routes successfully linked the Dutch trade sector to the massive expansion of slavery in Saint Domingue, which continued until the early 1790s when the revolution of the enslaved on the French part of that island ended slavery. Before that time, Dutch sugar mills processed tens of millions of pounds of sugar from the French Caribbean, which were then exported over the Rhine and through the Sound to the German and Eastern European 'slavery hinterlands'.[44] Coffee and indigo flowed through the Dutch Republic via the same trans-imperial routes, while the Dutch also imported tobacco produced by slaves in the British colonies, gold and tobacco produced in Brazil and small amounts of goods from the Danish West Indies. At the same time, the Dutch Republic exported cheese, gin and provisions for the slave trade in competing European nations. The value of all the different components of slave-based trade combined amounted to a sum of fl.57.3 million, more than 23% of all the Dutch trade in 1770. By far the largest part, equalling 19% of the value of all Dutch foreign trade, consisted of the import and re-export of sugar, coffee, tobacco and other commodities produced on Atlantic slave plantations. The Dutch moved slave-based goods not only to and from their own colonies, but all over the Atlantic basin and beyond.

However, trade statistics alone cannot answer the question about the weight of this sector within the economy. For this, it is necessary to find a procedure to relate the income derived from slave-based activities to the size of the economy as a whole. We have chosen to measure this weight in terms of GDP in current prices. The following sections explain the reason for this choice, outlines the procedure followed by us and presents our outcomes.

Methodology: slave-based activities and the Dutch GDP

GDP and GDP growth are frequently used measures of economic performance. GDP refers to 'the total market value of all final goods and services produced within a country in a given period of time (usually a calendar year)'.[45] GDP differs from Gross National Income (GNI), the other frequently used measure for the size of the national economy, in that it does not take into account the income that residents of a country draw from businesses they own outside that country. This is obviously important in the case of slavery, where plantation owners in the Netherlands drew substantial dividends from their investments and interest payments on their loans, while frequently also playing a key role in the trade in plantation goods. However, since so little is known about the annual return on plantation investments accruing to plantation owners and investors in the Netherlands, the extent to which capital was written off owing to the financial crisis of 1773 and the net results of Dutch foreign investments outside the plantation sector, GNI does not seem a suitable measure at this stage.[46]

No economic measure is perfect, and very few who know about the technical problems and ideologically loaded choices involved in the construction of a modern GDP, let alone a historical figure, would proclaim it to be the holy grail of national accounting.[47] The reason for relating slave-based activities to GDP in this article is that it provides a way to make meaningful estimates of the proportion of the Dutch *domestic* economy that revolved around Atlantic slavery from the moment a Dutch merchant came into possession of these goods at the place of production. One of the obvious downsides of using GDP as an indicator is that by its very nature it obscures the labour of the enslaved themselves on the plantation, since GDP does not account for production that takes place beyond a country's borders.[48] This is in part a technical issue (different economic indicators measure different things), but it is clear why it matters to provide a counterbalance. To do so, we have estimated the total amount of forced labour involved to produce the goods that entered the Dutch Republic based on the total volume of the sugar, coffee and tobacco that the Dutch imported in 1770. A simple calculation reveals that behind the flows of goods imported directly from the Atlantic colonies lie approximately 120,000 person-years of field labour on plantations in the Americas.[49] We can more easily envision the comparative size of this amount of labour if we keep in mind that the total size of the population of the Dutch Republic at the time was a mere 1.9 million, of whom about a million were gainfully employed.

There are many measures available to examine the ways in which the economy of the Dutch Republic profited from this massive amount of labour. We can only underline that calculating the contribution of slave-based activities as a proportion of GDP only provides a partial picture, which could be much enhanced by including other measures that were fruitfully employed in the British case, such as the contribution of capital transfers from the Atlantic plantation colonies to domestic capital formation. However, this would require considerable research. Looking at GDP allows us to get a clearer picture of the importance of the sectors of the Dutch economy that, while employing wage labour domestically, either worked for or depended on the labour performed on slave plantations across the Atlantic. This measure has the crucial advantage that it enables us to relate our estimates to the most complete reconstruction to date of the size of the economy of pre-industrial Holland: the GDP estimate compiled by Jan Luiten van Zanden and Bas van Leeuwen.[50] With some adjustment, this can be converted into an estimate for the GDP of the Dutch Republic as a whole. Van Zanden and Van Leeuwen followed an output model for reconstructing national accounts, in which the total size of GDP is arrived at by adding the net output (or value added) of each individual branch of the economy. They based their GDP estimates on data from two years for which relatively complete national accounts could be constructed (1510/14 and 1807), which they adjusted with the help of benchmark estimates for twenty-seven individual branches of the economy divided across the three main sectors, agriculture and fisheries, industry and services, for which time series could be created.

Apart from the paucity of data, a great methodological difficulty with this approach – even when applied to modern economies – is to properly account for the fact that, in an integrated economy, the output of one sector functions as input for another. This can easily lead to double counting, in which the value added for intermediary products is again included in the value added of end products.[51] Therefore, it is necessary to carefully separate the specific contribution made by each branch individually. This exercise demands special caution when dealing with linked trading activities, where, to give but one directly relevant example, trade goods imported through the Sound such as iron and linen were used to buy captives on the West African coast, the proceeds of their sale in Suriname being used to buy sugar, which was refined in the Dutch Republic and then re-exported across the Rhine to the German hinterland. Separating inputs from outputs becomes even more difficult when all we have to go on are aggregate figures on trade flows based on the value of goods in prices on the Amsterdam bourse. In fact, merchants made their profits through exploiting price differentials at every step in this complicated web of international trade movements.[52] Van Zanden and Van Leeuwen presented their methods in an elaborate annex that provides the basis for the many conjunctions and 'guesstimates' that the exercise of reconstructing net flows in every branch of the economy of necessity entails.[53] Our own annex provides more details on how we applied these methods to our data, as well as a test on the basis of the records of over one hundred voyages of the Middelburgse Commercie Compagnie (MCC), which provides confirmation of the realism of this model for the most important branch that is analysed in this article: the direct Atlantic trade (both slave trade and commodity trade).

What activities were slave-based?

While attempts to measure pre-industrial economies will remain highly contentious, using these existing estimates allows us to draw meaningful conclusions about the weight of slave-based activities within the Dutch economy as a whole. Importantly, relating our own data for each individual branch to the GDP of Holland through procedures that stay close to those followed by Van Zanden and Van Leeuwen creates a level of methodological consistency that guarantees our comparisons involve commensurable elements. This is an advance from methodologically naïve approaches, in which one category of economic data (e.g. the overall size of Atlantic imports) is compared without any intermediary steps to whatever measure for the size of the economy as a whole is available (e.g. GNI). Explaining every slave-based component of GDP is an elaborate task. We have done so in detail for the single year of 1770. Later in the article, we will enhance the snapshot that is thus created of the Dutch economy to create a more dynamic view for the mid- to late eighteenth century. The year 1770 provides a good starting point for such an exercise. The Surinamese slave sector, which formed the bedrock of Dutch slave-related economic activities, had already gone through its main phase of eighteenth-century expansion, and by 1770 it produced an output that would remain relatively stable in the period to come, despite violent interruptions in international trade.[54] On the other hand, within Europe large and relatively stable markets for coffee and sugar already existed. For many areas trading in slave-produced commodities, good data are available for either 1770 itself or the years immediately surrounding it.[55] The year 1770 is only a decade removed from Van der Oudermeulen's important observations on the structure of Dutch trade, but it is situated well before the American War of Independence, the Fourth Anglo Dutch War and the Haitian Revolution, all of which caused enormous volatility in the international trading system. The fact that 1770 was a peak year for the issuing of new plantation loans does not really affect GDP figures, since, as will be further explained below in relation to the financial sector, these only include income derived from banking fees and other fees for financial services on newly issued loans (which we rather conservatively calculate to have amounted to 0.2% of the GDP of Holland and as little as 0.07% of the GDP of the Dutch Republic as a whole).

The list of sectors that we consider slave-based is well aligned with international approaches.[56] It includes:

- the transatlantic slave trade and the direct imports from Atlantic colonies of commodities produced on slave plantations (most importantly slave-produced sugar and coffee);
- the production, export or re-export of goods to uphold the West Indian plantation colonies;
- financial services performed within the Netherlands for the West Indian plantation sector (including banking fees, but excluding returns on plantation-related foreign loans that contribute to GNI but not to GDP);
- the import of slave-produced commodities via European ports;
- the processing industry for slave-produced commodities within the Netherlands;
- the re-export of slave-produced goods to other parts of Europe;
- the transport of and trade in slave-produced commodities consumed in the Dutch Republic;
- domestic production, transport and trade of goods directly geared towards the trade in slaves and slave-produced commodities (such as ships, victuals and trade goods), as well as for the protection of this trade and the slave colonies, in as far as expenses were made in the Netherlands.[57]

This sequence of contributions not coincidentally greatly resembles a commodity chain. However, the commodity chain – or value chain – approach and GDP calculations are not entirely commensurable, because a commodity chain follows goods across national boundaries, whereas GDP is by definition about domestic product and only counts value added within national borders. Also excluded from the above list are the ample sums paid out to insurance companies who underwrote the slave trade. In our accounting method, this was a necessary step to avoid double counting, since Van Zanden and Van Leeuwen included the insurers' profits in the value added in the shipping sector. Furthermore, sceptical readers might wonder how military expenses paid out of custom taxes to protect the slaving sector could actually produce value added. This has to be deemed the case, because by definition domestic income derived from government spending counts towards GDP, provided that taxes are not included in the output of industry and trade.

Since at this stage we confine ourselves to assessing the importance of slave-based economic activities within the total economy for just a single year, there is no need for price adjustments. Furthermore, neither multiplier effects nor opportunity costs play a role at this stage of the analysis: they fall beyond static analysis of GDP in a single year and belong to a dynamic analysis of the impact of the growth or decline of a sector in consecutive years.[58] Once it has been established what proportion of the value added obtained in each of these sectors was derived from slave-based activities, it is possible to relate these proportions back to Van Zanden and Van Leeuwen's totals. Questions might arise about many of our calculating steps. The 30-page annex to this article aims to make these steps transparent, allowing for critique, nuance or readjustments. Readers can also use this annex to convince themselves that wherever faced with the necessity to make guesses, within the parameters of our chosen method, we have consistently chosen to err on the side of caution. We are therefore convinced that our resulting figures present a conservative estimate of the weight of Atlantic slave-based activities.

Our estimates

Following the method outlined, we have calculated that slave-based activities contributed 10.36% of the GDP in Holland in 1770. Table 3 presents a sectoral breakdown. The contribution to the Dutch GDP can be derived from this figure relatively easily, since our sectoral figures for the province of Holland were in most cases derived from aggregate figures for the Dutch Republic in the first place. As further explained in the annex, we estimate the contribution to the GDP of the Dutch Republic as a whole at 5.2%. Our calculations allow for broad conclusions about the kind of linkages that existed between the Dutch domestic economy and Atlantic slavery. The contribution of slave-related activities was massively concentrated in the service sector of the economy, especially in international trade (6.0% of the GDP of Holland) and shipping (1.5%). Smaller additions were made through auxiliary roles performed by Holland's financial sector, through banking activities (0.17%) and through notarial services (0.13%). Quite a substantial proportion of the service sector in Van Zanden and Van Leeuwen's calculations is provided by the government and the army and navy. Since the domestic staff of the various government organs involved in the management of slavery was negligible, we have not counted any contribution to GDP for this branch. Neither have we counted

Table 3. Contribution of slave-based activities to the GDP of Holland, 1770 (×1000 guilders).

Sector	Sector total	Branch	Branch total	Slave-based total	Slave-based total as % of branch total	Slave-based total as % of GDP
Agriculture and fisheries	19,919.6					
Industry	48,404.1					
		Of which: shipbuilding	3,071.15	974	31.74	0.55
		Of which: sugar refinery	696.39	682	98.00	0.39
Services	108,746					
		Of which: International trade	42,629.6	10,620	24.91	6.00
		Of which: International shipping	8,537.94	2,710	31.74	1.53
		Of which: Banking and financial services	910.78	296	32.51	0.17
		Of which: notarial services	1,777.95	222	12.50	0.13
		Of which: Army and Navy	6,393.76	334	5.23	0.19
Slave-related value added that falls under various sectors		Domestic production, trade and shipping		2,500		1.41
Total	177,069			18,340		10.36

military expenses for the protection of the slave plantations, which by the 1770s in Suriname involved substantial sums, because they were almost entirely raised and expended overseas. Within this branch, we have therefore only included expenditures on naval operations geared directly towards the protection of Atlantic trade, for which substantial expenses were made on wages and supplies that count toward the domestic economy (amounting to 0.19% of GDP). Technically, some of this belongs to other sectors, such as agriculture (for victuals) or industry (for warships), but since Van Zanden and Van Leeuwen treated all of them as part of the military branch of the service sector, we did so as well. As explained earlier, insurance companies were not treated as a separate branch by Van Zanden and Van Leeuwen, but following their approach the probably rather sizeable profits that insurers made on the slave trade and the trade in slave-produced commodities have been subsumed under international shipping.[59] Separating insurers' profits would not change the share of services in proportion to other sectors.

Since we are dealing with a part of the economy that revolved around production processes on slave plantations located far outside the borders of the Netherlands, the fact that such a large proportion of the domestic income derived from slavery was trade-related should come as no surprise. Nevertheless, it is important to note the extent to which this sector dominated. In Britain, domestic production for export to the Atlantic world became an important activity for export industries at the same time as slave plantations provided the raw material for the textile industry, which became one of the most dynamic parts of the home economy.[60] In the Netherlands, certainly more than half and perhaps as much as three-quarters of the goods exported to the slave colonies were not produced domestically, but imported from other parts of Europe. The Dutch imported textiles from the East Indies, guns from the Southern Netherlands and ironware from Sweden for the slave trade, building materials for the plantations from Northern Europe, wine from France and linen from Silesia for the trade with the Americas. A smaller proportion of the textiles, arms, foodstuffs, gin and clay pipes exported for use in the slave trade and for consumption by the slaves was produced at home.[61]

A substantial contribution to domestic industry, but one that was tied completely to the distributive function of Holland's economy within the larger European-Atlantic complex, was shipbuilding (0.55%). In Van Zanden and Van Leeuwen's approach, the value added in the shipbuilding sector is derived from the requirements for maintaining and expanding the merchant fleet, with the different components of this fleet being weighed according to the average tonnage of ships sailing on different routes as well as the distances sailed. This is a rather rough method.[62] Nevertheless, it is safe to say that with a substantial part of the fleet's total tonnage reserved either for direct Atlantic imports or the circulation of slave-produced goods within Europe, the size of this important domestic sector by the end of the eighteenth century was determined to a significant extent by the continuing role of the Dutch Republic in the slave-based commodity trade. Meanwhile, the main processing industry that was fully based on slave-produced goods was the Holland-based sugar industry (0.39% of GDP). It has been estimated that in 1770 Amsterdam alone housed 110 refineries, out of a total of 150 refineries in the province of Holland. These processed approximately 50 million pounds of raw sugar per year, employing over 4,000 workers.[63] Tied to Atlantic expansion, sugar refining remained the great exception to the general picture of stagnation presented by Holland's industrial sector, and it therefore 'loomed large in the eighteenth-century Republic's economic life'.[64] However, it never had the same potential to become the flywheel of a domestic Industrial Revolution as British textiles.

Some supporting activities for the export trade that were directed to the slave plantations clearly contributed to the domestic economy – such as the provisioning of ships that participated in the triangular trade – but are hard to pigeonhole into a single sector. For example, within the confines of our accounting method, it is almost impossible to determine what part of the value added in victualling belonged to the agrarian sector, what to food processing and what to domestic transport and trade. At the other end of the chain, coffee retail contained some elements of processing as well, such as roasting and grinding, which were not performed by a separate industry. We have taken the liberty of compiling all these activities that are hard to categorise into a single category (1.41%), outlining its contents in the annex. Estimating methods here, to a larger extent than in other posts, depended on conjunctions and guesstimates. We have tried to compensate for this by being conservative in the number of domestic activities that we included as slave-based, for example by leaving out the rather sizeable processing industry for indigo and all the ancillary activities for the European fleet carrying re-exported slave-produced goods. The MCC data presented in the online annex show the reliability of our estimates for international trade and shipping combined, which according to our calculation was alone responsible for almost three-quarters of the total contribution of slave-based activities to the economy of Holland. While we are fully aware of the extent to which any estimate of the weight of early modern economic activities remains tenuous, our results are therefore a good indication of the great importance of this sector for the late eighteenth-century economy.

From static observation to a more dynamic approach

So far, we have concentrated on reconstructing the contribution of slave-related activities to the Dutch economy in a single year, 1770. Our calculations have shown that 5.2% of the GDP of the Dutch Republic, and as much as 10.36% of the GDP of its most prosperous province, Holland, was derived from Atlantic slavery. We have further affirmed that by far the largest part of this contribution was concentrated in international trade and the shipping of goods produced by slave labour, both on plantations in the Dutch West Indies and within the plantation sector of other European Atlantic powers. In this section, we use this static observation as a starting point to investigate the importance of slavery for Dutch economic development in the eighteenth century. To do so, however, it is first necessary to establish that 1770 was not an exceptional year. We have already stated our reasons for assuming that this was not the case, but we can further investigate this by using the 1770 results to construct a time-series of the slave-based part of Holland's GDP for several decades around that year. We have done so by using a relatively simple set of calculations that are easy to follow.[65] We assumed that in some smaller sectors (notarial services, army and navy, and sugar refining, which was almost completely slave-based), slave-based activities developed in direct proportion to Van Zanden and Van Leeuwen's overall estimates for the development of these branches. For banking activities, we made the extreme assumption that before 1761 and after 1772, as a result of the collapse of the prevailing system of plantation loans, the value added drawn from financial services was either minimal or zero.[66] For the value added in the largest slave-based branches – those directly derived from the import from and export to the Atlantic plantation complex – we created two separate weighted indices for trade and shipping based on the total value of sugar and coffee imports. Given the great importance of these two goods within the total, we hold these indices to be a good measure of the overall fluctuations in slave-based international trade and shipping and the branches of the domestic economy that served them or depended upon them.

Figure 3 shows the incremental growth of slave-based activities during the middle decades of the eighteenth century, from representing around 4.5–6% of the GDP of Holland to well over 10% in most years after 1770. Of the twenty-four years for which we have more or less complete import data on which to base our indices, in five years (1761, 1762, 1777, 1778 and 1779) the share of slave-based activities in the GDP of Holland exceeded 14%. Incomplete trade data for the period after 1780 suggest that the slave-based contribution to Holland's GDP temporarily declined sharply as a result of the Fourth Anglo-Dutch War. Thereafter it resumed at a slightly lower level than the late 1770s peak period, but on a par with the average years given by our reconstruction for the years after 1761 (see Tables 4 and 5). That slave-based activities not only had substantial weight within the economy of Holland in the second half of the eighteenth century, but also had significant impact on economic growth as well, is suggested by the fact that while the economy of Holland grew by fl.51.9 million in the four decades from 1738 to 1779, the slave-based contribution to GDP alone grew by fl.20.5 million, thus contributing almost 40% of all growth generated in the economy of Holland in this period.

While these figures on the importance of slavery for the economy of the Dutch Republic might come as a surprise to some, the general trend that they express is confirmed by the literature. Klooster and others have shown that for most of the second half of the eighteenth century, the Dutch economy reaped great benefits from its policy of neutrality and the opportunities this created for Curaçao and St Eustatius in particular to act as entrepôts

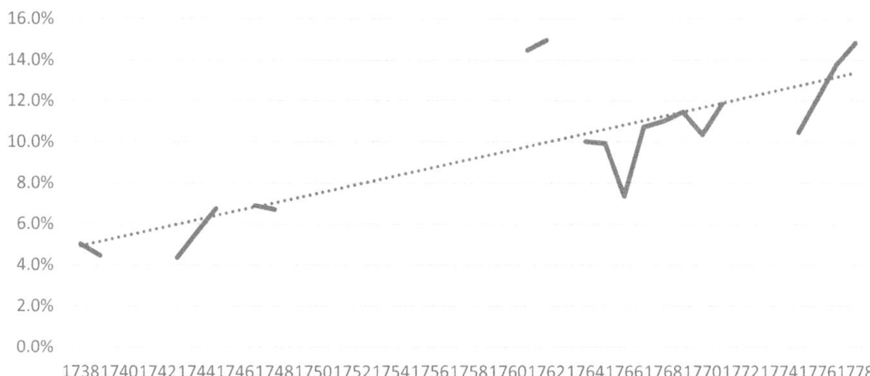

Figure 3. Slave-based activities as proportion of the GDP of Holland, 1738–1778, based on estimations 1770, indexing for fluctuations in slave-based international and domestic trade.
Sources and methods: see Annex.

Table 4. Dutch imports of sugar in lbs (1750–1790, excluding Asian imports).

Year	Suriname	Berbice	Ess/Dem	Curacao	St. Eustatius	France	Other	Totals
1750	24,646,800	526,384	1,839,912	100,000	2,663,526	30,000,000		59,776,622
1765	16,837,600	195,056	2,676,202		5,005,729	20,000,000		44,714,587
1775	18,632,024	681,615	3,918,518	400,000	4,802,400	34,400,000		62,834,557
1780	14,185,488	350,000	3,439,641	400,000	30,433,600	256,000		49,064,729
1786	14,716,512	350,000	4,295,145		2,766,900	38,730,340		60,858,897
1790	20,429,640	350,000	4,403,072		7,524,100	23,716,989	1,926,435	58,350,236

Source: Figures compiled by Gerhard de Kok. **Suriname**: J. Postma, *Dutch shipping and trade with Surinam, 1683–1795*. DANS. https://doi.org/10.17026/dans-zeh-h82t; **Berbice**: Klaas Kramer, 'Plantation Development in Berbice from 1753 to 1779: the shift from the interior to the coast', in Nieuwe West-Indische Gids 65, nr. 1/2 (Leiden 1991), 394–5; J. de Hullu, 'Memorie van den Amerikaanschen raad over de Hollandsche bezittingen in West-Indie in Juli 1806', in: West-Indische Gids 4, no. 1 (1923); **Essequibo and Demerara**: Henry Bolingbroke, A Voyage to the Demerary (Londen 1807), Appendix I, 397; NL-HaNA, WIC 1136, cargo manifests 1790; **Curacao**: Van der Voort, Westindische Plantages, 260–1; Klooster, Illicit Riches, 234, appendix 9; **St. Eustatius**: Klooster, Illicit Riches, appendix 5, 226-227; **France**: Van der Voort, Westindische Plantages, 260–1.

Table 5. Dutch imports of coffee in lbs (1750–1790, excluding Asian imports).

Year	Suriname	Berbice	Ess/Dem	Curacao	St. Eustatius	France	Totals
1750	3,593,423	69,976	120	99,370	148,638	1,500,000	5,411,527
1775	20,331,934	707,871	1,276,800	500,000	2,330,030	9,692,000	34,838,635
1780	11,363,077	1,572,785	5,305,710	500,000	10,075,920	612,000	29,429,492
1786	12,527,630	2,250,000	1,639,960		289,500	5,122,762	21,829,852
1790	14,815,275	2,250,000	4,233,770		288,070	4,142,596	25,729,711

Source: Figures compiled by Gerhard de Kok. **Suriname**: J. Postma, *Dutch shipping and trade with Surinam, 1683–1795*. DANS. https://doi.org/10.17026/dans-zeh-h82t; **Berbice**: Klaas Kramer, 'Plantation Development in Berbice from 1753 to 1779: the shift from the interior to the coast', in: Nieuwe West-Indische Gids 65, nr. 1/2 (Leiden 1991), 394–5; J. de Hullu, 'Memorie van den Amerikaanschen raad over de Hollandsche bezittingen in West-Indie in Juli 1806', in: West-Indische Gids 4, no. 1 (1923); **Essequibo and Demerara**: *Henry Bolingbroke, A Voyage to the Demerary* (Londen 1807), Appendix I, 397; NL-HaNA, WIC 1136, cargo manifests 1790; **Curacao**: Van der Voort, Westindische Plantages, 260–1; Klooster, Illicit Riches, 234, appendix 9; **St. Eustatius**: Klooster, Illicit Riches, appendix 5, 226–7; **France**: Van der Voort, Westindische Plantages, 260–1.

for slave-produced goods.[67] On the other hand, the collapse of Dutch Atlantic trade during the Fourth Anglo-Dutch War and after the French invasion of 1795 proved the vulnerability of this system. Nevertheless, it is important to emphasise that the second half of the eighteenth century contained many more years in which the Dutch economy profited from turbulence in the international system than years in which war interrupted its trade. It is certainly unwarranted to treat the period following the Fourth Anglo-Dutch War as the point of origin of terminal crisis or decline for the Dutch Atlantic.[68] In fact, as Tables 4 and 5 illustrate, the quantities of slave-produced goods exported to the Netherlands remained very large after 1784.

Although it is hard to deny that in the second half of the eighteenth century slave-produced Atlantic imports formed a major component of Dutch trade, some have tried to minimise the importance of slavery for the Dutch economy on the basis of counterfactual arguments, positing that slave-based activity could easily have been replaced by other activities that would have been as beneficial to the Dutch economy. The most vociferous proponents of this form of reasoning have been Eltis, Emmer and Lewis, who insisted that:

> In a market economy where prices adjust, ships and crews would have found employment, and guns, textiles, and other cargo would have been put to other uses. And investments in the Dutch Atlantic were almost never exclusively linked to the slave trade or to slavery. Without much difficulty, investors could transfer their money to other sectors of the economy.[69]

In their article, they never specify which branches of the by that time seriously depressed Dutch industrial sector or what new venues of trade should have absorbed 'without much difficulty' the capital and labour previously employed in slave-based activities. For international trade and shipping, as demonstrated earlier, this involved about one-fifth to one-quarter of all economic activities. Moreover, it is well known that in the eighteenth century the Dutch Republic already exported capital on a large scale because of the lack of investment opportunities in the domestic economy. The easy transferability of capital in the Dutch Republic therefore suggests a more likely counterfactual scenario. In specific areas of the Netherlands, most importantly the trading cities of Amsterdam, Rotterdam, Middelburg and Vlissingen, the immediate impact of the disappearance of slave-based activities would have been severe economic crisis.[70] In Holland, where alternatives were available to a certain extent, the initial shock might gradually have been absorbed by employment of merchant capital, ships and sailors on the considerably less profitable short-distance trading routes. The dependence on French, English and Iberian re-exports to Northern Europe would have increased, making the already embattled Dutch position in the European carrying trade even more vulnerable to international competition. Meanwhile, the opening up of the Rhine as a major trading route with the European hinterland, which in the German Ruhr region remained highly dependent on colonial goods until the Industrial Revolution, would have been slowed down, damaging the economic position of Amsterdam and Rotterdam.[71] Finally, some of the productive capital previously invested in the processing industry of slave-produced goods or of export goods for the Atlantic slave colonies might have found employment elsewhere in the Dutch Republic. But in all likelihood, an even greater part would have followed post-1740 trends in capital markets and been invested abroad, either in foreign government paper or in British industry, with all the detrimental effects for the size of Dutch GDP that this would have entailed.[72]

A more interesting question than what would have happened if the Dutch on a beautiful summer day in 1750 decided to completely opt out from all slave-based activities is the question of the distributive effects of their actual continued and growing involvement. The most important of these effects, of course, was the massive transfer of value produced by the enslaved in Dutch colonies, but also in English, French, Spanish, Portuguese and Danish overseas colonies, to the Dutch economy as a whole.[73] But our calculations also clearly show that the fruits of their forced labour were not distributed evenly throughout the Dutch economy. First, the benefits disproportionally flowed to certain areas within the Netherlands. As Gerhard de Kok has shown by tracking the forward and backward linkages of this trade within the urban and rural economy of the Zeeland island Walcheren, the local effects of the slave trade in that province were substantial.[74] However, the bulk of profits derived from slavery did not go to this province. By assessing the contribution of all slave-based activities, rather than just the slave trade, it can be proved that it was the Netherland's richest province Holland, and within Holland Amsterdam and Rotterdam, that benefited most from the Atlantic slave complex. The extent to which these benefits were drawn from international trade also underlines the centrality of slavery for the large merchant families that dominated Holland's economy and politics during the early modern period. Many slave-based activities provided income for, and allowed for participation by, groups in Dutch society below the elite.[75] But to an extent even greater than previously thought, slavery functioned to sustain the activities that augmented the wealth of those families that occupied the merchant houses along the canals of Amsterdam and the other trading cities of Holland.[76]

Conclusions

The question about how important slavery was for the economies of the European nations most involved in the Atlantic plantation complex has animated decades of academic and public debates. Most influentially elaborated in Eric Williams' *Capitalism and Slavery*, the thesis that the combined involvement in the slave trade and plantation slavery gave a significant push to the British Industrial Revolution has occupied several generations of scholars. As part of this wide-ranging problematic, economic historians have examined such diverse questions as the impact of the slave-based Atlantic trade on domestic industries, capital formation, financial systems, economic institutions and the world system at large, using a variety of different indicators. For the Netherlands, in as far as such questions were not deemed irrelevant because the country did not undergo an early Industrial Revolution, speculations on the economic importance of slavery have so far been based on figures for the slave trade alone, or subsumed without further qualification into debates on the impact of the Atlantic trade in general. In this article, we have presented the first systematic assessment of the contribution of all slave-based economic activities to the Dutch GDP in the second half of the eighteenth century, deriving our conclusions from a verifiable accounting method. The conclusions are significant for both Dutch and international debates.

Firstly, slave-based activities constituted 5.2% of Dutch GDP in the year 1770, and 10.36% of the GDP of Holland, the Netherlands' most wealthy province. We arrived at this conclusion by using the output approach to national accounting elaborated by Jan Luiten van Zanden and Bas van Leeuwen for the early modern economy of the province of Holland, and relating our own data to theirs using conservative estimates where there was any ground for doubt. The high proportion of GDP derived from slave-based activities reflects the important role attained by the Dutch Republic, and especially Holland, in international slave-based commodity chains. These chains ran from the export producers who supplied overseas colonies and the slave trade, to the slave traders who guaranteed the plantations their involuntary workforce, to the forced labour performed under the slave-owners' whip, and from there to European metropoles and hinterlands that in the eighteenth century became mass consumers of slave-produced goods such as sugar and coffee. These chains tied the Dutch economy to slave-based production in Suriname and other Dutch colonies, but also to the plantation complexes of other European powers, most crucially the French in Saint Domingue, as the Dutch became major importers and processers of French coffee and sugar that they then redistributed to Northern and Central Europe.

Secondly, the year 1770, for which we have made our detailed calculations, was representative for the economic trend of the second half of the eighteenth century. The explosive growth of production on slave plantations in the Dutch Guianas, combined with the international boom in coffee and sugar consumption, ensured that consistently high proportions (19% in 1770) of commodities entering and exiting Dutch harbors were produced on Atlantic slave plantations. The total share of the value of goods either deriving from or destined for the Atlantic slave complex stood at 23%. The Dutch economy profited from this Atlantic boom both as direct supplier of slave-produced goods and as intermediary between the Atlantic slave complexes of other European powers and the Northern and Central European hinterland. Based on two weighted indices, we project a growth of the importance of slave-based activities within the GDP of Holland from 4.5% to 6% in the 1740s to over 14% in the late 1770s. The speculative boom in plantation loans that ended in the financial crisis of 1771–1773 does not seem to have had a major direct impact on the continued supply of and demand for Atlantic commodities, or the continued benefits derived from this by the Dutch economy.

Thirdly, our breakdown of value added produced in different parts of the slave-based commodity chain allows for more precise conclusions about the proportion in which different kinds of slave-based activities contributed to the Dutch economy. Not the slave trade, but the trade in slave-produced commodities provided the main route through which Atlantic slavery contributed to Dutch incomes. Extrapolations from revenues drawn from the slave trade, however they are calculated, will always lead to a serious underestimation of the importance of the slave-based sector. The expansion of the trade in slave-produced sugar and coffee sustained Holland's international commerce throughout the difficult second half of the eighteenth century, opened up the Rhine trade with the German hinterland and to a lesser extent provided opportunities for the otherwise depressed industrial sector through the processing of raw sugar and the production of export goods, ships and provisions for the Atlantic trade.

Fourthly, since the value added derived from slave-based activities was so highly concentrated in international commodity trade and shipping, it should come as no surprise that the main beneficiaries of slavery could be found among the international merchants and merchant-financiers in Holland, especially Amsterdam. Activities related to the slave trade formed an important component of the income of the Zeeland trading towns Middelburg and Vlissingen, but in terms of their contribution to overall Dutch GDP, this was dwarfed by the revenues drawn in the Netherlands' most wealthy and politically most influential province. As the 1730s memorandum on the importance of Suriname for the Amsterdam economy cited in the introduction stated, here slave-based activities were ubiquitous.

Finally, the Dutch case adds a new dimension to international debates on the impact of slavery on European economies by providing a counter-example to the myopic approach that sees the economic contribution to slavery as important only if it fed into a domestic Industrial Revolution. The Dutch involvement in Atlantic slavery in the second half of the eighteenth century fulfilled altogether different functions. It helped to sustain the economy of one of Europe's most commercialised societies, provided new directions for trade and investment, and slowed down capital flight. This is not the place to investigate whether the increasing economic dependence on colonial trade, continuing well into the nineteenth century, closed off alternative routes of economic growth or helped to lay the foundations for them. Our aim was simply to lay bare to what extent Atlantic slavery contributed to the Dutch economy of the second half of the eighteenth century, a question that has increasingly been at the heart of heated academic and public debates in the Netherlands. Our conclusion is that both for the Dutch Republic as a whole, and for the province of Holland in particular, the economic importance of Atlantic slave-based activities was significantly larger than Dutch historians have so far assumed.

Notes

1. In this article, we use the term 'slave-based' for the activities involved in the trade in commodities produced on Atlantic slave plantations as well as the activities that sustained slavery on these plantations, including the transatlantic slave trade. Later in the article we explain which activities we have included under this header.
2. Eric Eustace Williams, *Capitalism and Slavery* (Chapel Hill: University of North Carolina Press, 1944).
3. It is important to note that while dealing specifically with the economic gains of Atlantic slave-based activities, the Dutch economy also drew substantial benefits from its involvement in Indian Ocean and Pacific Ocean slavery. For a long time, the Dutch East India Company was the main European power in that region and was heavily involved in both the slave trade and (plantation) slavery. However, since the knowledge of revenue streams connected to Asian slavery is still at a rudimentary state and our own research focused explicitly on Atlantic slavery, we will not examine this question further here. For the Dutch role in slavery in Asia, see Matthias van Rossum and Linda Mbeki, 'Private Slave Trade in the Dutch Indian Ocean World. A Study into the Networks and Backgrounds of Slavers and Enslaved in South Asia and South-Africa', *Slavery & Abolition* 38, no. 1 (2016): 95–116.
4. For the slave trade, see Johannes Menne Postma, *The Dutch in the Atlantic Slave Trade, 1600–1815* (Cambridge: Cambridge University Press, 1990); for an overview of the Dutch Atlantic plantation economy, see Wim Klooster, *Illicit Riches: Dutch Trade in the Caribbean, 1648–1795* (Leiden: KITLV Press, 1998); for an examination of the growth of the Dutch Atlantic trade sector in the eighteenth century, see Johannes Postma and Victor Enthoven, eds., *Riches from Atlantic Commerce. Dutch Transatlantic Trade and Shipping, 1585–1817* (Leiden and Boston: Brill, 2003).
5. Seymour Drescher pointed this out over two decades ago in an article that mostly deals with the late abolition of slavery in the Dutch West Indian colonies. S. Drescher, 'The Long Goodbye. Dutch Capitalism and Antislavery in Comparative Perspective', in *Fifty Years Later: Antislavery, Capitalism and Modernity in*

the Dutch Orbit, ed. G. Oostindie (Pittsburgh, PA: Pittsburgh University Press, 1996), 25–66.

6. Postma, *Dutch Slave Trade*, W.S. Unger, 'Bijdragen tot de geschiedenis van de Nederlandse slavenhandel', *Economisch-Historisch Jaarboek* 26 (1956): 133–74, and 28 (1961): 3–148; Karwan Fatah-Black and Matthias van Rossum, 'Beyond Profitability: The Dutch Transatlantic Slave Trade and its Economic Impact', *Slavery & Abolition* 36, no. 1 (2015): 63–83 (first published in Dutch in *TSEG*) and David Eltis, Pieter C. Emmer and Frank D. Lewis, 'More than Profits? The Contribution of the Slave Trade to the Dutch Economy: assessing Fatah-Black and Van Rossum', *Slavery & Abolition* 37, no. 4 (2016): 724–35.
7. Eltis, Emmer and Lewis, 'More than Profits?', 731.
8. J.G. van Dillen, 'Memorie betreffende de kolonie Suriname', *Economisch-Historisch Jaarboek* 24 (1950): 162–7.
9. Ibid., 167.
10. Jan Luiten van Zanden and Bas van Leeuwen, 'Persistent but not Consistent: The Growth of National Income in Holland 1347–1807', *Explorations in Economic History* 49 (2012): 119–30, and online annexes; building on estimates for the Netherlands as a whole presented in Edwin Horlings, Jan-Pieter Smits and Jan Luiten van Zanden, *Dutch GNP and its Components, 1800–1913* (Groningen: Groningen Growth and Development Centre, 2000).
11. B. Kuipers, *Het Rotterdam effect. De impact van mainport Rotterdam op de Nederlandse economie*, Erasmus UPT, 6 November 2018, 24.
12. Kevin Barefood, Dave Curtis , William A. Jolliff , Jessica R. Nicholson and Robert Omohundro, 'Defining and Measuring the Digital Economy', Working Paper, https://www.bea.gov/research/papers/2018/defining-and-measuring-digital-economy (accessed April 24, 2019). Under the digital economy, the authors include digital-enabling infrastructure, e-commerce, digital media, as well as the goods and services that go into producing those three.
13. Patrick O'Brien, 'European Economic Development: The Contribution of the Periphery', *The Economic History Review*, New Series 35, no. 1 (1982): 1–18; Joseph E. Inikori, *Africans and the Industrial Revolution in England: A Study in International Trade and Economic Development* (Cambridge: Cambridge University Press, 2002). Stanley L. Engerman, 'The Slave Trade and British Capital Formation in the Eighteenth Century: A Comment on the Williams Thesis', *The Business History Review* 46, no. 4 (1972): 430–44; Robin Blackburn, *The Making of New World Slavery: From the Baroque to the Modern, 1492–1800* (London: Verso, 1997), Part II, chap. 12 in particular; Daron Acemoglu, Simon Johnson and James Robinson, 'The Rise of Europe: Atlantic Trade, Institutional Change, and Economic Growth', *The American Economic Review* 95, no. 3 (2005): 546–79; Sven Beckert and Seth Rockman, eds., *Slavery's Capitalism: A New History of American Economic Development* (Philadelphia: The University of Pennsylvania Press, 2016). Dale Tomich, ed., *Slavery and Historical Capitalism during the Nineteenth Century* (Lanham, MD: Lexington Books, 2017).
14. In particular, in the context of claims and public debates over reparations, see Ana Lucia Araujo, *Reparations for Slavery and the Slave Trade: A Transnational and Comparative History* (London and New York: Bloomsbury Press, 2017); and Armand Zunder, *Herstelbetalingen. De 'Wiedergutmachung' voor de schade die Suriname en haar bevolking hebben geleden onder het Nederlands kolonialisme* (The Hague: Amrit, 2010).

15. Edward Long, *The History of Jamaica or General Survey of the Antient and Modern State of that Island with Reflections on its Situation, Settlements, Inhabitants, Climate, Products, Commerce, Laws, and Government* (London: T. Lowndes, 1774), vol. 1, 507–8.
16. See for Sheridan's quotation of Long 'The Wealth of Jamaica in the Eighteenth Century', *The Economic History Review*, New Series 18, no. 2 (1965): 292–311, 305. Also see Robert Paul Thomas, 'The Sugar Colonies of the Old Empire: Profit or Loss for Great Britain?', *The Economic History Review*, New Series 21:1 (1968), 30–45; R.B. Sheridan, 'The Wealth of Jamaica in the Eighteenth Century: A Rejoinder', *The Economic History Review*, New Series 21, no. 1: (1968), 46–61.
17. Ralph Davis, 'English Foreign Trade, 1700–1774', *The Economic History Review*, New Series 15, no. 2 (1962): 285–303, and here 292.
18. Sheridan, 'The Wealth of Jamaica', 292.
19. Engerman, 'The Slave Trade and British Capital Formation', 432.
20. Ibid., 440.
21. See William Darity Jr, 'British Industry and the West Indies Plantations', *Social Science History* 14, no. 1 (1990): 117–49.
22. Pieter C. Emmer, 'The Dutch and the Atlantic Challenge, 1600–1800', in *A Deus ex Machina Revisited: Atlantic Colonial Trade and European Economic Development*, ed. P.C. Emmer, O. Pétré-Grenouilleau and J.V. Roitman (Leiden/Boston: Brill, 2006), 151–77.
23. Solow, 'Caribbean Slavery and British Growth, The Eric Williams Hypothesis', *Journal of Development Economics* 17 (1985): 99–115, and here 105–6.
24. Ibid., 111.
25. Ibid., 113.
26. J.E. Inikori, 'Slavery and the Development of Industrial Capitalism in England', *The Journal of Interdisciplinary History* 17, no. 4 (1987): 771–93, 778–81, 788–9; Davis, 'English Foreign Trade', 291–2.
27. David Richardson, 'The Slave Trade, Sugar, and British Economic Growth, 1748–1776', *The Journal of Interdisciplinary History* 17, no. 4 (1987): 739–69, and here 750, 752 and 767.
28. O'Brien, 'European Economic Development', 18.
29. Patrick O'Brien, 'A Critical Review of a Tradition of Meta-Narratives from Adam Smith to Karl Pomeranz', in Emmer, Pétré-Grenouilleau and Roitman, *Deus ex Machina*, 5–24, 25. Also see Patrick O'Brien, 'Mercantilism and Imperialism in the Rise and Decline of the Dutch and British Economies 1585–1815', *De Economist* 148 (2000): 469–501.
30. Acemoglu, Johnson and Robinson, 'Rise of Europe', 572.
31. Nuala Zahedieh, 'Regulation, Rent-Seeking, and the Glorious Revolution in the English Atlantic Economy', *Economic History Review* 63, no. 4 (2010): 865–90.
32. Klas Rönnbäck, 'On the Economic Importance of the Slave Plantation Complex to the British Economy during the Eighteenth Century: A Value-Added Approach', *Journal of Global History* 13 (2018): 309–27.
33. For a critique of this narrow reading of the Williams thesis, see Pepijn Brandon, 'From Williams's Thesis to Williams Thesis: An Anti-Colonial Trajectory', *International Review of Social History* 62, no. 2 (2017): 305–27, and with specific reference to the argument on late industrialisation in the Netherlands, Pepijn Brandon, 'Rethinking Capitalism and Slavery: New Perspectives from American Debates', *TSEG/Low Countries Journal of Social and Economic History* 12, no. 4 (2015): 117–37.

34. For the slave trade, the main contributions are Unger, 'Bijdragen' I and II; Postma, *Slave Trade*; P.C. Emmer, *Geschiedenis van de Nederlandse slavenhandel* (Amsterdam: Nieuw Amsterdam, 2019; first edition 2003); and the recent debate between Karwan Fatah-Black and Matthias van Rossum, 'Beyond Profitability: The Dutch Transatlantic Slave Trade and its Economic Impact', *Slavery & Abolition* 36, no. 1 (2015): 63–83 and David Eltis, Pieter C. Emmer and Frank D. Lewis, 'More than Profits? The Contribution of the Slave Trade to the Dutch Economy: Assessing Fatah-Black and Van Rossum', *Slavery & Abolition* 37, no. 4 (2016): 724–35. For two contributions on the impact of the Atlantic trade that also cover the older literature, see Jan de Vries and Ad van der Woude, *The First Modern Economy: Success, Failure, and Perseverance of the Dutch Economy, 1500–1815* (Cambridge: Cambridge University Press, 1997); and Postma and Enthoven, *Riches from Atlantic Commerce*.
35. Emmer, *Slavenhandel*, 202.
36. Leading Eric Williams, often wrongly held responsible for the excessive focus on the profits from the slave trade, to the remark that 'Negro slavery['s] … origin can be expressed in three words: in the Caribbean, Sugar; on the mainland, Tobacco and Cotton.' Williams, *Capitalism and Slavery*, 23 (cited from the second edition, New York: Capricorn Books, 1966).
37. Fatah-Black and Van Rossum, 'Beyond Profitability', 79. To put this figure in perspective, our calculation will show that the value added from slave-based Atlantic trade and shipping alone in the single year 1770 amounted to fl.10.4 million.
38. Eltis, Emmer and Lewis, 'More than Profits?', 733.
39. Ibid. Eltis, Emmer and Lewis base their conclusion on the essentiality of this sector on Robert Fogel's argument that without the railroad the US GNP would have been 5% lower than it actually was at the end of the nineteenth century. One may question whether this figure makes the contribution of the railroads to the US economy insignificant, as the authors suggest. The argument that the entire slave sector in the Netherlands was of lesser impact than that seems to be based on an unrelated guesstimate made by Emmer elsewhere. In his *Slavenhandel*, 199, Emmer assumes that the total value of Dutch trade with the West Indies was fl.10 million, a figure he relates to De Vries and Van der Woude's calculation of the Dutch GNI to conclude that in an unspecified year in the second half of the eighteenth century, all slave-based activities amounted to 3%, or 5 guilders out of 162 guilders of per capita income. Also see P. Emmer, 'The Economic Impact of the Dutch Expansion Overseas, 1570–1870', *Revista de Historia Económica/Journal of Iberian and Latin American Economic History* 16, no. 1 (1998): 157–76, which however does not differentiate between slave-based and non-slave-based colonial trade.
40. Cornelis van der Oudermeulen, 'Iets dat tot voordeel der deelgenooten van de Oost-Indische Compagnie en tot nut van ieder ingezeten van dit gemeenebest kan strekken', in *Stukken raakende den tegenwoordigen toestand der Bataafsche bezittingen in Oost-Indië*, ed. G.K. van Hogendorp (The Hague and Delft: J.C. Leeuwestyn, 1801). Van der Oudermeulen put the value of direct trade with the Atlantic region below that with the East Indies, but his figure for Dutch exports to the East in particular is grossly inflated.
41. The most important tables and figures from our methodological annex, such as Table 2, are reproduced in the article in order to make it possible for readers to follow the main arguments without delving into the more technical discussion presented there, which will be appealing to specialists only. It is important to note that neither these trade figures, nor the ones constructed by Van Zanden and Van Leeuwen, include trade on Dutch ships that did not enter Dutch harbours, so that the potentially

significant carrying trade executed by the Dutch for other nations ('*voorbijlandvaart*') is not included in any of our calculations.

42. The former figure in De Vries and Van der Woude, *First Modern Economy*, 478, and the correction in Jan de Vries, 'The Dutch Atlantic Economies', in *The Atlantic Economy during the Seventeenth and Eighteenth Centuries: Organization, Operation, Practice, and Personnel*, ed. Peter A. Coclanis (Columbia: University of South Carolina Press, 2005), 1–29, 28, n.63.
43. G.M. Welling, *The Prize of Neutrality. Trade Relations between Amsterdam and North America 1771–1817. A Study in Computational History* (Amsterdam: Historisch Seminarium van de Universiteit van Amsterdam, 1998).
44. Silvia Marzagalli, 'The French Atlantic and the Dutch, Late Seventeenth–Late Eighteenth Century', in *Dutch Atlantic Connections, 1680–1800: Linking Empires, Bridging Borders*, ed. Gert Oostindie and Jessica V. Roitman (Leiden and Boston: Brill, 2014), 103–18; F. Brahm and E. Rosenhaft, eds., *Slavery Hinterland: Trans-Atlantic Slavery and Continental Europe, 1680–1850* (Woodbridge: Boydell & Brewer, 2016).
45. John Black, Nigar Hashimzade and Gareth Myles, *Oxford Dictionary of Economics*, 5th ed. (Oxford: Oxford University Press, 2017), online version: http://www.oxfordreference.com.vu-nl.idm.oclc.org/view/10.1093/acref/9780198759430.001.0001/acref-9780198759430-e-1403# (accessed February 24, 2019).
46. This aspect of the plantation economy is examined at length in Johannes Petrus van de Voort, *De Westindische plantages van 1720 tot 1795. Financiën en handel* (Eindhoven: Drukkerij de Witte, 1973); Alex van Stipriaan, *Surinaams contrast. Roofbouw en overleven in een Caraïbische plantagekolonie 1750–1863* (Leiden: KITLV Uitgeverij, 1993), especially chap. 7; Alex van Stipriaan, 'Debunking Debts. Image and Reality of a Colonial Crisis: Suriname at the End of the Eighteenth Century', *Itinerario* 19, no. 1 (1995): 69–84; and Bram Hoonhout, 'Subprime Plantation Mortgages in Suriname, Essequibo and Demerara, 1750–1800. On Manias, Ponzi Processes and Illegal Trade in the Dutch Negotiatie System', (MA thesis, Leiden University, 2012).
47. For two recent critical approaches to the over-reliance on GDPs in contemporary debates, see Dirk Philipsen, *The Little Big Number: How GDP came to Rule the World and What to Do about It* (Princeton, NJ and Oxford: Princeton University Press, 2015) and Eli Cook, *The Pricing of Progress: Economic Indicators and the Capitalization of American Life* (Cambridge, MA and London: Harvard University Press, 2017).
48. Klas Rönnbäck, 'The Economic Importance', has made the choice to include plantation production in his estimates on the significance of the British plantation complex. Of course, there are many reasons to do so. The problem for our current purposes is that this fundamentally changes what is measured. Rather than revealing the economic weight of slave-based activities *within* the British economy, this shows the importance of the plantation complex *in proportion to* the British economy. To treat activities in overseas colonies as parts of GDP, one would have to create a composite GDP that includes both the Dutch Republic and all the overseas areas under its control.
49. This figure is based on the imports of 56.9 million pounds of sugar, 23.8 million pounds of coffee and 32.8 million pounds of tobacco in the Dutch Republic in 1770 (sources mentioned in the online annex). In the late eighteenth century, the average coffee production per enslaved plantation worker amounted to 230 kilos in Saint Domingue and 219 in Suriname according to Van Stipriaan, *Surinaams contrast*, 133. M.-R. Trouillot, 'Motion in the System. Coffee, Color, and Slavery in Eighteenth-Century Saint-Domingue', *Review (Fernand Braudel Center)* 5, no. 3 (1982): 331–88

suggests an average production per slave in Saint Domingue of 225 kilos. We therefore took the figure of 225 kilos as an approximation. With regard to the sugar production per enslaved, figures vary widely depending on the grade of refining, but for raw sugar 420 kilos per enslaved worker on a late eighteenth-century plantation is a safe estimate. Van Stipriaan, *Surinaams contrast*, 139 and S.B. Schwartz, 'Introduction', in *Tropical Babylons. Sugar and the Making of the Atlantic World, 1450–1680*, ed. S.B. Schwartz (Chapel Hill: University of North Carolina Press, 2004), 1–26, 20. For tobacco, Menard presents figures of just over 1500 pounds per enslaved labourer in Maryland by the late seventeenth century. Russell Menard, 'Plantation Empire: How Sugar and Tobacco Planters Built Their Industries and Raised an Empire', *Agricultural History* 81, no. 3 (2007): 309–32, 320.

50. Van Zanden and Van Leeuwen, 'Persistent'. Datasets published at the website of the Centre for Global Economic History at Utrecht University, http://cgeh.nl/cgeh/research-projects/reconstruction-national-accounts-of-holland-1500-1800-2/ (accessed February 24, 2019).
51. As already spelled out in one of the foundational texts of the construction of national accounts according to the output method, Wassily W. Leontief, *The Structure of the American Economy, 1919–1929: An Empirical Application of Equilibrium Analysis* (Cambridge, MA: Harvard University Press, 1941), 19–20.
52. This is a classical problem in economic-historical literature. M. Morineau, *Pour une histoire économique vraie* (Lille: Presses Universitaires de Lille, 1985).
53. Note that here, as in other places in this article and the annex, net means deducting inputs, not deducting tax. The alternative method to estimate GDP is an income approach, based on factor incomes of all members of the economy. This is the more common method when investigating modern economies. The greatest difficulty in applying this method to the early modern period is the lack of reliable data on incomes in a period before the introduction of general taxation. While wages can be gauged using rough measures and indicators, a realistic estimation for profits and rents is prohibitively difficult. In practice, most calculations of GDP for the early modern period have to rely on creatively drawing on both methods, while trying to sail around the instances where they potentially clash, which is what we do as well.
54. The value of sugar, coffee and cotton imported from Suriname rose from slightly over fl.4 million yearly in 1740–1744 to over fl.8 million in 1765–1769, to remain constant at this level until the decade 1785–1794, when imports rose from fl.9.7 million to fl.10.3 million (current prices), to then collapse as a result of French occupation. Van Stipriaan, *Surinaams contrast*, 437.
55. Ibid.; and Klooster, *Illicit Riches*, 176; Enthoven, 'Assessment', 406.
56. Patrick O'Brien includes the following as 'profits to British capitalists engaged in trade and commerce with the periphery': 1. Imports from the periphery; 2. Exports to the periphery; 3. Re-exports of produce from the periphery; 4. Profits from imports accruing to shipping firms, brokers and commission agencies, and insurance companies; 5. Profits from exports accruing to shipping firms, brokers and commission agencies, and insurance companies; 6. Profits from re-exports accruing to the above groups; 7. Profits remitted to Britain on investments at the periphery; 8. Profits from the sale of services to the periphery; 9. Profits from commodities made or grown for export to the periphery. O'Brien, 'European Economic Development', 6. Guillaume Daudin uses the same selection for France in 'Do Frontiers Give or Do Frontiers Take? The Case of Intercontinental Trade in France at the End of the Eighteenth Century', in Emmer, Pétré-Grenouilleau and Roitman, *Deus Ex Machina*, 199–224,

201. Joseph Inikori rightly insists on the inclusion of processing industries located in Europe for which slave-produced inputs played a strategic role. Joseph E. Inikori, 'Slavery and the Revolution in Cotton Textile Production in England', in *The Atlantic Slave Trade: Effects on Economies, Societies, and Peoples in Africa, the Americas, and Europe*, ed. Joseph E. Inikori and Stanley L. Engerman (Durham, NC and London: Duke University Press, 1992), 145–82; and Inikori, *Africans and the Industrial Revolution*, 363.

57. Of course, in all these sectors the domestic economic activities ran on wage labour, not on slave labour. That is the reason why throughout this article we speak of the contribution of 'slave-based activities'. If one could only include the activities actually performed by the enslaved themselves in a GDP calculation, one would technically have to say that slavery only contributed to the GDP of early modern Suriname and contributed nothing to the GDP of the Dutch Republic, but this would make any GDP-based calculation of the weight of slave-based activities in the Dutch economy pointless from the outset.
58. It is necessary to emphasise this, since in some of the existing literature, knock-down arguments based on counterfactual reasoning are used to prima facie exclude entire branches of trade or processing of slave-produced goods. The proper order of reasoning, in our view, is to first establish what proportion of the economy actually did depend on slavery, before discussing whether things could have been different.
59. Karin Lurvink, 'The Insurance of Mass Murder. The Development of Slave Life Insurance Policies of Dutch Private Slave Ships (1720–1780)', *Enterprise & Society* 21, no. 1 (2020): 210–38.
60. Inikori, 'Slavery'; Sven Beckert, *Empire of Cotton: A Global History* (New York: Alfred A. Knopf, 2014).
61. Gerhard de Kok, 'Walcherse ketens. De trans-Atlantische slavenhandel en de economie van Walcheren, 1755–1780' (PhD thesis, Leiden University, 2019), which provides a detailed picture for the province of Zeeland, supports this argument. Note once again that our calculating method relies on singling out the proportion of value added on each separate leg of these linked trade movements, making sure that outputs of the first leg are not counted again as outputs in all the following legs.
62. This approach was developed by Jan Luiten van Zanden and Milja van Tielhof, 'Roots of Growth and Productivity Change in Dutch Shipping Industry, 1500–1800', *Explorations in Economic History* 46 (2009): 389–403. Both in calculating the costs of shipping and the value added in shipbuilding, a lot depends on the average size of ships on various routes. For bilateral trade between the Atlantic colonies and the Dutch Republic, the average size of ships used by them seems large. Smaller ships, and therefore a larger number of ships or voyages for the transport of a similar amount of commodities, would logically lead to an increase in the value added in the shipbuilding industry at the cost of shipping firms, but by how much remains unclear.
63. J.J. Reesse, *De suikerhandel van Amsterdam. Van het begin der 17e eeuw tot 1813* (Haarlem: J.L.E.I. Kleynenberg, 1908), 58. This will be further substantiated by Tamira Combrink's dissertation which is currently in preparation.
64. De Vries and Van der Woude, *First Modern Economy*, 328.
65. We have refrained from using our relatively limited data for more advanced cliometrical exercises, which not only fall outside our expertise but also of necessity remain highly speculative given the tentative nature of all assumptions on early modern economic trends. Such methods have of course been employed frequently in debates on

the economic impact of slavery, but their validity remains highly contested. The classical examples of the cliometrical approach to the history of slavery are Robert William Fogel and Stanley L. Engerman, *Time on the Cross: The Economics of American Negro Slavery* (Boston, MA: Little, Brown and Company, 1974); and Robert William Fogel, *Without Consent or Contract: The Rise and Fall of American Slavery* (New York: Norton, 1989). In the Netherlands, the prominent economist Jan Tinbergen modelled the impact of the twentieth-century colonies in the East Indies on Dutch national income. J.B.D. Derksen and J. Timbergen, 'Berekeningen over de economische beteekenis van Nederlandsch-Indië voor Nederland', *Maandschrift van het Centraal Bureau voor de Statistiek* 40, no. 10/12 (1945): 210–16, but our data do not allow for a similar approach, which depends on an incomes-based calculation of GDP.

66. This is an under-estimation. Van de Voort painted a highly pessimistic picture of the impact of the crisis of 1771–1772 on financial activities, leading to probably the majority of capital being written off, and interest payments dwindling after 1780. Van de Voort, *Westindische plantages*, 195. However, Van Stipriaan, 'Debunking Debts', has shown that actual capital destruction was far more limited and interest payments for many funds continued, albeit at a reduced level, right up to 1795. The financial service sector will have continued to play a substantial role in managing financial transfers for the plantation sector.
67. Klooster, *Illicit Riches*, 202; Enthoven, 'Assessment', 412–13.
68. As seems to be the position of Gert Oostindie, 'Dutch Atlantic Decline during the 'Age of Revolutions', in *Dutch Atlantic Connections, 1680–1800: Linking Empires, Bridging Borders*, ed. Gert Oostindie and Jessica V. Roitman (Leiden and Boston: Brill, 2014), 309–35.
69. Eltis, Emmer and Lewis, 'More than Profits?', 732.
70. For Zeeland, this is substantiated by Gerhard de Kok, 'Cursed Capital. The Economic Impact of the Transatlantic Slave Trade on Walcheren around 1770', *TSEG* 13, no. 3 (2016): 1–27.
71. Tamira Combrink, 'From French Harbours to German Rivers: European Distribution of Sugar by the Dutch in the Eighteenth Century', in *La diffusion des produits ultramarins en Europe. XVI–XVIII siècle*, ed. Marguerite Martin and Maud Villeret (Rennes: Presse Universitaire de Rennes, 2018), 39–56.
72. James C. Riley, *International Government Finance and the Amsterdam Market 1740–1785* (Cambridge: Cambridge University Press, 1980). Ironically, Emmer has previously flatly contradicted the counterfactual argument of Emmer, Eltis and Lewis, using arguments that are analogous to ours. P.C. Emmer, *The Dutch Slave Trade, 1500–1850* (New York and Oxford: Berghahn Books, 2006), 108, repeated in the latest edition of Emmer, *Slavenhandel*, 200.
73. See the contribution by Tamira Combrink in this special issue.
74. De Kok, *Walcherse ketens*.
75. For example, this is shown by the minority involvement of a shipwright, a captain and several artisans in underwriting slave insurances, although most underwriters remained professional insurers or rich merchants and financiers. Karin Lurvink, 'Underwriting Slavery. Insurance and Slavery in the Dutch Republic (1718–1778)', *Slavery & Abolition* 40, no. 3 (2019): 472–93.
76. Listed with names and addresses by Leo Balai, *Geschiedenis van de Amsterdamse slavenhandel. Over de belangen van Amsterdamse regenten bij de trans-Atlantische slavenhandel* (Zutphen: Walburg Pers, 2013), 109–33.

Acknowledgements

This article first appeared in Dutch as 'De betekenis van de Atlantische slavernij voor de Nederlandse economie in de tweede helft van de achttiende eeuw', *Tijdschrift voor Sociale en Economische Geschiedenis* 16, no. 2 (2019): 5–45. Only minor changes have been made in the English version. The article forms the synthesis of a project funded by the Dutch Council of Scientific Research (NWO), *Slaves, commodities and logistics. The direct and indirect, the immediate and long-term economic impact of eighteenth-century Dutch Republic transatlantic slave-based activities*, NWO Project Number 360-53-170 (principal applicants Marcel van der Linden, Karel Davids and Henk den Heijer). The data on which this article was based were reconstructed by Pepijn Brandon, Tamira Combrink, Gerhard de Kok and Karin Lurvink. A first version of this synthesis was discussed at an expert meeting involving scholars from inside and outside the Netherlands, to whom we owe our great gratitude. Our special thanks go to those who gave us elaborate oral or written comments: Cátia Antunes, Sven Beckert, Anthony Bogues, Guillaume Daudin, Karwan Fatah-Black, Dienke Hondius, Joseph Inikori, Sylvia Marzagalli, Linda Nooitmeer, Bas van Leeuwen, Ulrich Pfister, Matthias van Rossum, Peer Vries, Zach Wehrwein and Jan Luiten van Zanden, as well as to Tamira Combrink and Matthias van Rossum in their capacity of editors of this special issue and the anonymous reviewers of the *Tijdschrift voor Sociale en Economische Geschiedenis* and *Slavery & Abolition*.

Disclosure statement

No potential conflict of interest was reported by the author(s).

Funding

The article forms the synthesis of a project funded by the Dutch Council of Scientific Research (NWO): Slaves, commodities and logistics. The direct and indirect, the immediate and long-term economic impact of eighteenth-century Dutch Republic transatlantic slave-based activities, NWO Project Number 360-53-170 (principal applicants Marcel van der Linden, Karel Davids and Henk den Heijer).

OPEN ACCESS

Slave-based coffee in the eighteenth century and the role of the Dutch in global commodity chains

Tamira Combrink

ABSTRACT

This article discusses the development of eighteenth century commodity chain of coffee which was largely based on slavery. It highlights the role of the Dutch in this chain and in the intra-European trade. This study shows how the market for coffee was being expanded over the course of less than a century. It shows how consumption reached a mass scale and spread to inland regions on the European continent, notably to German regions along the Rhine river. The article aims to emphasise how this dynamic of market expansion was linked to the expansion of slavery in Dutch Guiana and the French West Indies, especially the rapid growth of Saint Domingue. Finally, this article highlights the importance of this coffee expansion to the Dutch economy. Based on collected data from numerous sources, this article calculates that the share of coffee in Dutch trade value grew from 1% to 9.5% over the course of the eighteenth century and was pivotal to the changing orientation of Dutch foreign trade during this period.

Introduction

There is a direct connection between the expansion of consumption and new consumer culture in Europe on the one hand and the expansion of plantation slavery in the Caribbean on the other. As Sidney Mintz has already pointed out in his classic book *Sweetness and Power. The Place of Sugar in Modern History*, it is important to link these connected developments firmly. Global commodity chain analysis offers a tool for achieving this as it studies the whole chain of activities from initial production to final consumption. For the most part, however, studies of the development of European consumption and demand, and European regional distribution, have been conducted quite separately from the study of slave-based production, colonial expansion and Atlantic empires at large.[1]

In studies dealing with the intra-European trade and the Atlantic trade, the phenomena of overseas trade and colonial production are still too often perceived as being two different circuits. The first field prefers to speak about 'global goods', 'new consumption items' or at best 'colonial products', but hardly ever refers to slavery, or to the origins and production processes of the consumer goods. Such framing clouds the relation that these intra-European processes have with the violent processes of the increasing European control of production. The second field, the study of the Atlantic empire and its plantation colonies usually stops its analysis at the arrival of goods in any European harbour: what happened with the products afterwards is beyond the scope of study. In this way, colonial enterprise is readily perceived as not having much of a link to the common economy of the European mainland.

As this article will argue, however, these circuits were interconnected and their interdependence increased over time. Slave-based commodities formed a large part of intra-European trade, especially in the case of the Dutch Republic, and the expansion of one was not possible without the expansion of the other. This article focuses on the global commodity chain of coffee in the eighteenth century and the part the Dutch played in this. By taking a global commodity chain approach, this article does not just look at this slave-based commodity as a plantation export or a colonial import but also follows it from its final consumption back to its slave-based production. This approach goes beyond focusing on transnational connections, and it is especially suitable to overcome methodological nationalism, since it takes production, trade and consumption together as one process, one unit of analysis.[2] Unlike studies focusing on international actors, such as transnational trade networks, this study zooms out from the spiders and shows their webs, connecting local actors around the globe, touching on elements of their material daily cultures that matter to them.

Coffee is key to understanding the Atlantic world in the second half of the eighteenth century. Demand for this commodity led to an enormous expansion of slave-based production in the West Indies. Not only did it do so by leading to an increasing number of new coffee plantations, but also by expanding sugar production, which was partly dependent on the coffee boom. As coffee was often consumed with it, the spread of the daily consumption of coffee over continental Europe caused a further increase of demand for sugar.[3] To place a commodity at the centre of an academic study implies having to look across national boundaries and to connect the economies involved. By following this approach, it will be shown that slave-based coffee was more important to the Dutch economy than previously thought. That it was important to the Dutch in the eighteenth century should not be controversial, but this article will substantiate this importance and add to the existing historiography in three new ways.

First, Atlantic trade in coffee was more important to the Dutch than current historiography suggests. Although the Vereenigde Oostindische Compagnie (VOC) and East Indies have received much more attention in Dutch historiography than Atlantic trade, Victor Enthoven and Johannes Postma have argued that in the eighteenth century the growth of Atlantic trade surpassed that of the East in value.[4] This article strengthens the call for attention to the great importance of Atlantic trade for the Dutch. While Enthoven and Postma's argument is based on approximate trade figures, this article provides more detailed figures for the Dutch coffee trade. It also aims to colour in the picture: the dynamics of what large and increasing Atlantic trade meant for the Dutch, and those connected by them, with respect to coffee.

Second, coffee culture and its expansion at this stage depended a great deal on slavery. This article highlights this and urges historians not to ignore the significant fact that Atlantic trade was mostly slave-based. In historiography on the continental European economy or daily consumer culture, the role of slavery is not emphasised. There has been hardly any research to date on the actual size and share of slave-based activities in the Dutch economy.[5] My research is part of a larger project aiming to address this omission and within this, this article focuses on slave-based commodity chains. This brings into the discussion the value added to the European economy by European processing and services related to the slave-based commodities before their final consumption. This value also includes the intra-European trade in slave-based commodities. Since added value by processing had only limited importance for coffee, as no separate processing industry existed yet in the eighteenth century, this article therefore focuses on including intra-European trade in a narrative on the importance of slave-based coffee to the Dutch economy.[6]

Third, by connecting growing overseas production to the growth of consumption in the Rhine region, coffee was also key in changing the orientation of the Dutch economy during this period. It is, of course, known that coffee drinking increased in this period, that Surinam produced a lot of coffee and that coffee was traded from France to Holland. Furthermore, it has already been remarked that German coffee drinking habits were beneficial to Dutch merchants.[7] This study shows how the market for coffee was being expanded over the course of less than a century, in waves, to greater geographical regions and larger groups of the population. It also shows how this dynamic of market expansion was linked to the expansion of slave-based production in Dutch Guiana and outside the Dutch empire.

In doing so, it shows an important connection between inland Germany and the Atlantic and slavery. These connections have been studied by Klaus Weber, and recently in the book *Slavery's Hinterland*, as well as in a joint research project on 'globalized peripheries' by Klaus Weber, Jutta Wimmler, Anka Steffen and Torsten dos Santos Arnold (see also the contribution of Anka Steffen in this issue).[8] Northern Germany has been better studied in this respect, while the Rhine region has received relatively little attention. At the same time, there are various indications that the upstream-Rhine trade in this period was increasing.[9] However, this has hardly been put into the perspective of larger Atlantic developments.[10] This article affirms that the growth of the upstream-Rhine trade in this period was largely slave-based and explains this development by indicating its connection with the coffee boom.

Maintaining a transnational perspective, Dutch developments will be discussed in relation to, in interaction with and in comparison with the French role in slave-based coffee chains. Coffee at that time was almost exclusively a French and Dutch trade. The Dutch had a large share in the world's coffee production, with the Dutch Guianas producing one third of all coffee consumed in Europe between 1738–67.[11] The French–Dutch intertwinement in their Atlantic trades has been noted before.[12] J.P. van der Voort has suggested that it was the failure by Dutch planters to provide protection against the French competition that hit the planters hard in Surinam eventually. This line of argument has received far less attention in Dutch historiography than the other aspect in J.P. van der Voort's study, which looks into the debt-crisis of these plantation mortgage funds. This is a mistake as this article will show that in order to understand Dutch Atlantic developments in the eighteenth century, it is crucial to look at the Dutch–French intertwinement. By looking at the example of coffee, it becomes clear how directly the French and Dutch were competing with each other in this respect.

Proceeding where J.P. van der Voort ended, this study also adds a different dimension: by not stopping at the arrival of commodities in the Atlantic harbour and adding the Rhine trade, it becomes clearer where all the Dutch imports went and what the role of demand was. In addition, it will be argued that the phenomenal growth of Saint Domingue was partly made possible by the export market along the Rhine that was opened up by the Dutch Republic. Bringing together production figures, trade data and data on consumption and dissemination, this article maps the slave-based commodity chain of coffee in its entirety, providing insight into the chronology and geography of supply and demand.

Coffee times: the chronology of Dutch and French coffee development

Coffee was important to the eighteenth-century Atlantic world and may be to some extent a symbol of the changes that occurred during that time period. It was a relatively new phenomenon in Europe. The European trade in coffee was dominated by Dutch and French actors; West Indian production soon exceeded the oriental imports to Europe.[13] A coffee boom that started in the 1750s increased the growth of the world's coffee production: it was mostly the French colony of Saint Domingue, modern Haiti, that was responsible for the rapid growth of coffee production in the second half of the eighteenth century, but Dutch West Indian coffee production accelerated it as well.

The Dutch and French were rivals in the domination of the western coffee market and were well aware of it. From the very beginning of the European mastery of coffee cultivation, the French and Dutch were competing. Popular narratives still disagree as to who mastered the cultivation first. There is typically a Dutch and a French version of the 'origin of coffee' tale – which is a clear sign of the long competition between the nations in this commodity's business.[14] At first they were both competing with the Levant and Indian Ocean trade and, as coffee was planted in Java and on the island Bourbon (currently Réunion), with the Indian Ocean production (the VOC, Marseille merchant houses and Compagnie des Indes). But early in the eighteenth century, the Dutch and French began production in their respective West Indian colonies, in Surinam and Martinique. In the decades that followed the Dutch and French West Indies would produce most of the coffee for the expanding European consumer market.

At the beginning of the eighteenth century, coffee was still a very exclusive product in Europe. Yemen had been the centre of world coffee production in the preceding centuries, when most coffee was consumed on the Ottoman market.[15] Coffee was introduced to Europe in the seventeenth century: following the Turkish example, coffee houses had been selling it for half a century and more of them were opening up in all the major towns of Europe. It was a popular drink among the urban bourgeois.[16] As the beverage of the coffee house, where merchants exchanged news and politics was discussed, it has been described as being associated with modern, rationalistic values and the Enlightenment. At the same time coffee was also viewed as being related to the home and women, as Bach's *Coffee Cantata* (Leipzig, 1732) illustrates, and in the German speaking world the *Kaffeekränzchen* may have been at least as common as the coffee house was.[17]

Coffee consumption started to spread further, as supplies became more regular from the 1690s onward. From the late 1720s, with more and more successful harvests from West Indian slave plantations coming in, the price of coffee decreased significantly, and it started to become affordable by a wider group of people. As early as 1726 a Dutch contemporary observer wrote that 'coffee had broken through so generally in our land that maids and seamstresses now had to have their coffee in the morning or they could not put their thread through the eye of their needle'.[18] Research into inventories in the Netherlands proves that the common people owned coffee-making utensils from the second quarter of the eighteenth century onward. The consumption of coffee was especially widespread among the urban commercial and artisanal classes and spread later in rural areas.[19] For many artisans and maids, coffee (with sugar) replaced beer as a common beverage to start the day. While beer prices were rising at that time, this substitution proved to be a persistent cultural change. Coffee was part of the 'invention of breakfast'.[20]

From the late 1750s the volume of Atlantic coffee production once again increased significantly. It was at that time that the habit of drinking coffee spread further inland, beyond the coastal regions, including sections of the middle and lower classes in Rhineland Germany. This was true for many urban centres along the coast in western and northern Europe, but also increasingly for inland Germany, because its urban centres and some of its rural areas were connected to the global market.[21] This created a discussion about the morality of coffee drinking in the German regions. At the Prussian court, King Friedrich II feared the moral degradation of the common people and called for the return to having traditional '*biersuppe*' for breakfast.[22] There were also some local efforts to prohibit coffee drinking or the selling of roasted coffee beans.[23]

Over the course of the eighteenth century coffee consumption grew to massive proportions. In some places coffee had already become a product of mass consumption: the average person from the poorest tax-paying classes in the Dutch province of Friesland in the north was buying 2.8 kilograms of coffee per year around 1786. [24] With this amount, they could drink a cup of coffee a day, perhaps more, since it was common to mix coffee with roasted rye or chicory. Although its consumption may not have been as widespread as the tea–sugar complex in Britain, there certainly was a similar 'coffee–sugar complex' in continental Europe, and, while it reached some regions later than others, its spread during the eighteenth century was extensive.

This expansive dissemination of coffee consumption is confirmed by research in probate inventories,[25] by the growing numbers of retailers selling coffee in many towns,[26] by rural pedlars carrying coffee,[27] but also by the sheer volume of coffee traded through Europe. The total amount of coffee imported to Europe (excluding the Italian Levant trade) was less than 4 million pounds per year during 1723–7 and rose to almost 100 million pounds per year around 1788 (see Table 1).[28] While Dutch coffee imports rose from over 6 million pounds in 1753 to over 28 million in 1790 (with a peak of 35 million in the middle of the 1770s),[29] Dutch exports of coffee to the north and over the Rhine grew from about half a million pounds in 1753 to over 22 million pounds in 1790.[30]

Lastly, the growth of demand for coffee is apparent from the price movements: although world coffee production kept expanding at a remarkable pace in the second half of the eighteenth century, despite two temporary price drops lasting a few years, coffee prices did not structurally decrease further over those decades (see Figure 1). Apparently, demand rose even faster than production. Drinking coffee had become a new daily habit, a cultural practice that would stay.[31] Alongside and partly replacing beer and wine, it is

Table 1. Coffee on the European market, volume in pounds.

Yearly average	Dutch Guianas	Dutch East	French West	Other	Total**
1723–1727	81,254	3,595,930	10,897		3,688,081
1733–1737	1,659,996	4,326,175	1,045,302		7,031,473
1743–1747	3,039,135	3,111,131	3,475,158	31,680	9,657,104
1753–1757	4,699,330	3,196,174	6,364,741	67,080	14,327,325
1763–1767	13,010,702	3,417,893	9,755,403	100,420	26,284,417
1773–1777	19,519,656	5,250,250	35,294,922	808,260	60,873,088
1783–1787*	13,887,195	5,116,691	79,138,144	1,154,880	99,296,910

Sources: **Dutch West Indies**: On Surinam: J. Postma (2009): Dutch shipping and trade with Surinam, 1683–1795. DANS database. https://doi.org/10.17026/dans-zeh-h82t, on Berbice: Klaas Kramer, 'Plantation Development in Berbice from 1753 to 1779: The Shift from the Interior to the Coast', *Nieuwe West-Indische Gids* 65, no. 1–2 (1991): 51–65.; On Essequibo: Henry Bolingbroke, *A Voyage to the Demerary* (London 1807), Appendix I, 397. **Dutch East Indies**: VOC auctions in Amsterdam *2, derived from Pim de Zwart, *Globalization and the Colonial Origins of the Great Divergence. Intercontinental Trade and Living Standards in the Dutch East India Company's Commercial Empire, c. 1600–1800* (Leiden: Brill, 2016); I checked this and missing years are from the VOC Boekhouder Generaal Asian exports to Holland, Judith Schooneveld-Oosterling, Gerrit Knaap (2013) *Bookkeeper-General Batavia; the circulation of commodities of the VOC in the eighteenth century (BGB)* Database hosted by Huygens ING: https://bgb.huygens.knaw.nl/. **French West Indies**: French import data, national + local best guess in Toflit18 database: Loïc Charles, Guillaume Daudin, Guillaume Plique and Paul Girard, TOFLIT18 website (consulted June 2018). Retrieved from http://toflit18.medialab.sciences-po.fr; Added to this are data of coffee smuggled via St. Eustatius and Curacao to Holland: Wim Klooster, *Illicit Riches*, 226–227, appendix 5, but for the years 1775, 1780: Van der Oudermeulen, 'Iets dat tot voordeel', 333, appendix L. Bales and tierces are converted into pounds using Van der Voort, *Westindische Plantages*, 260. **Other**: Jamaica, Brazil and Cuba: production data collected by Mario Samper, 'appendix' in: Clarence Smith, W. C. and S. Topik, eds., *The global coffee economy in Africa, Asia, and Latin America 1500–1989* (Cambridge 2003) 412 Table a.1.

* 5-year averages are calculated based on the years reported within the period; for various origins some years are missing. In the case of French West in the 1783–1787 all years are missing, the figure presented here is the figure for 1788 – it is from a different source than most other French import data and may represent production rather than imports.

** Missing in this total is European imports from the Levant.

***Also note that not all Caribbean coffee production went to Europe: The French West Indies produced more coffee than France imported in 1750s, 1760s and 1770s (see J. Tarrade, *Le commerce colonial de la France à la fin de l'Ancien Régime. L'évolution du régime de l' "Exclusif" de 1763 à 1789. Tome I* (Paris: Presses Universitaires de France, 1972) p. 413, and Michel-Rolph Trouillot, 'Motion in the System: Coffee, Color and Slavery in Eighteenth--Century Saint--Dominique', *Review (Fernand Braudel Center)* 5, no. 3 (1982): 331–88.). Some of this has been smuggled to Europe, but as far as this was via Dutch Caribbean Islands this is included in the figure presented above. Some of it may have been consumed in the Americas. The difference between European imports of French West Indian production (as estimated by French import data and Dutch imports of French coffee from the Windward islands) and estimates of French total Caribbean production is over 13 million in the 1770s.

the most accepted and regular drink in continental Europe up to the present day.

A slave-based coffee boom and new markets

Coffee started booming in both the French and Dutch West Indies in the 1750s. The 1750s saw a sudden further growth of coffee plantations and trade. Surinamese coffee production roughly doubled in those years and French West Indian production soared as well. Around 1755 already almost 80% of the European-consumed coffee was West Indian, and about a third of the total production for the European market was Surinamese. This expansion followed a period of high coffee prices at the end of the Austrian succession wars. The increase in production was set in motion early in the 1750s, but, as coffee trees take four to

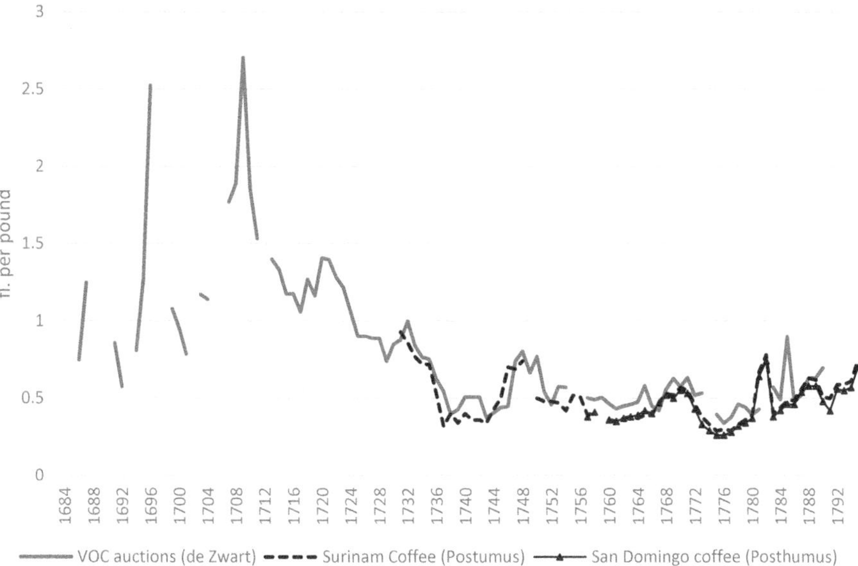

Figure 1. Coffee prices in Amsterdam. Sources: Pim de Zwart, Globalization and the Colonial Origins of the Great Divergence. Intercontinental Trade and Living Standards in the Dutch East India Company's Commercial Empire, c. 1600–1800 (Leiden: Brill, 2016); N.W Posthumus, Nederlandsche Prijsgeschiedenis. (Leiden: Brill, 1943).

five years to come to full maturation, traders had to find consumer markets for the first large harvests from 1756 onward.

The harvest boom coincided with the outbreak of the Seven Years' War (1756–63), where France was at war with Britain in the Americas and at the same time, allied with Austria, fighting against Prussia on the continent. This war impeded French shipping, and also France depended heavily on Baltic supplies for colonial supplies and armaments.[32] This made France rely on neutral parties, such as the Dutch and the Danish. As a result, for several years French colonial production reached Europe mostly via the Dutch Caribbean island of St. Eustatius (and this went on even after the British occupation of nearby Guadeloupe), as well as via the Danish island St Croix.[33] Thus, in these years, the Dutch shipped about 40%, or possibly more, of the French West Indian booming coffee production to Holland, while Surinamese coffee exports were also soaring.[34] Much of this coffee was re-exported but not so much overseas, where the Dutch were troubled by the British who did not accept the Dutch shipping for the French. During this period the Dutch made more use of an ancient trade route inland over the Rhine river. Outside periods of war, the Dutch kept shipping one-fifth to one-quarter of the increasing French coffee production, mostly importing it from Bordeaux, and re-exporting this, along with Surinamese coffee, predominantly over the Rhine river (see Figure 2, and Figure 3 for French and Dutch market shares).[35]

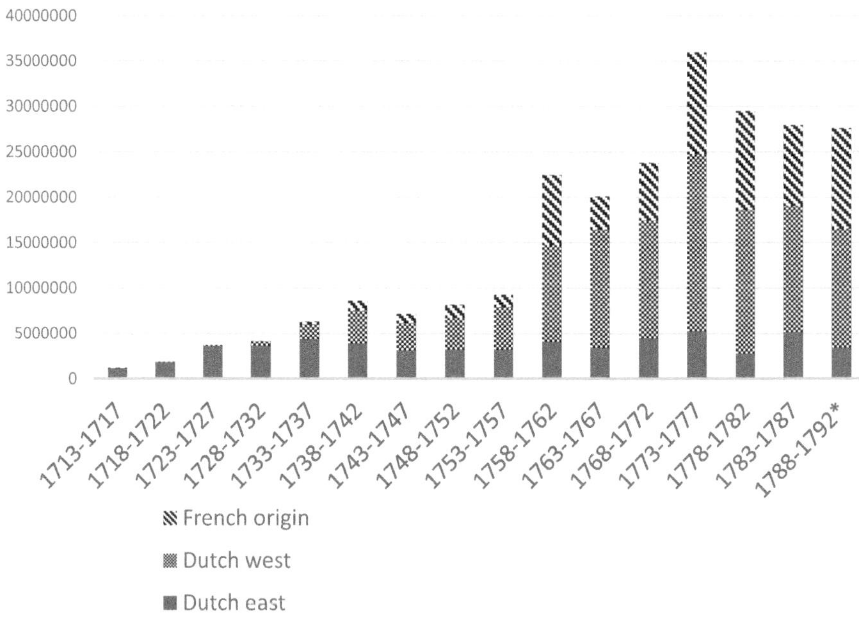

Figure 2. Dutch coffee imports. Sources: **French origin**: French origin is both French exports to Holland and Dutch imports from St. Eustatius: French import data, local best guess, adjusted for minimum values with national best guess in Toflit18 database: Loïc Charles, Guillaume Daudin, Guillaume Plique and Paul Girard, TOFLIT18 website (consulted June 2018). Retrieved from http://toflit18.medialab.sciences-po.fr. This is completed for missing years with Welling Paalgeld database G.M. Welling,'The prize of neutrality: trade relations between Amsterdam and North America 1771–1817', doctoral thesis 1998, University of Groningen,and data from Dutch customs Convoyen en Licenten, as published in the following four publications: P.J. Dobbelaar, 'Een statistiek van den in- en uitvoer van Rotterdam c. a. in 1753', *Economisch-Historisch Jaarboek* 7 (1921); L. van Nierop, 'Uit de bakermat der Amsterdamsche handelsstatistiek', in *Amstelodamum 13 and 15, bijlagen* (Amsterdam, 1915 and 1917); Joh. de Vries, 'De statistiek van in- en uitvoer van de admiraliteit op de Maaze 1784–1793, II: de statistiek van uitvoer', *Economisch-Historisch Jaarboek* 60 (1965; Added to this are data of coffee smuggled via St. Eustatius and Curacao to Holland: Wim Klooster, Illicit Riches, 226–227, appendix 5, but for the years 1775, 1780: Van der Oudermeulen, 'Iets dat tot voordeel', 333, appendix L. I converted bales and tierces into pounds using Van der Voort, Westindische Plantages, 260. **Dutch West Indies**: All colonies on the Wild Coast, the Dutch Guianas: On Surinam: J. Postma (2009): Dutch shipping and trade with Surinam, 1683–1795. DANS database. https://doi.org/10.17026/dans-zeh-h82t, on Berbice: Klaas Kramer, 'Plantation development in Berbice from 1753 to 1779 : the shift from the interior to the coast', *Nieuwe West-Indische Gids* 65, no. 1–2 (1991), 51–65.; On Essequibo: Henry Bolingbroke, *A Voyage to the Demerary* (London 1807), Appendix I, 397. **Dutch East Indies**: VOC auctions in Amsterdam *2, derived from Pim de Zwart, Globalization and the Colonial Origins of the Great Divergence. Intercontinental Trade and Living Standards in the Dutch East India Company's Commercial Empire, c. 1600–1800. (Leiden: Brill, 2016); This is checked with, and missing years are from, the VOC Boekhouder Generaal Asian exports to Holland: Judith Schooneveld-Oosterling, Gerrit Knaap (2013) Bookkeeper-General Batavia; the circulation of commodities of the VOC in the eighteenth century (BGB) Database hosted by Huygens ING: https://bgb.huygens.knaw.nl/.

This temporary extra-large Dutch distribution seemed to have opened up new markets for the consumption of coffee and sugar in its wake. Up till the 1750s the quantities of coffee exported by the Dutch had been moderate.

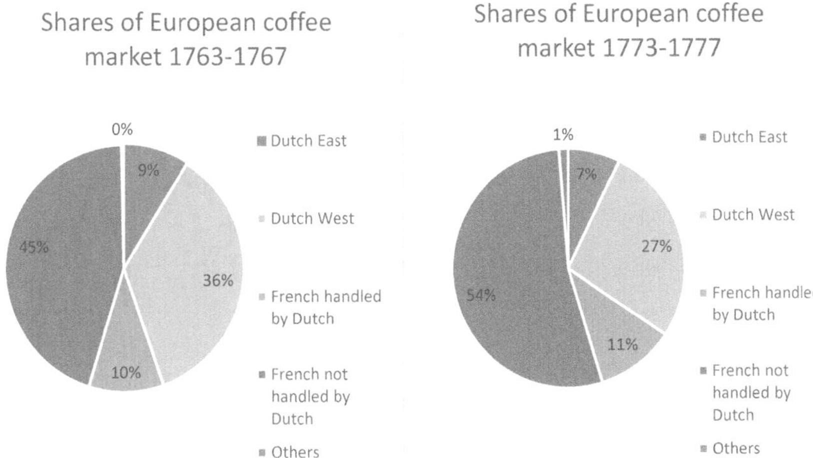

Figure 3. Sources: see Table 1. Sources: shortened reference: **Dutch West Indies**: Postma Dutch shipping DANS database; Kramer, 'Plantation development in Berbice', 51–65.; Bolingbroke, A Voyage, Appendix I, 397**;** De Zwart, Globalization and the Colonial; Schooneveld-Oosterling, e.a., Bookkeeper-General Batavia (BGB) Database: https://bgb.huygens.knaw.nl/. **French West Indies**: Charles, Daudin, e.a., TOFLIT18 database http://toflit18.medialab.sciences-po.fr; Klooster, Illicit Riches, 226–227, appendix 5, Van der Oudermeulen, 'Iets dat tot voordeel', 333, appendix L. Van der Voort, Westindische Plantages, 260. **Other**: Clarence Smith, W. C. and S. Topik (eds.), The global coffee economy, 412 Table a.1.

Dutch domestic consumption of coffee was already about 6 million pounds a year and had spread to the common people.[36] However, in the German markets that functioned as the Dutch hinterland, coffee was still primarily a luxury item. The late 1750s marked a change in this. In this period during the Seven Years War, Dutch exports to the German hinterland over the Rhine river increased to a significantly higher level. The years of West Indian coffee production expansion coincided with a substantial expansion in the volume of Dutch Rhine trade (see Figure 4).[37]

All the available evidence points to coffee playing an important part in this: the data that survives for later periods shows that coffee was a very large part of the upstream Rhine trade. In 1780 the Rhine toll in Emmerich reported that a quarter of this volume passing upstream was coffee. In 1790 the Convoyen of de Maze (Rotterdam region) and Amsterdam region together registered that almost half of the value of exports over the Rhine was coffee.[38] Coffee was also increasingly mentioned as being part of the load in the Rhine toll registers in the non-quantified remarks of bookkeepers of various Dutch Rhine tolls.[39] Also Dutch newspapers in the period immediately following commented on the increased coffee consumption by German regions, and on the Dutch merchants' increased success in selling coffee there. For instance, this report on the Leipziger Messe in *Middelburgse Courant*, written in Juna on 5 May 1766 states:

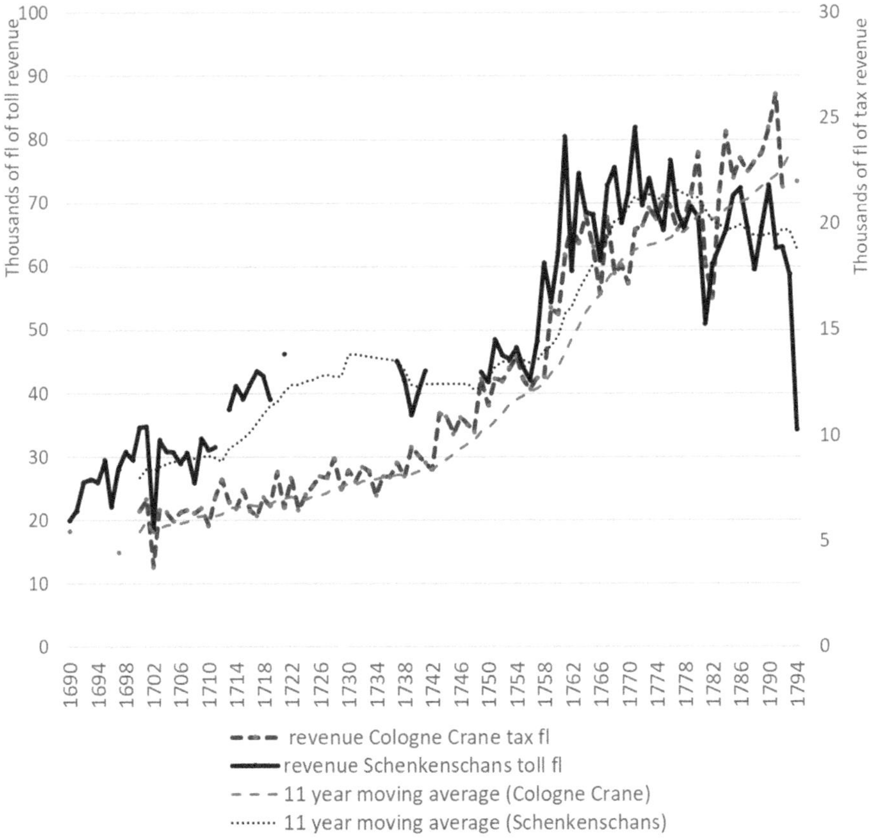

Figure 4. Comparison of Rhine trade proxy's (based on toll or crane tax). Sources: M. M. Verheul 'Anderhalve eeuw Rijnvaart: een kwantitatieve studie naar de Rijnhandel met het Duitse achterland op basis van de tolregisters van schenkenschans 1650–1800' (unpublished thesis, University of Utrecht, 1994); Ulrich Pfister, 'The Quantitative Development of Germany's International Trade during the Eighteenth and Early Nineteenth Centuries', *Revue de l'OFCE* 2015/4 (N°140): 175–221, on p 184, data collected by Wilfried Paul Feldenkirchen, 'Der Handel Der Stadt Köln Im 18. Jahrhundert (1700–1814)' (dissertation Bonn University, 1975), 286–8.

> According to our Merchants, the Leipzig Misse has not been very advantageous for the Hamburger Merchants, which brought Sugar, Tabacq, Coffy, Tea & c. there, because those of Holland had outdone them by sending a considerable multitude of these products over Frankfort down there.[40]

The opening of new markets in the Baltic and German states seems to have created a continuously increasing demand for coffee. Although a wave of increased supply caused a short period of lower prices, overall, this huge expansion of supply did not cause a continued decrease of coffee prices in the second half of the eighteenth century. Prices reacted to the boom of the 1750s, but the fall in prices during the supply boom of the 1750s did not last for very long: from 1761 onward prices were already rising again. The rising prices in the 1760s encouraged more investment in coffee in Dutch Guiana and the start of new plantations in Saint Domingue. This occurred to such an extent that this boom produced a new, more severe price drop in the first half of the 1770s. The price drop of the 1770s was deeper but was followed by a longer period of rising prices again. Coffee prices are volatile and react to market circumstances, and prices are influenced by war and by speculations on it.[41] But with coffee, there also seems to be a cyclical movement of high prices stimulating an over-production crisis in the following decade.[42] Although cyclical price movements can harm individual businesses in global coffee supply chains, they do not harm all the participants equally and do not stop expansion. The craving for coffee on the European continent stimulated an enormous expansion of production in the slave plantation colonies.

Plantation expansion, two coffee colonies

Up until the middle of the eighteenth century French West Indian production grew at a similar pace to Surinamese production. The pace of expansion on Saint Domingue was higher than in Surinam in the 1750s and kept increasing. The French windward islands, Martinique and Guadeloupe, did not grow in terms of total production between 1765–88. It was Saint Domingue, where there was still space left to expand, that was growing so quickly. Production in Saint Domingue skyrocketed and surpassed all the others, so that this colony provided 60% of all the coffee in the world by 1789.[43] Also, the Dutch colony of Surinam grew substantially up until the late 1770s, when it stagnated and even declined a little (see Figure 5).

In the light of the growing demand for coffee in continental Europe and the large market share supplied by the Dutch, the stagnation of coffee expansion in Surinam was somewhat unexpected. Answers to both Surinam's standstill and Saint Domingue's exceptional expansion should be sought within a comparative perspective. Both French and Dutch coffee merchants operated basically in the same market: French and Dutch colonies produced coffee for the same coffee markets. A large part of this continental European market did not have its own colonies and depended on the import of coffee via the French and Dutch. Additionally, the Dutch did not have a protective tariff wall to block French coffee from their markets. They did block free access from the Rhine to the sea and vice versa, but they did not protect the coffee production in Dutch colonies from the French competition on the home market and hinterland.

Unfortunately, little comparative work has been published so far. However, Rafael de Bivar Marquese is doing exciting comparative research and his work in progress has influenced and strengthened my argument here.[44] In Dutch historiography, there is a focus on failing financial instruments. In French historiography, the 'Dutch problems' are considered to be the slave revolts (the Boni-maroon wars).[45] Both, indeed, troubled Surinam in the 1770s, but it does not completely explain why plantation expansion did not recover when coffee

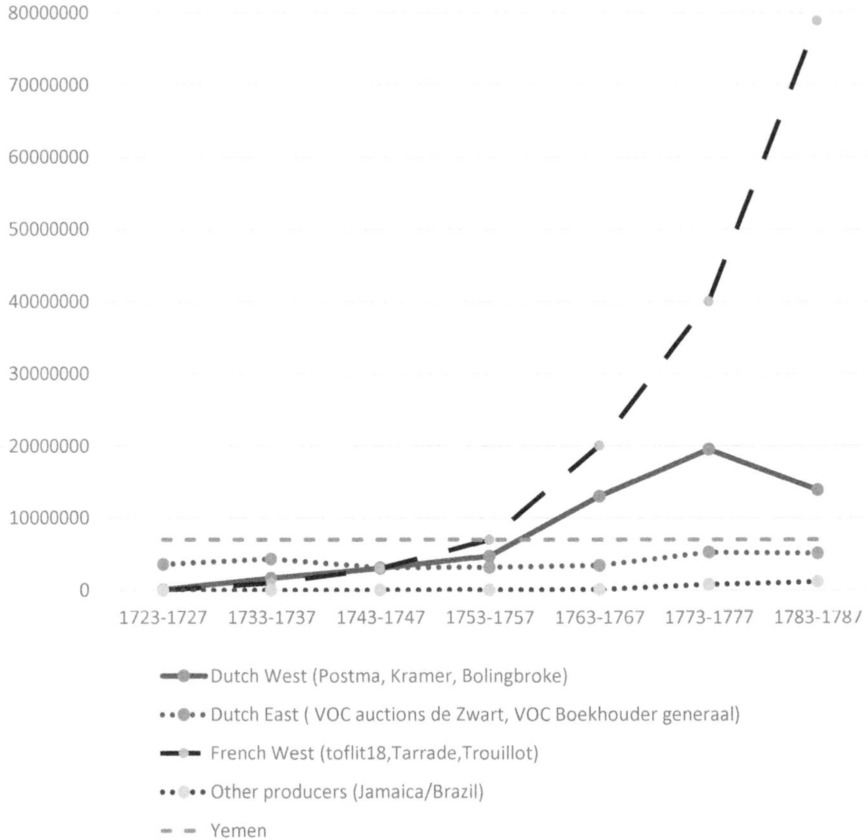

Figure 5. Coffee trade for the European market. Sources: **Dutch West Indies**: On Surinam: J. Postma (2009): Dutch shipping and trade with Surinam, 1683–1795. DANS database. https://doi.org/10.17026/dans-zeh-h82t, on Berbice: Klaas Kramer, 'Plantation Development in Berbice from 1753 to 1779 : The Shift from the Interior to the Coast', *Nieuwe West-Indische Gids* 65, no. 1–2 (1991): 51–65.; On Essequibo: Henry Bolingbroke, *A Voyage to the Demerary* (Londen 1807), Appendix I, 397. Data for the Dutch west is trade data and therefore smuggled production for American market may be missing in the later years. **Dutch East Indies**: VOC auctions in Amsterdam *2, derived from Pim de Zwart, *Globalization and the Colonial Origins of the Great Divergence. Intercontinental Trade and Living Standards in the Dutch East India Company's Commercial Empire, c. 1600–1800*. (Leiden: Brill, 2016); Missing years are from the VOC Boekhouder Generaal Asian exports to Holland, Judith Schooneveld-Oosterling, Gerrit Knaap (2013) *Bookkeeper-General Batavia; the circulation of commodities of the VOC in the eighteenth century (BGB)* Database hosted by Huygens ING: https://bgb.huygens.knaw.nl/. **French West Indies**: J. Tarrade, *Le commerce colonial de la France à la fin de l'Ancien Régime. L'évolution du régime de l' "Exclusif" de 1763 à 1789*. Tome I (Paris: Presses Universitaires de France, 1972), 413, and Michel-Rolph Trouillot, 'Motion in the system: Coffee, colour and slavery in eighteenth--century Saint--Dominique', *Review (Fernand Braudel Center)* 5, no. 3 (1982): 331–88; completed with French import data, form the Toflit18 database: Loïc Charles, Guillaume Daudin, Guillaume Plique and Paul Girard, TOFLIT18 website (consulted June 2018). Retrieved from http://toflit18.medialab.sciences-po.fr. **Other**: Jamaica, Brazil and Cuba: production data collected by Mario Samper, 'appendix' in: Clarence Smith, W. C. and S. Topik, eds., *The Global Coffee Economy in Africa, Asia, and Latin America 1500–1989* (Cambridge 2003), 412 Table a.1. **Yemen**: Michel Tuchscherer, 'Coffee in the Red Sea Area from the Sixteenth to the Nineteenth Century', in *The Global Coffee Economy in Africa, Asia, and Latin America 1500–1989*, eds. W. G. Clarence Smith, and S. Topik (Cambridge: Cambridge University Press, 2003), 55.

prices rose again. Yet, as Marquese pointed out, there are a few comparative comments in the literature that suggest that Surinam's disadvantage was ecological, and for coffee as a plantation crop specifically this had very different social and financial implications.[46] The Guianas are wet and in Surinam it was necessary to make polders and maintain waterworks. These additional costs aside, this meant that to start a coffee plantation in Surinam required significantly more involvement than was needed for a coffee plantation elsewhere in the Caribbean. This caused the structure of Dutch coffee expansion to be very different from that in Saint Domingue.

In Saint Domingue, coffee was planted in the hills. These were typically small-scale plantations, comprising just a few cheap acres of land, which were unsuitable for growing sugar, and just a few slaves (the average in 1789 was 40 enslaved people per plantation, but most plantations had fewer than 25). It was partly driven by the local population (*petit blanc, gens de couleur*) and immigrants (Canadians, retired soldiers) with relatively small amounts of capital.[47] In Surinam, coffee plantations, although smaller than sugar plantations, still consisted on average of about 90 enslaved people. Investment mostly came from creditors in Holland. This ecological difference, leading to social and financial differences in both colonies, may have played an important role in making coffee expansion on Saint Domingue more resilient to the overproduction crisis of the 1770s than Surinam.

The run on West Indian bonds in the 1760s led to a wave of investments in the colony of Surinam. However, when in the 1770s returns were less than expected, problematic financial instruments were revealed, maroon attacks were at their height causing damage and war costs to planters, and a few bankruptcies occurred. The image of coffee from Surinam as a good investment opportunity was damaged and a new wave of investment did not materialise in the following decades.[48] Surinam's rapid expansion stagnated. Investors may have been right: coffee did not seem to do so well in Surinam and there was a real risk of maroon attacks that was greater in the Guianas, where land and forests were so abundant and successful free maroon groups had already set an example.

The story of the rise of coffee in the eighteenth century is also intrinsically connected to the expansion of Atlantic slavery in that century, and also, in certain ways, to the partial collapse and subsequent transformation of Atlantic slavery at the end of the eighteenth century. France made use of the Dutch 'troubles' to expand its market share and coffee production in Saint Domingue, which accelerated at an exponential rate. 'Never before and perhaps never since has the world seen anything proportionately so dazzling as the last years of prerevolutionary San Domingo.'[49] At that time on Saint Domingue, just before the French Revolution, Toussaint l'Ouverture was reading the work of Abbé Raynal mentioning the two successful colonies of fugitive blacks in Surinam: 'those lightnings announce the thunder'.[50] And the thunder came.

The 1790s and beginning of the nineteenth century saw an enduring shortage of European coffee, and the completely changed geopolitical settings had profoundly disturbing influences on the global commodity chains. The wars and blockades following the French revolution, including the French occupation of the Dutch Republic, largely cut off France and Holland from direct access to the coffee supplies of their colonies. This caused the trade routes for coffee to change and also stimulated other locations of production, giving a role to Jamaican producers, and to Britain, North America and Hamburg as traders, as well as a role to European producers of substitutes such as chicory. But the demand for coffee on the continent, among the Dutch and a growing group of German consumers, had not diminished.

The French had lost their prominent market share, although Martinique and Guadeloupe kept on producing coffee. Moreover, independent Haiti still produced coffee, but never again at such a level as previously. Some coffee production had shifted to Jamaica, which had also received investments and immigrants from former Saint Domingue planters, and was quick to fill the supply gap that the Haitian revolution had caused. Brazil had started expanding coffee production, slowly building up to a very impressive level starting in the 1830s.[51] Surinam continued to supply coffee for a few decades, although it was facing diminishing productivity from its soil and trees, but Dutch investors seemed to have had new hopes set on Java, which had started to expand its coffee production late in the eighteenth century.[52] After the introduction of a new form of colonial labour exploitation on Java in 1830, the Dutch would come back to dominate a large share of the world market for coffee, selling the coffee from Amsterdam via the same routes along the Rhine to mostly German consumers.[53]

The share of the Dutch economy

The absolute growth of slave-based coffee production and coffee trade in the Dutch realm was undeniable and remarkable, even though Surinam's production was dwarfed by Saint Domingue and stagnated after the 1770s. Coffee occupied a new and very important position in Dutch trade: around 1770 and around 1790, coffee alone represented almost 10% of Dutch trade (both imports and exports). When leaving out the Javanese coffee that was based primarily on tributary labour exploitation and not chattel slavery, slave-based coffee represented 7.5% of Dutch trade value. Together with the slave-based production of sugar this represented about 16% of Dutch trade (see Table 2).[54] This is a strong indication that Atlantic slavery – especially the coffee-with-sugar complex – played an important part in the trade-based growth of the Dutch economy in this period.

The Dutch had a large share of the world's coffee production and trade, with the Dutch Guianas producing over a third of the coffee consumed in Europe

Table 2. Dutch trade value and the share of coffee.

	Imports		Exports		Total trade	
	1720	1770	1720	1770	1720	1770
Coffee trade in value (million guilder)	2.5	13	0.5	9.3		
Slave-based coffee trade		10		7.5		
Total trade in value (million guilder)	108	143	90	100		
Coffee as % of total trade	2.3%	9.1%	1%	10%	1.4%	9.5%
Slave based coffee as % of total trade	0%	7%	0%	8%	0%	7.4%

Sources : **Imports**: N.W Posthumus, *Nederlandsche Prijsgeschiedenis* (Leiden: Brill, 1943). (prices), Postma, Kramer, Bolingbroke (west), VOC boekhouder generaal (east), toflit18 + , Klooster (French). **Exports**: Figures from convoyen and licenten 1790: projected back to 1770 on the basis of general Rhine trade proxies (Pfister and Verheul), adjusted for share of Baltic trade (on basis of Veluwenkamp). Calculated to value (in prices from Posthumus). **Total trade value**: as estimated by Jan de Vries, and A. M. van der Woude. *The First Modern Economy: Success, Failure, and Perseverance of the Dutch Economy, 1500–1815* (Cambridge: Cambridge University Press 1997), table 10.13, 577.
See the appendix for full annotation and the calculations and figures underlying this table.

between 1738 and 1767. The Dutch were the first Europeans to bring coffee cultivation under European control: they organised a more regular and significant supply, and they expanded the market to new social groups and new parts of Europe. Additionally, the Dutch regularly shipped and traded about one fifth of French coffee. Moreover, the Dutch played a crucial role in shipping French coffee at war times, especially when coffee first started booming and the Seven Years' War broke out. The Dutch flooded the Rhine region with coffee and sugar, creating a lasting demand for both commodities, as the two are typically consumed together. Coffee became a booming business from the 1750s until the Haitian revolution.

Conclusions and implications

By following the commodity chain, this article has highlighted how the emergence of the German coffee tradition is rooted in Atlantic slavery. Additionally, it has also indicated that the Dutch shift in its orientation of international trade away from the traditional Baltic trade towards the German hinterland is related to the boom of slave-based production in Surinam and Saint Domingue.[55] The commodity chain approach used here helped identify intra-European trade connections and to come up with a more inclusive account and figure of the importance of coffee in Dutch trade. It has argued that coffee also had a notable influence on the Dutch economy: a new commodity grew to equal 9.5% of its total trade value within fifty years and remained important in the following century. Moreover, slave-based coffee production also played a crucial role in the shift in orientation of the Dutch economy that occurred in the eighteenth century, from the Baltic–Mediterranean trade towards the trade-axis and from colonies to the German hinterland.

There seems to be a growing consensus among Dutch economic historians that the Dutch economy experienced trade-based growth in the second half of the eighteenth century, while other sectors remained stagnant or were declining.[56] In the light of this, a large and increasing share of slave-based coffee production within this growing Dutch trade is significant. This narrative places this production at the heart of one of the few dynamic sectors in the economy of this period and has shown its centrality to an important reorientation of the Dutch economy developing around that time.

This article also adds to our understanding of an important chapter in the global history of coffee. William Gervase Clarence Smith's and Steven Topik's collected volume is an important contribution to the global overview of the history of coffee and contains global comparative studies on coffee with an excellent collection of data by Mario Samper. While they note that Dutch and French West Indian production took coffee out of the hands of monopolistic trading companies, they pay relatively little attention to the role of slavery, and the role of Saint Domingue in particular, in the history of coffee.[57] This article has argued that the history of the slave-based coffee production in Surinam and Saint Domingue was pivotal in starting the mass consumption of coffee in Europe. Slavery thus had a significant part to play in an important phase of the history of coffee.

Acknowledging the role of slavery raises the question as to why slavery played such a role in coffee expansion. Slave-based coffee production was also crucial during the brief importation of coffee from Jamaica, following the Haitian revolution, and most prominently in Brazil during the 'second slavery', where slavery existed on an enormous scale and was reshaped in the world's biggest coffee producing country during the nineteenth century. Clarence-Smith and Topik's comment that slavery was 'a myopic system that probably delayed' progress in coffee production does not help to explain the large part it played. Answers should perhaps be sought not in the later years of slavery in Brazil, but in the earlier phase of the use of this dehumanising system in coffee planting in Surinam and the French colonies (including the islands in the Indian Ocean). If one focuses on this phase, a possible new source of explanation might be found by looking at factors of production in a market which made the expansion of production for the market 'possible' and relatively flexible. These factors also made it possible to be organised largely by the capital of the international merchant-bankers that were governing the global coffee chains.

This article began by stating that the European distribution of exotics and the Atlantic expansion of slave-based production are usually treated as separate. By discussing the case of coffee in the eighteenth century, the article has shown how developments in production, consumption and distribution are firmly related and are better understood together. Changing consumer habits, growing demand for coffee and the opening up of the new market along the Rhine all developed in interaction with the rapid expansion of the slave-based production of coffee in the French and Dutch West Indies.

It is this aspect of expansion that makes the study of coffee history so fascinating – as Topik underscores in an article on the long history of coffee.[58] Coffee was a relatively 'new' product to Europeans: in one century coffee changed from being an exotic novelty for the rich in trendy capitals to a daily necessity of many common people in the hinterlands of the European continent. By bringing this addictive product to new geographical areas and at a low price, new groups of people could afford it and the market for coffee expanded, demand grew and the market was able to grow even more. I am not the first to stress that the development of consumer culture is an important aspect of the development of capitalism, but the case of coffee is quite stunning as it demonstrates how easily new markets are created and how easily areas and groups of people become incorporated into them. In fact, the market for caffeinated beverages including cola has been continuously growing.

In order to supply this mass craving for coffee, world coffee production had to be expanded. Whether it was because merchants in Mocha did not aim for expansion or did not succeed in expanding the Yemenite coffee production further, in the eighteenth century they did not provide for more than the already considerable Ottoman demand. Nor did production expand considerably after the initial planting of coffee in Java. The VOC at first did not seem interested in expansion: when prices started falling in the late 1720s, the VOC even demanded cutting down coffee trees in an attempt to control overproduction and the subsequent decline in prices.[59] However, the VOC could not control the market. Planters in the West Indies, fuelled by merchant capital from Europe, entered the coffee market, made it a competitive one and sought profit in its expansion, producing more and more coffee for more and more consumers. Slavery proved a system well-fit to organise the expansion of production by investing money in it: buy labour power in the form of enslaved human beings, let them plant trees and do all the work, and then sell the coffee. The Dutch merchant-bankers organised coffee investment, enslavement, and planting and selling; while not leaving the town of Amsterdam, they took this merchant-capital-led production system to quite an extreme.

While some believe that all capitalist expansion ends in crisis, this one certainly did – a crisis caused by uprisings and revolutions, most notably, the Haitian one. Yet the Germans still liked coffee. And the Dutch colonial merchant-banker elite had learned something about expanding markets and expanding production, and perhaps also something about the role of the state in labour control: as soon as they could, they sent Johannes van der Bosch to Surinam and Java in order to solve the labour issues and expand the colonial production of coffee.

Notes

1. Notable exceptions are the classics Sidney Mintz, *Sweetness and Power: The Place of Sugar in Modern History* (New York: Penguin Books, 1985) and, more recently, Sven Beckert, *Empire of Cotton: A New History of Global Capitalism* (New York: Penguin Books, 2014). See also the remark on the lack of a link between studies of different parts of the commodity chain of cotton, on page xx of Beckert's book.
2. For a discussion of definitions and uses of the commodity chain approach, see the introduction in Jennifer Bair, ed., *Frontiers of Commodity Chain Research* (Stanford, CA: Stanford University Press, 2009). The origin of the term is from Terence K. Hopkins and Immanuel Wallerstein, 'Commodity Chains in the World-economy prior to 1800', *Review* 10, no. 1 (1986): 157–70, 159. See also Gary Gereffi and Miguel Korzeniewicz, eds., *Commodity Chains and Global Capitalism* (Westport, CT: Greenwood Press, 1994), 17.
3. See also J. Tarrade, *Le commerce colonial de la France à la fin de l'Ancien Régime. L'évolution du régime de l'"Exclusif" de 1763 à 1789*, vol. 1 (Paris: Presses Universitaires de France, 1972), 34.
4. Victor Enthoven, 'An Assessment of Dutch Transatlantic Commerce', in *Riches from Atlantic Commerce*, eds. Johannes Postma and Victor Enthoven (2003), 445. See also Jan de Vries, 'The Limits of Globalization in the Early Modern World', *Economic History Review* 63, no. 3 (2010): 710–33 – this article makes the point that early modern European trade with Asia, through a number of constraints, had relatively little impact: its argument shows that in comparison, Atlantic trade was larger and growing faster (see figure on page 720, and for Dutch trade data see table on page 729).
5. See the article by Brandon and Bosma appearing in this same issue. There is a narrow focus on the slave trade, for which there are some contested figures. See the call for broadening the discussion on the slave trade to include the impact of slavery at large in K. Fatah-Black and M. van Rossum, 'Beyond Profitability: The Dutch Transatlantic Slave Trade and its Economic Impact', *Slavery & Abolition* 36, no. 1 (2015): 63–83.
6. Roasted beans cannot be conserved for long without modern vacuum packaging techniques, so the final processing was done mostly at home by retailers or in coffee houses. I look at processing at the retail level in my dissertation, but because most of this happened outside the Dutch Republic I have left it out of this article for the sake of conciseness. For the importance of the added value to sugar, see also the contribution of Klass Rönnbäck in this issue.
7. On coffee consumption: Anne McCants, 'Exotic Goods, Popular Consumption, and the Standard of Living: Thinking about Globalization in the Early Modern World', *Journal of World History* 18, no. 4 (2007): 433–62 and Anne McCants, 'Poor Consumers as Global Consumers', *Economic History Review* 61, no. S1 (2008): 177; P. Reinders and Th. Wijsenbeek, *Koffie in Nederland. Vier eeuwen cultuurgeschiedenis* (Delft, 1994). On coffee production in Surinam: Alex van Stipriaan, *Surinaams Contrast: roofbouw en overleven in een Caraïbische plantagekolonie 1750–1863* (Leiden: KITLV, 1993). On French colonial exports to Holland: M. Morineau, 'La balance du commerce franco-néerlandais et le resserrement Economique des Provinces-Unies au XVIIIe siècle', *Economisch-Historisch Jaarboek* 30 (1965), 170–235; P. Butel, *Les négociants bordelais, l'Europe et les Iles au XVIIIe siècle* (Paris : Aubier, 1974); J.P, van der Voort, *De Westindische Plantages. 1720–1795 Financiën en handel* (Eindhoven: De Witte, 1973); Pierrick Pourchasse, *Le commerce du Nord:*

les changes commerciaux entre la France et l'Europe septentrionale au XVIIIe *siècle* (Rennes: Presses Universitaires de Rennes 2006). On German consumption of Dutch-traded coffee: Joh. De Vries, 'De problematiek der Duits-Nederlandse "economische betrekkingen in de negentiende eeuw"', *Tijdschrift voor Geschiedenis* 78 (1965): 23–48.

8. K. Weber, *Deutsche kaufleute im Atlantikhandel 1680–1830* (Munich: C.H. Beck, 2004), 192; see A.S. Overkamp, 'A Hinterland tot the Slave Trade? Atlantic Connections of the Wupper Valley in the Early Ninetheenth Century', in *Slavery Hinterland: Transatlantic Slavery and Continental Europe, 1680–1850*, eds. Felix Brahm and Eve Rosenhaft (Woodbridge: Boydell & Brewer, 2016); 'Globalized Peripheries. New Approaches to the Atlantic World 1680–1850', Conference held 05.07.2018–07.07.2018 in Frankfurt an der Oder, by Klaus Weber, Jutta Wimmler, Anka Steffen and Torsten dos Santos Arnold.
9. Ulrich Pfister, 'The Quantitative Development of Germany's International Trade during the Eighteenth and Early Nineteenth Centuries', *Revue de l'OFCE* 2015/4 (N °140), 175–221; De Vries, 'De problematiek der Duits-Nederlandse, 23–48.
10. Tamira Combrink, 'From French Harbours to German Rivers. European Distribution of Sugar by the Dutch in the Eighteenth Century', in *Le diffusion des produits ultramarine en l'Europe dans le XVIIIe siècle*, ed. Maud Villeret (Rennes: Presses Universitaires de Rennes, 2018), 39–56.
11. See table in appendix (underlying sources of data: Postma, Kramer, Bolingbroke, Boekhouder general for Dutch coffee production; Tarrade, Trouillot and Toflit18 for French; Samper in Topik for Jamaican and Brazilian).
12. Most recently by Sylvia Marzagalli, 'The French Atlantic and the Dutch, Late Seventeenth - Late Eighteenth Century', in *Dutch Atlantic Connections, 1680–1800*, eds. Jessica Roitman and Gert Oostindie (Leiden and Boston: Brill, 2014), 103–18 and Pourchasse, *Le commerce du Nord*. Originally by Morineau, 'La balance du commerce franco-néerlandais et le resserrement économique des Provinces-Unies au XVIIIe siècle', 170–235; Butel, *Les négociants bordelais, l'Europe et les Iles au XVIII*[e] *siècle* ; and Van der Voort, *De Westindische plantages.*
13. See Figure 1. Also see 'Introduction' by S. Topik and 'Appendix' by Mario Samper in Clarence Smith, W. C. and S. Topik, eds., *The Global Coffee Economy in Africa, Asia, and Latin America 1500–1989* (Cambridge: Cambridge University Press 2003), 412 Table a.1.; Michel-Rolph Trouillot, 'Motion in the System: Coffee, Color and Slavery in Eighteenth-century Saint Dominique', *Review (Fernand Braudel Center)* 5, no. 3 (1982): 331–88.
14. Most nationalistic tales have their roots in the nineteenth century, but the older M. Brevet, *Essai sur la Culture du Cafè* (Port-au-Prince, Associés de l'Imprimerie Royale, 1763), 5, gives credit to the Dutch for taking the plant from Mocha to Batavia and from Batavia to Amsterdam. But after the mayors of Amsterdam gave it as a gift to the French king in 1714, it was a French military officer who took it from Paris' botanical gardens to Martinique and this was the origin of coffee in the French West Indies. Van Stipriaan, *Surinaams Contrast*, 146, asserts that coffee was planted in Surinam first, in 1712, and retells, without affirming its truth, the story that the first coffee crop was planted along the Cottica river and came from Hortus Medicus in Amsterdam. These accounts are not mutually exclusive: both stories could be true.
15. Michel Tuchscherer, 'Coffee in the Red Sea Area from the Sixteenth to the Nineteenth Century', in *The Global Coffee Economy in Africa, Asia, and Latin America 1500–*

1989, eds. W. G. Clarence-Smith and S. Topik (Cambridge: Cambridge University Press, 2003), 55.

16. P. Reinders and Th. Wijsenbeek, *Koffie in Nederland. Vier eeuwen cultuurgeschiedenis* (Zutphen: Walburg Pers, 1994), 108.
17. H.J. Schulze and Alfred Mann 'Ey! Wie Schmeckt der Coffee Süsse: Johan Sebastian Bach's Kaffee-kantate in Ihrer Zeit' *Bach* vol 2. (2001), 1–117.
18. Anne McCants, 'Poor Consumers as Global Consumers', *Economic History Review* 61, S1 (2008), 177. Also referred to by Jan Breman, *Mobilizing Labour for the Global Coffee Market: Profits From an Unfree Work Regime in Colonial Java* (Amsterdam: Amsterdam University Press, 2019), ch. 3, note 13, original F. Valentijn, *Oud en Nieuw Oost-Indiën* (Dordrecht, J. Van Braam 1726), 190.
19. Th. Wijsenbeek, 'Van Medicijn tot Statussymbool', in *Koffie in Nederland. Vier Eeuwen Cultuurgeschiedenis*, eds. P. Reinders and Th. Wijsenbeek (Zutphen: Walburg Pers, 1994), 113–15, found coffee-making utensils in 50% of the poor (Pro-Deo) classes and 95% of the middle classes in Delft between 1735 and 1760. She also states that between 1740 and 1782 about 52% of the probate inventories of the Amsterdam Municipal Orphanage (Burgerweeshuis) mentioned coffee-making utensils (a selection made up from the working poor, craftsmen and petty shopkeepers) rising for all households at the end of the century. For this, she refers to Julie Ledoux's and Simone Baksteen's unpublished master's thesis (UvA 1992). Anne McCants found coffee-making utensils in 90% of all inventories (belonging to beer brewers, linen weavers, and farmers) of Weesp, Doesburg, and Maassluis from 1730: Anne McCants, 'Exotic Goods, Popular Consumption, and the Standard of Living: Thinking about Globalization in the Early Modern World', *Journal of World History* 18, no. 4 (2007): 444; See for rural data: J.A. Kamermans, *Materiële Cultuur in De Krimpenerwaard in De Zeventiende En Achttiende Eeuw: Ontwikkeling en Diversiteit* (Hilversum: Verloren, 1999). This study showed that coffee had already spread to parts of the village middle classes but had spread further in rural areas in the second half of the 18th century.
20. Woodruff D. Smith, *Consumption and the Making of Respectability, 1600–1800* (New York: Routledge, 2002), 183–7.
21. M. Zeuske and J. Ludwig, Amerikanische Kolonialwaren und Wirtschaftspolitik in Preuβen und Sachsen: Prolegomena (17./18. und frühes 19. Jahrhundert)', *Jahrbuch für Geschichte Lateinamerikas* 32, no. 1 (1995): 257–301; H.E. Bödeker, 'Le café allemand au XVIIIe siècle: une forme de sociabilité eclairée', *Revue d'histoire moderne et contemporaine* 37, no. 4 (1990): 571–88; P. Albrecht, 'Kaffeetrinken. Dem Bürger zur Ehr' – dem Armen zur Schand', in *Das Volk als Objekt Obrigkeitlichen Handelns*, ed. R. Vierhaus (Tübingen: Niemeyer, 1992), 57–100.
22. Zeuske and Ludwig, 'Amerikanische Kolonialwaren', 268. 'Die Leute sollten Biersuppe geniessen' is a phrase from Friedrich II in an attempt to temper the selling and consumption of coffee. See also: William H. Ukers, *All about Coffee* (New York: The Tea and Coffee Trade Journal, 1922) 'On September 13, 1777, Frederick issued a coffee and beer manifesto, a curious document, which recited: "It is disgusting to notice the increase in the quantity of coffee used by my subjects, and the amount of money that goes out of the country in consequence. Everybody is using coffee. If possible, this must be prevented. My people must drink beer. [...]"'
23. See for instance: Prohibition in Kassel especially threatens coffee consumption with punishment in rural areas in 1766: 'DUITSLAND en aangrenzende RYKEN',in *Leydse courant*' 7 March 1766, Leyden (viewed in Delpher, 2 July 2018, http://resolver.kb.nl/resolve?urn=ddd:010911330:mpeg21:p001). Tarrade also mentions

French merchants being worried about 'northern princes' prohibiting coffee around 1770; Ukers, *All About Coffee*, mentions a prohibition on selling roasted coffee in Cologne in the 1780s. Also Albrecht 'Kaffeetrinken', mentions unsuccessful attempts at repressing coffee.

24. Pim Reinders, *Thera Wijsenbeek-Olthuis* and Steven Braat, *Koffie in Nederland: Vier Eeuwen Cultuurgeschiedenis* (Zutphen: Delft: Walburg Pers; Gemeente Musea Delft, 1994) mentions Frisan tax records on page 113.
25. For the rural evidence, see especially the ongoing inventory research in Münster led by Christine Fertig: Henning Bovenkerk presented the first results showing poor rural regions connected through textile production that did have coffee-making tools, while richer rural regions without those longer-distance connections did not (work in progress presented at *EURHO* September 2019 in Paris). Earlier version: 'Sweet Coffee, Pretty Scarves: Global Goods and Rural Households in 19th Century (Northwestern Germany)', conference paper at ESSHC 2018 in Belfast. Published work: Christine Fertig and Ulrich Pfister, 'Coffee, Mind and Body. Global Material Culture and the Eighteenth-century Hamburg Import Trade', in Anne Gerritsen and Giorgio Riello (ed.), *The Global Lives of Things. The Material Culture of Connections in the Early Modern World* (London: Routledge, 2016), 221–40.
26. For Frankfurt: Alexander Dietz, *Frankfurter Handelsgeschichte*, vierter band (Frankfurt am Main: Verlag von Hermann Minjon1925), 205–15; for Amsterdam and Rotterdam see Pim Reinders. Thera Wijsenbeek and Steven Braat, *Koffie in Nederland*<shortened, is mentioned above. For smaller Dutch towns see D. van den Heuvel and E. van Nederveen Meerkerk, 'Households, Work and Consumer Changes. The Case of Tea and Coffee Sellers in 18th-Century Leiden', Mems Working Papers No. 2 (2012).
27. M. Häberlein, 'Savoyische Kaufleute und die Distribution von Konsumgütern im Oberrheingebiet, ca. 1720–1840', in *Geschichte des Konsums. Erträge der 20. Arbeitstagung der Gesellschaft für Sozial- und Wirtschaftsgeschichte 23.–26. April 2003 in Greifswald*, ed. R. Walter (Stuttgart: Steiner 2004). Albrecht, 'Kaffeetrinken. Dem Bürger zur Ehr' – dem Armen zur Schand', 57–100.
28. French coffee imports in Toflit18 and as reported by Tarrade, Troulliot were 78 million pounds in 1788, adding Dutch imports for a five-year average during the years 1783–7, as estimated by the Amsterdam VOC sales *2 as reported by Pim de Zwart, Postma Database on Surinam exports, Bolingbroke on Essequibo exports, Kramer on Berbice exports, Klooster on Dutch Antillian exports, adding production or exports in Jamaica, Brazil and Cuba as collected by Mario Samper, totals 99 million pounds (an estimate based on the VOC Boekhouder Generaal (Asian exports to Holland) for that year would be higher and bring it to 102 million pounds). The 1720s estimate is based on the same sources – taking either one reported year or averaging several reported years between 1723 and 1727.
29. Ibidem for the five-year averages. For the years 1753 and 1790 import figures are from Van der Voort, *De Westindische Plantages.*
30. Figure based on Convoyen and Licenten by taking together the figures from the Amsterdam-region and Rotterdam-region, as published in the following four publications: P.J. Dobbelaar, 'Een statistiek van den in- en uitvoer van Rotterdam c. a. in 1753', *Economisch-Historisch Jaarboek* 7 (1921); L. van Nierop, 'Uit de bakermat der Amsterdamsche handelsstatistiek', *Amstelodamum* 13 and 15, bijlagen (Amsterdam, 1915 and 1917); Joh. de Vries, 'De statistiek van in- en uitvoer van de admiraliteit op de Maaze 1784–1793, II: de statistiek van uitvoer', *Economisch-Historisch Jaarboek* 60 (1965).

31. McCants, 'Exotic Goods, Popular Consumption', 433–62 and McCants, 'Poor Consumers as Global Consumers', 177.
32. See the work in progress by Pernille Røge for more information on the Danish (and Swedish) role in French colonial expansion. Pernille Røge, *Northern Pillars of Empire: The Baltic and the French Atlantic Colonies, 1615–1815* (Harvard Talk, 2018; publication of an article is in preparation).
33. Daniel Baugh, *The Global Seven Years War 1754–1763: Britain and France in a Great Power Contest* (New York: Longman, 2011), 281, 324, 385.
34. The figure 40% is based on a production estimate from 1765 (Tarrade, *Le commerce colonial de la France*, 413), combined with trade data on Dutch imports for the year 1760: Toflit18 data on French exports to Holland, combined with Klooster's estimates for St. Eustatius and Curacao exports of coffee (Wim Klooster, *Illicit Riches : Dutch Trade in the Caribbean, 1648–1795* (Leiden: KITLV Press, 1998), 226–7, appendix 5.
35. Combined sources of Tolfit18, Tarrade, Trouillot for production figures, Klooster for St. Eustatius trade and additional data from Dutch convoyen.
36. Estimate is based on the import and export figures of Convoyen and Licenten, as published in the following four publications: Dobbelaar, 'Een statistiek van den in- en uitvoer van Rotterdam c. a. in 1753'. van Nierop, 'Uit de bakermat der Amsterdamsche handelsstatistiek', de Vries, 'De statistiek van in- en uitvoer van de admiraliteit op de Maaze 1784-1793, II'.
37. Combining U. Pfister's Rhine trade proxy based on the cranetax in Cologne, with Verheul, Rhine trade proxy based on Lobith's Rhine tolls, the two politically independent tolls and taxes show an increase in exactly the same period. M. M. Verheul 'Anderhalve eeuw Rijnvaart: een kwantitatieve studie naar de Rijnhandel met het Duitse achterland op basis van de tolregisters van schenkenschans 1650–1800' (unpublished thesis, University of Utrecht, 1994); Pfister, 'The Quantitative Development of Germany's International Trade during the Eighteenth and Early Nineteenth Centuries', 175–221, on p 184, data collected by Wilfried Paul Feldenkirchen, 'Der Handel Der Stadt Köln Im 18. Jahrhundert (1700–1814)' (dissertation Universitat Bonn, 1975), 286–8.
38. Almost half in value in 1790, about a quarter in volume in 1780. M. Scholz-Babisch, *Quellen zur Geschichte des Klevischen Rheinzollwesens vom 11. bis 18 Jahrhundert* (Wiesbaden, Steiner 1971), 1001–12. Convoyen and Licenten as published in P.J. Dobbelaar, 'Een statistiek', L. van Nierop 'Uit de bakermat' and Joh. de Vries, 'De statistiek van in- en uitvoer'.
39. M.M. Verheul, 'Anderhalve eeuw Rijnvaart' (Master thesis University of Utrecht,1994), 24. She counted for the sample years 1715, 1752, 1780, 1800. I counted commodities in a database I constructed by taking a sample from the Groote Gelderse tollen te Arnhem: 'rekeningen van Jasper Schulder' (1747) in the archive of the Rekenkamer in Gelders Archief, GA:0012:2410, and the published toll accounts for the years 1801–5 by R.A.J. Dix, ed., *De grote Gelderse tol te Arnhem en IJseloord. Deel 1, 1801–1805* (Arnhem, Nederlandse Genealogische Vereniging, Genealogische Werkgroep Gelderland, 1995).
40. My translation. 'DUITSCHLAND'. *Middelburgsche courant*, Middelburg, 20 May 1766 (viewed in Delpher, 28 June 2018).
41. Pierre Gervais, 'Facing and Surviving War: Merchant Strategies, Market Management and Transnational Merchant Rings', in *Merchants in Times of Crises (16th to mid-19th Century)*, eds. Andrea Bonoldi, Markus Denzel, Andrea Leonardi and Cinzia Lorandini (Stuttgart: Franz Steiner Verlag, 2015), 79–94. He gives an account of a (sugar)

merchant's market control and speculation on the basis of upcoming events in Canada in Bordeaux 1755.

42. This cyclical movement of stimulation and overproduction for coffee prices is still noticeable today (in the twentieth century a group of coffee-producing countries tried to regulate this with quotas, and now there are coffee futures, but farmers suffer): see Jeff Neilson and Bill Pritchard, *Value Chain Struggles: Institutions and Governance in the Plantation Districts of South India* (Chichester, UK and Malden, MA: Wiley-Blackwell, 2009).
43. Trouillot, 'Motion in the System', 337 (he claims this without a reference; data underlying figure 1 suggest 66% in 1788).
44. Rafael de Bivar Marquese, 'A Tale of Two Coffee Colonies', paper presented in ICLASA, Barcelona, May 2018.
45. Van der Voort, in *Westindische Plantages*, paid ample attention to *negotiatiefondsen*. More recently, Bram Hoonhout, 'The Crisis of the Subprime Plantation Mortgages in the Dutch West Indies, 1750–1775', *Leidschrift* 28:2 (2013), 85–100. For a broader and more balanced account see A. van Stipriaan, 'Debunking Debt. Image and Reality of a Colonial Crisis. Surinam at the end of the 18th century', *Itinerario*, 19:1 (1995), 69–84, and G. Oostindie, 'The Economics of Surinam Slavery', *Economic and Social History in the Netherlands* 5 (1993), 1–18. French historiography mentioning Surinam and its crisis caused by the revolt: Tarrade, *Le commerce colonial de la France*, 418. Morineaux in *Deus ex machina*, Trouillot, 'Motion in the System'. These remarks are based on the French ministers' correspondence about the matter in 1775, as well as on Stedman and on active references to Surinam's revolts by French contemporary philosophers such as Raynal.
46. Many thanks to Rafael de Bivar Marquese, who sent me his paper that pointed out this insight to me (that the difference in scale was essentially an ecological difference): Rafael de Bivar Marquese, 'A Tale of Two Coffee Colonies', paper presented in ICLASA, Barcelona, May 2018. See for this Van Stipriaan, *Surinaams Contrast*, especially the chapter on water management and the paragraphs on coffee. See also Oostindies' paragraph comparing coffee explicitly with Saint Domingue and Brazil. See also Trouillots comments on ecological and social circumstances that were specific to coffee on Saint Domingue, Oostindie, *Roosenburg en Mon Bijou. Twee Surinaamse plantages, 1720–1870* (Dordrecht: Springer, 1989). See Debien for more details on coffee plantations in Saint Domingue: G. Debien, 'L'établissement d'une caféière dans un quartier neuf de Saint-Domingue à la fin du XVIIIe s.', *Bull. Soc. Arch, et hist. de Nantes et de la L. inf* 80 (1940): 141–51.
47. See Trouillot, 'Motion in the System', 356; Tarrade, *Le commerce colonial de la France*, 19 and 147; and Debien, 'Plantations et esclaves a saint domingue, sucrerie cotitineau', 16 and 22. See also Debien, 'L'établissement d'une caféière'. To contrast with investments in sugar, see Natasha Bonnet, 'L'investissement colonial au XIIIe Siècle: l'exemple de quatre plantations sucrières à Saint Domingue', *Entreprises et histoire* 3, 52 (2008): 46–55.
48. Van der Voort, *Westindische Plantages*; Hoonhout, 'The Crisis of the Subprime Plantation Mortgages', 85–100. See also the reading of Karwan Fatah-Black, *Societeit van Suriname 1683–1795: Het bestuur van de kolonie in de achttiene eeuw* (Zutphen: Walburg Pers, 2019), 139–41; Van Stipriaan, 'Debunking Debt', 69–84.
49. Quoted in Cyril Lionel Robert James,. *The Black Jacobins: Toussaint L'Ouverture and the San Domingo Revolution*, 2nd rev. edn (New York: Vintage Books, 1989), 55.
50. As cited by James, *Black Jacobins*, 25.

51. Samper, in Clarence-Smith and Topik, *The Global Coffee Economy in Africa, Asia, and Latin America 1500–1989.*
52. See also Breman, *Mobilizing Labour for the Global Coffee Market*, 83, about doubling of production from 1789 onward. (As coffee trees take four years to grow to maturation, the investments must have started just after the fourth Anglo-Dutch war – although possibly the production has always been higher, and it was more an issue of Dutch control that was further enforced from 1789 onward – as a new governor made a point of securing the coffee supply. See Breman, *Mobilizing Labour for the Global Coffee Market*, 84 and 95 [a new instruction from 1789 by Rolff]).
53. Mark Jakob and Laura Rischbieter, 'A Matter of Location? Traders and Manufacturers of Colonial Goods in the 19th Century Rhine Economy', in *The Rhine: A Transnational Economic History*, eds. Ralf Banken and Ben Wubs (Nomos: Baden-Baden, 2017).
54. Calculations based on de Vries and vd Woude's total trade value estimates, combined with estimates on coffee imports and exports as assembled by me: exports from Rhine trade proxies for an estimate of 1770 based on the trend between 1750 and 1790, convoyen en licenten for 1750 and 1790, imports by combining: Postma, Kramer, Toflit18, VOC boekhouder generaal, Klooster. Prices from Posthumus 1944.
55. See the argument by Jan de Vries, and A.M. van der Woude. *The First Modern Economy: Success, Failure, and Perseverance of the Dutch Economy, 1500–1815* (Cambridge: Cambridge University Press 1997) on this important reorientation of the Dutch trade-axis.
56. J.L. van Zanden and Bas van Leeuwen, 'Persistent But Not Consistent', *Explorations in Economic History* 49 (2012): 119–30; J.L. van Zanden and A. van Riel, *Nederland 1780–1914. Staat, instituties en economische ontwikkeling* (Amsterdam,Balans 2000), 31. See de Vries and van der Woude, *The First Modern Economy*, 490, 500 and 681–3.
57. Clarence-Smith and Topik, *The Global Coffee Economy in Africa, Asia and Latin America, 1500–1989*, 9–10.
58. Steven Topik, 'Historicizing Commodity Chains', in *Frontiers of Commodity Chain Research*, ed. Jennifer Bair (Stanford, CA: Stanford University Press, 2009), 39. Quote: 'Why study coffee? [...] Because "coffee itself has been central to the expansion of the world economy"'.
59. Breman, *Mobilizing Labour for the Global Coffee Market.*

Disclosure statement

No potential conflict of interest was reported by the author(s).

Appendix: Addendum to Table 2: Calculation of coffee trade values and shares of Dutch trade

Step 1: Dutch export figures known

Total exports according to Dutch customs (convoyen en licenten), as published in parts by Dobbelaar, de Vries and van Nierop (in 4 publications):

Table A1. Dutch export of coffee in pounds.

pounds	Coffee
1753	458,082
1790	22,443,302

Source: Convoyen en Licenten. Figures calculated by taking together the figures from the Amsterdam-region and Rotterdam (de Maze)-region, as published in the following four publications: P.J. Dobbelaar, 'Een statistiek van den in- en uitvoer van Rotterdam c. a. in 1753', *Economisch-Historisch Jaarboek* 7 (1921); L. van Nierop, 'Uit de bakermat der Amsterdamsche handelsstatistiek', *Amstelodamum* 13 and 15, bijlagen (Amsterdam, 1915 and 1917); Joh. de Vries, 'De statistiek van in- en uitvoer van de admiraliteit op de Maaze 1784–1793, II: de statistiek van uitvoer', *Economisch-Historisch Jaarboek* 60 (1965).

Step 2: An estimate for the year 1770

Calculation of an estimate for exports of coffee in 1770 estimate by a reasoned interpolation. Reasoning the formula for interpolation: on the basis of Rhine trade proxies (see Figure 3) can be estimated that 90% of the growth of Rhine exports between 1753 and 1790 took place before 1770. Approximately 70% of all coffee exports are over the Rhine river, but 30% is to other destinations (based on Convoyen en Licenten) – for this part, a simple interpolation assuming linear growth is used.

Formula of interpolation:

1: 0.7 Rhine exports * 0.9 + 0.3 other destinations * 0.5 = 0.78
2: export 1753 + ((export 1790 – export 1753) * 0.78) = 1770 estimated export of coffee

Table A2. Dutch exports of coffee including interpolated estimate for 1770.

pounds	Coffee
1753	458,082
1770	17,606,554
1790	22,443,302

Sources: see table i.

Step 3: Calculate trade value on the basis of prices

The trade value of coffee is calculated on this basis are the Surinamese coffee prices in Amsterdam as reported by Posthumus. Most exported coffee was from Surinam, but also Javanese coffee and San Domingo coffee were exported, although how much of each kind is unknown. Coffee from Saint Domingue was a little cheaper in Amsterdam, but in German sources there was no price difference, or the difference is reversed. Javanese coffee was much more expensive, but it accounts for a smaller part of the exports. In the calculations of slave-based coffee, this type of coffee is subtracted in pounds.

Table A3. Coffee price on the Amsterdam bourse, presented in 5-year averages.

	Surinam price per lb (until 1732 equalled that of Java coffee)	San Domingo coffee price per lb	Java coffee price per lb
1718–1722			1.1
1748–1752	0.55		0.645

(*Continued*)

Table A3. Continued.

	Surinam price per lb (until 1732 equalled that of Java coffee)	San Domingo coffee price per lb	Java coffee price per lb
1768–1772	0.526	0.506	0.6
1788–1792*	0.57	0.524	0.678

Source: N.W Posthumus, *Nederlandsche Prijsgeschiedenis.* (Leiden: Brill, 1943).

Table A4. Dutch export of coffee in volume and value.

	export in million pounds	exports calculated in million guilders
1750	0.5	0.3
1770	17.6	9.3
1790	22.4	12.8

Sources: Convoyen en Licenten for export volume: P.J. Dobbelaar, 'Een statistiek van den in- en uitvoer van Rotterdam c. a. in 1753', *Economisch-Historisch Jaarboek* 7 (1921); L. van Nierop, 'Uit de bakermat der Amsterdamsche handelsstatistiek', *Amstelodamum* 13 and 15, bijlagen (Amsterdam, 1915 and 1917); Joh. de Vries, 'De statistiek van in- en uitvoer van de admiraliteit op de Maaze 1784–1793, II: de statistiek van uitvoer', *Economisch-Historisch Jaarboek* 60 (1965)., 1770 is an interpolation see step 3, N.W Posthumus, *Nederlandsche Prijsgeschiedenis.* (Leiden: Brill, 1943).for prices

Step 4:

There is much more data available about the Dutch import of coffee: many more years and origins are known (with combined data from various sources on the Dutch import of coffee in value and in volume). Also it can be reconstructed what share of this is West-Indian slave-based coffee.

Table A5. Dutch imports of coffee, in total and slave-based.

	Slave-based coffee	Coffee
in guilder	Total value of Dutch slave-based coffee imports	Total value of Dutch coffee imports
1718–1722		2,012,900
1748–1752	2,746,273	4,802,501
1768–1772	10,047,693	12,726,721
1788–1792	13,297,612	15,595,744

Sources: **French origin**: Loïc Charles, Guillaume Daudin, Guillaume Plique and Paul Girard, TOFLIT18 website (consulted June 2018). Retrieved from http://toflit18.medialab.sciences-po.fr; Welling Paalgeld database G.M. Welling,'The prize of neutrality: trade relations between Amsterdam and North America 1771–1817', doctoral thesis 1998, University of Groningen; P.J. Dobbelaar, 'Een statistiek van den in- en uitvoer van Rotterdam c. a. in 1753', *Economisch-Historisch Jaarboek* 7 (1921); L. van Nierop, 'Uit de bakermat der Amsterdamsche handelsstatistiek', *Amstelodamum* 13 and 15, bijlagen (Amsterdam, 1915 and 1917); Joh. de Vries, 'De statistiek van in- en uitvoer van de admiraliteit op de Maaze 1784–1793, II: de statistiek van uitvoer', *Economisch-Historisch Jaarboek* 60 (1965); Wim Klooster, *Illicit Riches*, 226–227, appendix 5; Van der Oudermeulen, 'Iets dat tot voordeel', 333, appendix L;Van der Voort, *Westindische Plantages*, 260. **Dutch West Indies**: J. Postma (2009): *Dutch shipping and trade with Surinam, 1683–1795.* DANS database. https://doi.org/10.17026/dans-zeh-h82t; Klaas Kramer, 'Plantation Development in Berbice from 1753 to 1779 : The Shift from the Interior to the Coast' *Nieuwe West-Indische Gids* 65, no. 1–2 (1991): 51–65.; Henry Bolingbroke, *A Voyage to the Demerary* (London, 1807), Appendix I, 397. **Dutch East Indies**: Pim de Zwart, *Globalization and the Colonial Origins of the Great Divergence. Intercontinental Trade and Living Standards in the Dutch East India Company's Commercial Empire, c. 1600–1800* (Leiden: Brill, 2016); Judith Schooneveld-Oosterling, Gerrit Knaap (2013) *Bookkeeper-General Batavia; the circulation of commodities of the VOC in the eighteenth century (BGB)* Database hosted by Huygens ING: https://bgb.huygens.knaw.nl/.

(For more information on the processing of these data from these sources into value and five year averages, please contact author, reference data file 'coffee clean tables').

Step 5:

On the basis of known import data, trends for Dutch total exports over the Rhine, and what is known about trends and volume of domestic consumption, the export figure for coffee in 1720 can be estimated, and the share of slave-based coffee in the exports can be estimated.

Table A6. Dutch coffee trade in volume and value.

		in million pound		*in million guilder*	
		import	export	import value according to divers detailed trade serials	export value calculated
1720	coffee	2.1		2.0	
	slave-based coffee	0.1		0.0	
1750	coffee	8.2	0.5	4.8	*0.3*
	slave-based coffee	5.0		2.7	
1770	coffee	23.8	17.6	12.7	9.3
	slave-based coffee	19.4	*14.4*	10.0	*7.5*
1790	coffee	28.3	22.4	15.6	12.8
	slave-based coffee	24.3	*19.3*	13.3	*11.0*

Sources: combined sources (see Table v for imports, see tables i and ii for exports, see Posthumus, *Nederlandsche Prijsgeschiedenis*,for prices).

Sources: Loïc Charles, Guillaume Daudin, Guillaume Plique and Paul Girard, TOFLIT18 website (consulted June 2018). Retrieved from http://toflit18.medialab.sciences-po.fr; Welling Paalgeld database G.M. Welling,'The prize of neutrality: trade relations between Amsterdam and North America 1771–1817', doctoral thesis 1998, University of Groningen; P.J. Dobbelaar, 'Een statistiek van den in- en uitvoer van Rotterdam c. a. in 1753', *Economisch-Historisch Jaarboek* 7 (1921); L. van Nierop, 'Uit de bakermat der Amsterdamsche handelsstatistiek', *Amstelodamum* 13 and 15, bijlagen (Amsterdam, 1915 and 1917); Joh. de Vries, 'De statistiek van in- en uitvoer van de admiraliteit op de Maaze 1784–1793, II: de statistiek van uitvoer', *Economisch-Historisch Jaarboek* 60 (1965); Wim Klooster, *Illicit Riches*, 226–227, appendix 5; Van der Oudermeulen, 'Iets dat tot voordeel', 333, appendix L;Van der Voort, *Westindische Plantages*, 260. J. Postma (2009): Dutch shipping and trade with Surinam, 1683–1795. DANS database. https://doi.org/10.17026/dans-zeh-h82t; Klaas Kramer, 'Plantation Development in Berbice from 1753 to 1779 : The Shift from the Interior to the Coast', *Nieuwe West-Indische Gids* 65, no. 1–2 (1991): 51–65.; Henry Bolingbroke, *A Voyage to the Demerary* (London, 1807), Appendix I, 397; Pim de Zwart, *Globalization and the Colonial Origins of the Great Divergence. Intercontinental Trade and Living Standards in the Dutch East India Company's Commercial Empire, c. 1600–1800* (Leiden: Brill, 2016); Judith Schooneveld-Oosterling, Gerrit Knaap (2013) *Bookkeeper-General Batavia; The Circulation of Commodities of the VOC in the Eighteenth Century (BGB)* Database hosted by Huygens ING: https://bgb.huygens.knaw.nl/.

The estimate of 0.5 million guilder coffee exports in 1720 is based on the export volume of 1750 combined with the higher prices of the period (458,082 pound x 1.1 guilder = 502,8902 pounds is 0.5 million pounds). The estimate of 7.5 million guilder exports of slave-based coffee in 1770 and the estimated 14.4 million pounds of slave-based coffee exported in 1770 is an estimate assuming the same mix of origins in the export as in the import. As there is no reason to assume that the mix in origins of exported coffee was different between the exports and the imports in one direction or the other.

A cloth that binds: new perspectives on the eighteenth-century Prussian economy

Anka Steffen

ABSTRACT

The active participation of Eastern European lands in European overseas expansion has not been studied properly. This article therefore focuses on the province of Silesia and its highly productive rural household linen processing. Special attention is given to the mutual impact of the trade in Silesian linen fabrics and the Atlantic slave-related markets during the long eighteenth century. The endogenous and exogenous factors which shaped the specific economic development of the Silesian linen region will be identified. It will also present an approximate calculation of the share of slave-based activities in the economic performance of Silesia and Prussia respectively during the second half of the eighteenth century.

Introduction: a new approach to Silesian economic history

The slave trade, or the forced labour of African slaves on plantations around the Atlantic basin, not only contributed to the profits made by individuals, but actually supported the industrial advancement of *Western* Europe.[1] In the case of England, Joseph E. Inikori tried to quantify the impact of its overseas trade on the country's development and concluded that 'Africans made an invaluable contribution to the Industrial Revolution in England'.[2] However, detailed studies on the impact of Africans and their labour on processes taking place in *Eastern* Europe have remained unwritten. Here, research about the Silesian linen trade can offer interesting insights.

As early as the 1960s, the Polish economic historians Marian Małowist (1909–88) and Witold Kula (1916–88) pursued the idea that trade relations between Western and Eastern Europe were to some extent economically complementary. It is striking that both scholars found themselves wanting to know what role maritime trade played in Eastern Europe's economic development while examining Poland's industrial advancement from different perspectives. While Małowist was a trade theorist who emphasised the advantages Western Europe drew from the economic integration of Eastern Europe into maritime trade, especially because of grain shipments to Portugal and the Netherlands since the fifteenth century, Kula dealt with the regional agricultural system, which was boosted by endogenous factors, notably land abundance and labour shortage.[3] Meanwhile, Zsigmond Pál Pach (1919–2001), a Hungarian historian, asked the important question of the manner and extent to which the appearance of overseas colonies and their linkage to world trade affected the economic relations between Western and Eastern Europe.[4] Unfortunately, these pioneering reflections did not find their way into the broader sphere of economic research and no one has yet paid sufficient attention to the role of Eastern Europe in European overseas expansion.[5] This article argues that while all three historians provide intriguing intellectual starting points, a combination of their approaches is required to form a frame that can adequately explain why household-based linen processing became a major industry in Silesia and how its unique features could shape the economic development of the region for centuries.

The argument here is that Silesian linens, a commodity not yet scrutinised in the highly advanced field of research on early-modern global trade, were not only a pivotal factor as a barter commodity within the transatlantic exchange for slaves, but were also in demand for use as clothing material for slaves and for ordinary white settlers in the overseas colonies.[6] Despite increasing competition from other major textiles traded across the Atlantic, especially English woollens and Indian cottons, this fabric sparked an ever-rising demand in distant markets from the sixteenth century, and had a significant, long-lasting impact on the economic development of Silesia and on the conditions under which the region's rural population produced the cloth.[7] But exogenous influences alone would not have had as much of an impact if endogenous factors had not ensured that the demand could be met. Silesia's spinning and weaving sector could prosper (and the linen industry could dominate the region's economy well into the nineteenth and twentieth centuries) because the local organisation of labour under serfdom within the system of 'Gutsherrschaftsgesellschaft' ('landlord-society') made it possible to provide cheap but qualitatively suitable linen that satisfied seaborne demand.[8] This article proposes a new framework for examining the economic development of the historical region of Silesia and of the Prussian state during the 'long' eighteenth century. Taking both exogenous and endogenous determinants into account broadens the perspective on the economic performance of Silesia and Prussia and, as a consequence, brings to light the depth of the repercussions which slave-based activities had on Europe beyond its narrow coastal stretch. While it may seem self-evident, this topic will be explored in detail for the first time.

The article is structured in three parts. First, it introduces the main Silesian linen processing region and explains the socio-economic conditions of the region within the context of international developments. Second, the early phases of the linen export trade are described, together with the impact on the further socio-economic development of the province. Finally, the article estimates the contribution of slave-based activities to the Silesian economy and the revenues of the Prussian state during the second half of the eighteenth century.

From the Giant Mountains to the Atlantic Ocean

In 1698, a letter sent from the Silesian town of Glatz (Kłodzko) reached Matthias Giesque, a Hamburg-born merchant living in London. Ignatius Gruber's remote location in the Kłodzko Valley (Kotlina Kłodzka), surrounded by the Western Sudetes, had been no hindrance to his forming a business relationship with the well-connected merchant in the city on the Thames. Gruber supplied Giesque with linen fabrics with blue and white stripes through the trading company Planck & Volckmann, which received the linen wares in Hamburg and had them shipped to London. In return, Gruber was supplied with luxury items such as clocks made by David Lestourgeon of London or beaver hats, which he intended to sell in Breslau (Wrocław). In addition, he was involved in importing exotic goods such as pepper, sugar and logwood. Giesque also corresponded with Johann Christian von Knorr of Breslau and Daniel Buchs of Hirschberg (Jelenia Góra), both of whom also dealt in Silesian linen cloth.[9] These fabrics were headed to Jamaica, where Benjamin Willet either traded them for cotton and indigo, or sold them for cash. Willet also kept Giesque informed about the 'Guinea Trade' and the latest price developments for slaves arriving in Port Royal.[10]

This short example of how business relations unfolded between the English metropolis, major trade cities in Silesia and the distant colony of Jamaica, illustrates that Silesia participated early on in the maritime trade, even if indirectly. Such commercial activities were not exceptional in the seventeenth century but were part of an already regular pattern of business.

From the map of Europe we can see their share of the coastline gave the Portuguese, Dutch and English the advantage over the inland masses of continental Europe when it came to development of seaborne trade. It is not surprising, therefore, that the nobility of Eastern Europe invested in land and grew grain for export to support their lifestyles. In Silesia, in contrast, climatic conditions favoured the cultivation of hemp and flax. Hence, on the foothills of the Giant Mountains, production of linen cloth, mainly for export, had begun in the sixteenth century.

Johannes Ziekursch (1876–1945), a German historian interested in the social history of Silesia under Prussian rule, identifies ten administrative districts in Silesia as the main linen processing zone. The narrow finger of land in the immediate vicinity of the Sudetes was termed by him as the 'Grenzstreifen' ('border strip') and included the organisational districts of Goldberg-Hainau

(Złotoryja, Chojnów), Löwenberg-Bunzlau (Lwówek Śląski, Bolesławiec) and Bolkenhain-Landeshut (Bolków, Kamienna Góra); the precincts of the towns of Hirschberg, Leobschütz (Głubczyce), Neisse (Nysa), Neustadt (Prudnik), Reichenbach (Dzierżoniów) and Schweidnitz (Świdnica); and the county of Glatz.[11] In this border strip, where soil fertility was poor, the cultivation of cereal was undertaken only on a limited scale. Except for the area surrounding Schweidnitz, all the districts had to import grain to sustain their populations.[12] It is no wonder that landowners supplemented the lucrative but limited cultivation of grain with flax, another cash crop (Illustration 1).

When the influx of new settlers into the eastern parts of Central Europe dried up during the fourteenth century and the Black Death caused a demographic breakdown, noble landowners who held extensive arable land promising an increase in future income faced a diminishing number of people sowing, planting and harvesting crops. To prevent further losses of agricultural workers, landowners gradually imposed restrictions on the mobility of the rural population. This long-term process included seizures of property and limitations on the utilisation of common meadows, pastures and forests, and led to a gradual impoverishment of the rural population. In consequence, by the beginning of the seventeenth century extensive estates had been established where peasants were increasingly liable to fulfil obligations imposed upon them by their landlords.[13]

During the same period, different processes could be observed in the western part of the continent. Since the success of Vasco da Gama's first voyage to the East Indies in 1498, Portugal's share of the spice trade grew. The city of

Illustration 1. The border strip of Silesia with the present-day south-western borderline of Poland. © Anka Steffen, based on d-maps.com.

Antwerp was chosen as a hub for selling exotic imports to Northern Europe. At the same time, the Portuguese had to stock up on barter commodities that could be exchanged for gold on the African coast. Large numbers of brass and copper goods meant for African consumption were brought to Antwerp by southern German merchant houses such as the Fuggers, the Welsers and the Imhoffs; woollens and linen cloth were supplied by English and Dutch merchants.[14] Thus, contacts between merchants from Portugal, Brabant, Flanders, the Hanse and Upper Germany strengthened in Antwerp in the early years of the sixteenth century, and knowledge of popular commodities started to circulate widely.

Naturally, the Dutch and English textile industries followed the trend, producing the lighter fabrics for hot climates overseas. However, the 'new draperies' produced in both countries differed. While the Dutch concentrated on the production of expensive, high-quality linen, woollen or mixed linen-wool cloths, the English produced predominantly woollens.[15] The demand for a variety of textiles grew steadily, chiefly because Europeans were increasingly engaged in the African trade and sailing repeatedly to the Americas to establish lucrative plantations worked by forced migrants (indentured servants and slaves). Apart from cheap clothing fabrics, low-priced sail cloths and packaging materials were also sought. This presented a new problem for the maritime powers: while the trade, flourishing since the early sixteenth century, had increased their purchasing potential, the required barter commodity – durable good-quality, but low-priced linens – could not be provided in sufficient amounts by their own domestic production. Therefore, they had to seek other sources. Unsurprisingly, German fortune seekers saw this opening as an opportunity.

Entangled economies: Silesia and the Atlantic

Southern German merchants from Nuremberg and Augsburg, as well as Dutch and English factors, desperately in search of inexpensive textiles, initially provided capital for the rural production of linens in Silesia. They took firm control of the cloth trade from the mid- sixteenth century.[16] As weaving had been, at first, organised in urban craft guilds, foreign merchants approached the guilds and signed collective contracts directly with them. Usually the merchants advanced the money for their orders and specified the amount, quality and measurements of the cloth they wished to purchase.[17] The foreign firms soon brought in their own employees, some of whom settled permanently in Silesia. They organised the acceptance of goods and transport to market.

One such employee was Johann Christian, born in 1578 in Breithardt (near Frankfurt am Main), who was hired in 1599 by the Nuremberg Viatis family. Before settling down as a factor in Greiffenberg (Gryfów Śląski) in 1603, he had studied book-keeping in Leipzig. Christian died aged 66 in 1644, having worked a full 45 years for the company of Viatis & Peller in Silesia. In his obituary, the Greiffenberg priest Christian Adolph depicts him as a 'Schatzkasten' ('treasure chest') for many people, particularly for local linen weavers, who had found good earning opportunities while he administered the trade.[18] Twenty-eight years earlier, the London-born merchant Thomas Cheswright had passed away in the same Silesian town and was buried in the local cemetery. The printed funeral oration indicates that Cheswright had been active since around 1606 as a linen textile buyer in Silesia. Five other English merchants were present at his funeral: Humfrid Tomkins, Thomas Johnson, Jacob Hawley, Samuel Seymer and Nathanael Jackson.[19] It seems reasonable to assume that all of them were at that time in the vicinity of Greiffenberg to purchase linens.

The foreign merchants took the risks of journeying into distant parts of Europe to build up their stocks of cloth, knowing that high profits could be achieved. Between 1593 and 1607, the Dutch alone carried around 200,000 ells (c. 120,000 metres) of Silesian linens to the Gold Coast.[20] Pieter de Marees mentioned in his travel account published in 1602 that the Dutch brought great amounts of 'Sleser Lywaet' to the West African coast and that African merchants and noblemen were dressed in white linens.[21] In this way, Western European merchants linked East Central European production zones with West African consumer markets as early as the mid-sixteenth century. Only when the turmoil of the Thirty Years' War (1618–48) cut off the trade routes connecting foreign merchants with Silesia did Silesian retailers and assimilated migrant merchants start to supervise the production process themselves and come to successfully monopolise the linen trade to Western port cities.[22]

The years of warfare devastated the province. Alongside severe damage to the road network, farms and peasant dwellings, the number of inhabitants shrunk to one-third of its pre-war size.[23] Under these circumstances, it is not surprising that the process of binding the peasant work force to the land ('Bauernlegen') continued and worked out in favour of the landowners.[24] Refugees, who had fled the devastated areas, settled in the safer accessible mountain regions, as a result of which the spinning and weaving handicrafts became decentralised.[25] The town guilds lost their power. Ultimately, Silesian noble landholders grew into entrepreneurs, dealing in raw materials or semi-finished manufactures, such as linen yarn, which were forcibly delivered to them for pre-determined prices by the peasants living on their land.[26] The decentralisation of the production sites were thus of no concern to them.[27] This feudal system allowed landowners to exploit the people working on their estates, which further drove down the already low Silesian labour costs, which had been prevented from rising for a long time.[28] The few people who managed to avoid forced labour had little power to demand more money for their produce. Since they were not allowed to trade their merchandise for their own account and had no option but to deliver it to privileged buyers who dictated prices, their income was equally low.[29] Because their business relationships with foreign merchants were not as strong as those of the new mercantile elite, the noble landowners soon withdrew from the linen trade. Yet their position as chief 'providers' of hemp and flax and 'suppliers' of cheap yarns remained uncontested.[30] Concurrently, local merchants in turn secured a monopoly on buying and selling linen cloth with the freshly established merchant guilds ('Kaufmanns-Societäten'), as in Hirschberg in 1658 and Landeshut in 1677.[31] By 1700, Silesian merchants such as Ignatius Gruber, Daniel Buchs and Johann Christian von Knorr were firmly established at the top of the linen supply-chain, taking advantage of local and international conditions. African markets were major outlets for Silesian cloth, and plantations in the Caribbean and the Americas proved to be attractive complements.

The situation changed in the later seventeenth and eighteenth centuries, as the population grew again and the landowners of the border strip were faced with a new problem to be solved. They had to ensure the existence of a minimum number of larger peasant plots to secure the basic reproduction of draught animals to meet the need for future plough and carriage services.[32] All other working hands, however, were of best use to them if they manufactured as much marketable yarn or cloth as possible and did not waste time engaging in time-consuming yet financially unrewarding subsistence farming. As such, the number of people who were not able to sustain their families from what little land they were allotted or who were left landless increased. The hierarchy within the strata of the rural population became much more complex and rigid.

Peasants, who owned their own houses and farms, and who had enough land at their disposal to keep cattle and horses, were at the top. Next came those who did not have enough land to gain much from farming and kept only a few animals, typically chicken or geese. Because their plots were no bigger than gardens, they were called 'gardeners' ('Gärtner'). 'Cottagers' ('Häusler') in turn did not have any property other than their huts, but they were still better off than 'lodgers' ('Einlieger'), who had to rent rooms in other peoples' houses. The extension of the landlord's rights had fundamentally determined the makeup of this rural hierarchy. In the second half of the eighteenth century, peasants made up only approximately 21.5% of the population of the border strip, while the group of more or less strictly bonded serfs, who had little or no land, reached approximately 67%.[33] Markus Cerman has described this transformation as a change from a 'peasant society' into a 'sub-peasant society' ('unterbäuerlich').[34] Clearly, more than half the population had to spin and weave in order to survive. In a sense, Silesian linens bound the fates of the miserable on both sides of the Atlantic together. Silesian serfs were bound to land they did not own, enslaved Africans were bound to land they did not even call home.

The benefits of low labour costs were gradually skimmed off by the merchants entering the linen trade and profiting from the beginning of the boom in overseas demand. Careful study of the records of the Royal African Company of England, preserved in the National Archives in London (Kew), show that during the last decade of the seventeenth century and first twenty to thirty years of the eighteenth century, the African market gave a boost to the linen trade – something not noted by research to date. A plausible reason could be the price development of Silesian linens. The prices per piece for all textiles traded by the Royal African Company show that Silesian linens and Indian cottons competed with each other in the middle- and lower-price segments. The appeal of Silesian linen grew even more when their prices started to decline around 1700, as a result of serfdom being solidly institutionalised in the Eastern European province (Figure 1).[35]

In summary, the socio-economic setting all but predestined the exploitation of the province's rural population and the booming demand for linen for the overseas trade made it much easier for young merchants to decide to try their luck in Silesia and to partake in the exploitation. It is therefore not surprising that the offspring of financially sound merchants from distant places settled permanently in the major trading towns of the region once the disastrous effects of the Thirty

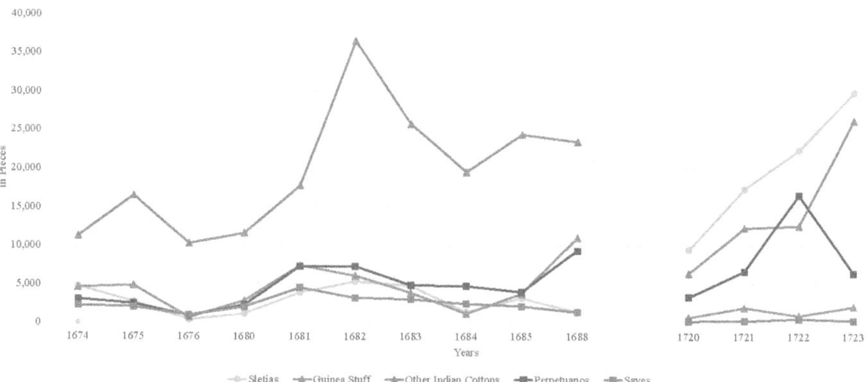

Figure 1. Export of 'Sletias' by the Royal African Company of England Compared with English Woollens and Indian Cottons Exports. Source: The National Archives (TNA), London (Kew), T 70/910–923. The years included in the graph recorded ships sailing from London to West Africa during at least six months of the respective year. The time between 1688 and 1720 saw the 'Glorious Revolution' in England (1688–1689), the so called 'Komenda Wars' (1694–1700) and the War of the Spanish Succession (1701–1714) which essentially interrupted the seaborne trade of the Royal African Company during those years. Sletias = linens labelled as, for example, 'Sletias', 'Sleties' and 'Sleazies'. Guinea Stuff = Indian cotton cloth produced specifically for the African market, usually coloured white and blue. Other Indian Cottons = different sorts of Indian cottons varying in quality and price, here summed together. Perpetuanos and Sayes = coarse and finer woolen textiles. The discrepancies between the number of pieces counted by the author of this paper and the numbers offered by Kenneth G. Davies for the time period 1674–1704 are minimal. Compare Kenneth G. Davies, *The Royal African Company* (London: Longmans, Green & Co., 1957), 350–357.

Years' War had been largely overcome. For example, Johann Jäger (1680–1751), native of Nuremberg, and Johann Martin Gottfried (1685–1737), a former resident of Großenhain in Saxony, both settled in Hirschberg in 1715.[36] A rather unusual entry in a visitors' book, then on display at the top of Śnieżka, the highest peak of the Sudetes, hints at the early arrival of Hannß Brünnß/ Primbß from Schiffbeck near Hamburg. The visitor's book shows that he and two other Hamburg merchants, Johann Hieronymus Classen and Gottfried Christoph Frichen, had been on a hiking tour there in 1711.[37] His son, Johann David Brünnß/ Primbs, married in 1714 and settled down in Landeshut.[38] Hannß Brünnß/ Primbß must have died when his son was not yet of age, because Claus Claussen is mentioned in the wedding records as his foster father.[39] Claussen himself arrived during the early 1690s from Brunsbüttel near Hamburg and also established a business in Landeshut.[40]

The memberships of the merchant guilds grew steadily as a consequence of the increasing number of new arrivals. Between 1660 and 1760, the Hirschberg guild grew from 18 to 148 members.[41] To safeguard their monopoly over trade, the already established merchants asked the authorities in Breslau to pass into law more restrictive rules of entry to the guild. Finally, in 1726, they agreed on more restrictive admission criteria for obtaining the right to trade. Six years of apprenticeship, two years of experience as a commercial clerk and at least two years of training in commerce abroad, as well as significantly higher admission fees, were among the requirements newcomers now had to meet before they could enter the business.[42]

It did not take the merchants long to identify an additional way to reduce production costs and retain even more of the business. The sources show a peculiar trend of ennoblements among merchant families; it seemed only logical to cut out the nobility as middlemen in the provision of raw materials. The easiest way to achieve this was to have knighthood conferred on the merchants themselves by the emperor. Christian von Kluge (1679–1732) was made a Bohemian knight by the Austrian emperor around 1726 for his achievements in growing the Silesian linen trade.[43] The son of Daniel Buchs (I), Daniel (von) Buchs (II, 1676–1735), received a similar honour in 1731.[44] Being part of the aristocracy, von Kluge acquired no fewer than six villages: Ober Adelsbach (Struga), Nieder Adelsbach, Liebersdorff (Lubomin), Frölichsdorff (Cieszów), Zeißberg (Cisów) and Neu Laßig.[45] Daniel von Buchs (III, 1707–79), purchased three manors: Eichberg, Schildau (Wojanów) and Boberstein (Bobrów).[46] In this way they set a precedent for others and eventually it ceased to matter whether they were ennobled or not: for example, Gottfried Glafey (1656–1720), Christian Mentzel (1667–1748) and George Friedrich Smith (Schmidt, 1703–57), all became merchant–landowners without a noble title. Thus, the new mercantile landholder-elite slowly but surely surpassed the established pure aristocratic proprietors of land as rivals in the retail business of hemp and yarn, while adopting the established mechanisms of tight control over the countrified work force.

The example of linen merchant Christian Mentzel (1667–1748) is a good illustration of the situation in Silesia in the mid-eighteenth century. Some 2,481 people lived on his estates Ober Berbisdorf and Nieder Berbisdorf (today both make up Dziwiszów) and Lomnitz (Łomnica) in 1786, among them 67 peasants, 109 tenant farmers and 118 cottagers with their families.[47] The overwhelming number of cottagers and tenants (227) in comparison with peasants (67) is not surprising. These numbers match the general breakdown of these groups in the whole region, as explained earlier. A preserved copy of the urbarium issued by Christian Mentzel for his Lomnitz estate in 1742 records the duties of the fief holder toward his subjects and also lists in great detail all the long-established obligations of the villagers toward the merchant–landlord. It consists of three main parts: the largest lists all duties and services of thirty-two individual serfs (thirty-two pages). The second part lists all the compulsory labour that all peasants, tenants and cottagers had to perform (seven pages). The last part lists all taxes, rents and fees to be paid by the people living on the Lomnitz estate (seven pages).[48] Unfortunately, there is no urbarium preserved for Ober Berbisdorf and Nieder Berbisdorf, but we may be certain that a similar set of regulations was enacted in those two places as well.

The routine obligations of yarn spinning assigned to all people under servitude is of special interest. Cottagers had to deliver four pieces of yarn a year and unmarried women had to make two pieces of yarn per year. One piece of yarn was usually approximately 14,400 Silesian ells long, or roughly 8,640 kilometres. Each male cottager – or his wife – had to spin around 34,560 kilometres of yarn per year.[49] This meant about one month of compulsory spinning annually (apart from all other duties).[50] Given that 14,400 Silesian ells of yarn were needed to weave one piece of an average Silesian linen cloth designed for export, each male cottager produced enough yarn for four regular pieces of linen.[51] All 118 (male) cottagers living on the three properties of Mentzel, therefore, delivered enough yarn for 472 pieces of linen, which the merchant could sell without having to bear any additional costs. Additionally, all yarn spun by the unmarried women during the off-season had to be delivered to him as well. Thus, Mentzel received considerably more yarn free of charge than set out above. Furthermore, he profited from the yarn spun by his subjects in their spare time. They were not obliged to deliver this yarn to him for free but were forced to sell it to him for a fixed price of six silver Groschen per piece.[52]

Linen merchants within the border strip owned not only estates, but estates encompassing entire villages, and secured their assets in immovable property while benefiting from the lowest production costs possible. It was the low fabrication costs that allowed them to sell Silesian linens at unbeatably low prices to international purchasers, who then re-exported them to Atlantic markets. At the same time, having imposed strict regulations of entry to their guilds, the merchants efficiently guarded their monopoly over linens produced in the province. Foreign businessmen who wanted these cheap and essential textiles had no choice but to order them from authorised members of a guild.

The success of these merchants in squeezing out more from their serfs than one might believe possible was observed by John Quincy Adams (1767–1848). The ambassador to Berlin and future sixth president of the United States of America (1825–29) travelled the province in 1800 and noted that a Silesian serf is 'compelled to labour for his lord, more days than there are. [...] [H]e is often obliged to furnish ten days work in a week'. Adams' summary of his observations made on the estates he visited is a pointed one: 'The manufactories of linens, in particular, which raise large fortunes to the merchants who export them from the cities, scarcely give bread to the peasants, who do all the valuable part of the work'.[53]

These general observations demonstrate how serfdom allowed the low production costs of linen textiles that enabled Silesian linen merchants to sell their wares as cheaply as they did, while meeting demand. The fortunate coincidence of endogenous and exogenous factors pointed the way for Silesian economic development and shaped the region as a 'prospering' one. Obviously, the division of labour between a large group of underprivileged manufacturers of the best-selling product and the relatively small body of overprivileged merchants trading the merchandise led to a lopsided distribution of the financial gains.

Silesian slave-related linen trade and Prussian state revenues

The first two parts of this article demonstrated how Silesian socio-economic conditions that evolved over the 400 years leading up to the eighteenth century favoured the production of linen textiles for export. They explained how the growing demand for cheap textiles in Atlantic markets, either for the purchase of slaves or to clothe them, paved the way for Silesian merchants to invest in land and, at the same time, forced their tenants into spinning and weaving for survival. Without question, both endogenous and exogenous factors closely integrated the Silesian economy with the Atlantic commercial system in general, and the slave trade and exploitation of slaves on plantations in particular.

In order to estimate the share of slave-based activities in the Silesian economy, however, it is necessary to have meaningful statistical data. Luckily, Frederick the Great believed in statistics and was fond of statistical tables which provided an overview of the economic power of his monarchy. Therefore, on the one hand, there are sets of figures relating to the demography and trade of Silesia in comparison to the other provinces of the Prussian state for the second half of the eighteenth century, readily available in published collections, most prominently perhaps in Otto Behre's *Geschichte der Statistik in Brandenburg-Preussen* (History of statistics in Brandenburg-Prussia).[54]

Similar compilations for the period under Habsburg rule are, as far as I am aware, not existent. On the other hand, using the extant figures for the purpose of comparison is problematic, since the territory of the Prussian state changed over time and the design of the surveys differed, if only slightly.[55] Additionally, customs duties of Prussian provinces varied greatly during the second half of the eighteenth century, especially in regard to the textile industry.[56] Another important factor is that merchants at the time managed to avoid customs duties or at least tried to pay the lowest possible tariff on the merchandise, which was mostly taxed according to its value or quality.[57] Despite these shortcomings in the data, the general picture of Prussia's trade patterns remains the same.

We are indebted to the Silesian geographer and Prussian civil servant Friedrich Albert Zimmermann (1745–1815) for his impressive thirteen-volume book series about his native province, *Beyträge zur Beschreibung von Schlesien* ('Contributions for the Description of Silesia'). The books were published between 1783 and 1796 and include detailed information based on official records. It is striking that Zimmermann considered not only the bigger administrative districts, but took each single village, town and city into account, and noted the geographical locations, specifics of flora and fauna, livestock numbers, inhabitants, marriages, and so on. Also valuable is the compilation of export statistics for linen textiles from Silesia to different countries for the years 1748–49 to 1787–88 by Alfred Zimmermann (1859–1925), first published in the 31st volume of the journal *Schlesische Provinzialblätter* in 1800.[58] Figures giving an account of the demographic profile of the border strip are provided by Ziekursch in *Hundert Jahre schlesischer Agrargeschichte* ('One Hundred Years of Silesian Agrarian History'), published in 1927.[59] These sources serve as the basis for the following explanations.

Before the share of slave-based activities in Silesian and Prussian economic development can be estimated, the contribution of Silesia to the overall income of the Prussian state has to be clarified. Comparable statistical data are available for the years 1775–76, 1785–86 and 1793.[60] Accordingly, in the fiscal year 1775/6, Silesia contributed 25% to the country's revenues, leading the eleven other provinces by a wide margin: Kurmark was second, with close to 17%, closely followed by East Prussia (together with Lithuania) with a share of 14% (see Table 1). Ten years later, Silesia was responsible for close to 37% of the total revenue of the Prussian state. Again, Kurmark was second with slightly over 10%.

Silesia's huge share can be explained by the profits of each province in exports, both to other provinces and for long-distance trade. While Silesia, unlike Kurmark, Neumark or the city of Magdeburg, did not export any considerable quantity of goods to other Prussian provinces, its contribution to Prussia's total profits in the export trade to foreign countries approached nearly 50% in 1785–86. Specifically, Prussia exported manufactures worth a

Table 1. Contribution of each province to the total Prussian state revenue, 1775/76.

Provinces	Contribution to the Prussian state revenue	Share in %
East Prussia with Lithuania	2,000,133	14.2
West Prussia with Warmia and Netzte District	1,633,506	11.6
Kurmark (Electoral March)	2,342,788	16.6
Neumark (New March)	464,861	3.3
Pomerania	901,073	6.4
Magdeburg	969,995	6.9
Halberstadt-Hohnstein	475,213	3.4
Minden, Ravensberg, Tecklenburg-Lingen	511,689	3.6
Cleves, Mark, Meurs, Geldern	939,914	6.7
East Frisia	306,255	2.2
Neuchâtel		
(Prussian) Silesia	3,546,548	25.2
Total Prussian State Revenue	**14,091,975**	**100**

Source: 'Der Anteil der Provinzen an den Staatseinnahmen Preußens, 1775/76', in *Geschichte der Statistik in Brandenburg-Preussen bis zur Gründung des Königlichen Statistischen Bureaus*, ed. Otto Behre (Berlin: Carl Heymanns Verlag, 1905), 102.

total of 22,361,916 thalers. Subtracting the amount of money spent on importing products, the Prussian state had a trade surplus of 8,560,429 thalers in 1785–86, with Silesia contributing half, or 4,044,075 thalers (see Table 2).

The last figures of note illustrate the productivity of the Prussian provinces in 1793. The total value of all manufactured goods in that fiscal year came to 37,144,993 thalers. Silesia produced goods worth 12,603,318 thalers (34%), slightly ahead of the provinces of Kurmark and Neumark, which had a combined output worth 12,404,154 thalers (33%). The share of linen textiles is remarkable. While all of Prussian linen wares were valued at 9,521,680 thalers (26% of all manufactured goods in Prussia), Silesian linen cloth alone accounted for 7,456,754 thalers, 78% of overall Prussian linen textile production and approximately 60% of all Silesian manufactures (see Table 3).

From this data, three things are clear: first, that Silesia played a significant role in overall Prussian state revenues; second, that the province derived its financial means mainly from the production of linen cloth; and, third, that these Silesian linens were chiefly exported to foreign countries. This last point is underlined by the export figures provided by the *Schlesische Provinzialblätter* in 1800 and republished by Alfred Zimmermann in 1885. Fortunately, the fiscal year 1775/6 is also included, which makes it easier to see in light of the Prussian statistics discussed above. While Silesia contributed 25% to the state revenues in that year, the province exported linen wares valued at 5,062,291 thalers, of which 86% were sold to England, Holland, France, Spain, Portugal and the West Indies.

During the thirty-nine years between 1748–49 and 1787–88, on average 76% of all Silesian linen textiles were headed to these places. The rest went to Italy, the Nordic countries (Sweden, Denmark, and Russia), Poland, Hungary and the Ottoman Empire, as well as the Austrian lands, Saxony, Switzerland and other German-speaking territories. Only during years of major international disturbances in trade did the share of exports to north- and south-western European

Table 2. Balance sheet, June 1st 1785 – May 31st 1786 (extract).

Provinces	Export of Prussian manufactures to foreign countries in Thaler	Share in %	Profits of the royal provinces gained from the export of its manufactures to foreign countries in Thaler	Share in %	Profits of the royal provinces gained from the export of its manufactures to other Prussian provinces in Thaler	Share in %	Total profits of the royal provinces in Thaler	Share in %
East Prussia	1,793,525	8	801,945	9.4			801,945	7.3
West Prussia	1,983,256	8.9	866,580	10			866,580	7.9
Kurmark	2,134,725	9.5			1,118,651	46	1,118,651	10.2
Neumark	591,684	2.6	155,245	1.8	660,058	27	815,303	7.4
Pomerania	849,285	3.8	465,735	5.4	49,342	2	515,077	4.7
Magdeburg	556,842	2.5	43,241	0.5	521,382	21	564,623	5.1
Halberstadt	608,601	2.7	326,326	3.8			326,326	3
Minden	1,275,494	5.7	612,357	7.2			612,357	5.6
Cleves, Geldern, Meurs	1,217,386	5.4	505,578	6			505,578	4.6
Mark	1,376,550	6.2	606,399	7.1	96,578	4	702,977	6.4
East Frisia	938,485	4.2	132,948	1.6			132,948	1.2
(Prussian) Silesia	9,036,083	40.4	4,044,075	47.2			4,044,075	36.7
Prussia total	**22,361,916**	**100**	**8,560,429**	**100**	**2,446,011**	**100**	**11,006,440**	**100**

Source: 'General-Balance wie sich die aus Se. Königl. Majestät von Preußen gesammten Staaten vom 1. Juni 1785 bis ult. May 1786 dem Werthe nach, nach fremden Landen und nach anderen Königl. Provinzen ausgegangenen Landesproducte und Fabriquen-Waaren gegen die von daher wieder hereingekommenen und zur Consumtion verbliebenen fremden und inländischen Waaren gegen einander verhalten' [extract], in *Geschichte der Statistik in Brandenburg-Preussen bis zur Gründung des Königlichen Statistischen Bureaus*, ed. Otto Behre, (Berlin: Carl Heymanns Verlag, 1905), 348.

Table 3. Overview of the manufacturing out-put of the Prussian provinces, 1793 (extract).

	(East and West) Prussia	Kur- and Neumark	Pomerania	Magdeburg and Halberstadt	Westphalia	Rhine Province	East Frisia	(Prussian) Silesia	Prussia total
Value of Linen Wares in Thaler	194,446	461,602	46,147	236,599	858,462	238,065	29,605	7,456,754	**9,521,680**
Value of all manufactures in Thaler	3,131,938	12,404,154	913,043	2,891,488	1,229,067	3,581,669	390,316	12,603,318	**37,144,993**

Source: 'Generaltableau von der Nationalfabrikation in sämtlichen Provinzen im Jahre 1793' [extract], in *Geschichte der Statistik in Brandenburg-Preussen bis zur Gründung des Königlichen Statistischen Bureaus*, ed. Otto Behre (Berlin: Carl Heymanns Verlag, 1905), 350–1.

port cities drop below the 50% mark. Such a time of severe crisis occurred during the last years of the Seven Years War, in 1761–62, when only 48% of linens were exported to the European maritime powers. However, one must note that the overall volume exported also declined during such periods. Other countries like Poland, Russia, Austria or the riparian countries of the Baltic did not function as substitute markets. Whereas the value of exported linen textiles amounted to 5,419,336 thalers in total in 1774–75, when England, France and Spain ordered close to 90% of all Silesian linen products, the total sum of exported linens in 1761–62 shrank to only 1,123,338 thalers (see Table 4).

Evidently, the eagerness of the colonial powers to purchase linens proved favourable for Silesia, since they bought on average more than two-thirds of Silesia's annual provincial output during the second half of the eighteenth century. Since customs duties on Silesian linens were enormously high in Spain and Portugal, the import of foreign linen wares for home consumption was completely forbidden in France, and the 'draw back' explicitly encouraged the re-export of Silesian linens from English ports (while the Irish and Scottish production of linens was supported), one can conclude that nearly all linen textiles purchased by the British, Dutch, French, Spanish or Portuguese were destined for either the slave trade, their own colonial possessions, or for smuggling into the colonies of their rivals. In all these sectors of trade linens played a crucial role.[61] Therefore, since on average more than two-thirds of the linen manufactured in Silesia was channelled through Atlantic-oriented European ports (76%), one can assume that the overwhelming majority of the annual provincial linen production was connected to trade circuits related directly or indirectly to slavery. Less than one-third of the fabrics remained on the European continent and that was more in the central and eastern parts than in the west. For this reason, one can be certain that, if there was free and secure transportation of goods to places where slave-based activities were the major driver for European presence, Silesia's economy fared well. In times of war and disruption to Atlantic traffic, though, when overseas markets for the sale of linens were out of reach and orders did not come in, the Silesian economy declined considerably.

In order to quantify this, I offer the following estimate: the average advantage Silesia drew from slave-based activities for its own economy matched the average share of the linen textiles exported from the province to colonial powers, that is 76% on average in the second half of the eighteenth century (1748–49 to 1787–88) as stated above. Assuming that in 1793 the average of 76% remains valid, Silesian linen fabrics worth 5,667,133 thalers were shipped overseas, since the overall production of linen wares in the province was worth 7,456,754 thalers. That means that at least 15% of the total value of all manufactures produced in the Prussian state in 1793, worth 37,144,993 thalers, was connected to slave-based activities in that year. The available

Table 4. The Silesian linen export in Thaler (extract).

Year	Linen Wares	to England, Holland, France, Spain, Portugal and the West Indies	to Italy	to Sweden, Danmark, Norway, Russia	to Poland, Hungary, Transylvania and Turkey	to Austria and Switzerland	to Saxony	to other Territories of the German Empire	to other Prussian Provinces	in total
1748/49	Bleached linen	1,432,198	73,134	13,121	329,290	192,168	172,780	19,436	130,370	
	Unbleached linen	204,154	3,392	2,323	332	90,248	23,782	2,838	24,074	
	Battiste (Schleyer)	692,454	58,415	12,618	14,527	40,599	15,803	52	4,700	
	Total	**2,328,806**	**134,941**	**28,062**	**344,149**	**323,015**	**212,365**	**22,326**	**159,144**	**3,542,811**
	Share in %	**66**								**100**
1761/62	Bleached linen	470,963	6,493	27,184	475,471½	20,267	9,523	3,049	13,423½	
	Unbleached linen	64,457	–	–	2,366	120	5	–	1,624	
	Battiste	6,971	900	900	8,580	6,801	2,004	24	3,112	
	Total	**542,391**								**1,123,338**
	Share in %	**48**								**100**
1774/75	Bleached linen	3,824,766	44,890½	50,230	258,024	10,326	44,246½	3,537	79,674¾	
	Unbleached linen	152,167	1,100	1,100	2,526	531	2,825⅔	–	11,092	
	Battiste	857,098	37,266½	6,936	4,450	6,202	12,554	497	8,395	
	Total	**4,834,031**								**5,419,336**
	Share in %	**89**								**100**
1775/76	Bleached linen	3,560,862	57,580	64,802	248,410	13,893	50,478	5,007	139,319	
	Unbleached linen	278,957	5,720	5,720	687	508	5,600	355	8,365	
	Battiste	489,548	89,983	6,334	4,085	5,878	10,435	2,321	13,159	
	Total	**4,329,367**								**5,062,291**
	Share in %	**86**								**100**
1787/88	Bleached linen	3,990,038	120,282	76,115	423,741⅝	10,163½	65,600½	64,883¾	177,487¾	
	Unbleached linen	162,916	4,922	1,650	754	60	7,108½	3,690¾	6,991	
	Battiste	443,943	167,421¾	3,036	56,240	17,608	46,729	2,781	52,085⅓	
	Total	**4,596,897**								**5,906,248**
	Share in %	**78**								**100**

Source: Alfred Zimmermann, *Blüthe und Verfall des Leinengewerbes in Schlesien. Gewerbe- und Handelspolitik dreier Jahrhunderte* [extract] (Breslau: Verlag von Wilh. Gottl. Korn, 1885), 460–467.

statistical data does not allow similar calculations for other time spans. However, during peace-years of high demand from Atlantic-bound trade, the slave-based stimulus for the Prussian economy might have been even higher than 15%.

Especially in the border strip, where the soil did not favour cereal farming and people were forced to earn an additional income from spinning and weaving, any disruption in trade had dire consequences. Since the serfs had no chance of negotiating prices to their advantage during peace time, when demand for linens was high, they had no savings to support themselves with in times of crisis. While the merchants based in the urban centres were forced to withdraw from trade, most of them could patiently wait for better conditions even though they had no major returns during that period. In comparison, the merchant–landlords could comfortably renounce trade and live from the revenues of their estate(s). The roughly 6% of the Silesian population who lived in the border strip, laboriously spinning, weaving and bleaching, made up the major production force behind the enormous volumes of linen fabrics exported overseas.[62] While they were the ones driving the large revenues accumulated by the Silesian merchants and claimed by the Prussian state, their own conditions oscillated between bad and worse. Serf-based activities in this region most certainly contributed to the advancement of slave-based activities, and vice versa.

Conclusion: different paths of economic development

The importance of Silesia to Atlantic markets was not based on the high price of the linen that the region produced, but on the indispensability of Silesian linen cloth for the maritime powers purchasing it. Linens of all qualities were in high demand. Linens of good quality produced in Silesia were a crucial barter commodity on the African coast, helping to facilitate the purchase of slaves and making them cheaper because of their comparatively low selling prices. Coarser linens provided clothing for both enslaved black people and poor whites in the colonies. Other types of linen fabrics were used as sail cloth for trade vessels and slave ships.

Thus, Silesia supplemented the array of goods for countries directly involved in the Atlantic trade, whose domestic linens were not available at such low prices. This firmly established Silesia as one of the multipolar nodes of an increasingly interconnected world economy. The province's development can only be satisfactorily understood if analysed against this overarching backdrop of Atlantic trade, while also considering the conditions of the Silesian linen trade. Only then does the interconnectedness of slave-based activities and serf-based activities become evident.

This perspective puts the Silesian linen merchants in a whole new light as well. They were not, as some authors suggest, narrow-minded traditionalists who refused to make changes to the production process (for example investing in expensive machinery) or trading system as others elsewhere did in the early phase of industrialisation.[63] On the contrary, they simply exploited the conditions to the maximum, and even shaped them further to their advantage. For instance, their push to become estate-owners allowed Silesian merchants to control both the rural labour force and the raw material production, which allowed them to maximise their profits, just as the noble elite had done earlier. They amassed enough wealth to live a comfortable life while 'merely' supplying those in the more uncertain business of sending cargo overseas. The relation between trade routes, trade strategies and local production realities that shaped socio-economic circumstances, therefore, deserve a closer look from historians writing about 'economic development'. This approach would most certainly help go beyond the postulated dichotomy within Europe, between an 'industrially advanced' western and a 'backward' eastern part. Likewise, this approach could help to understand why commercial elites in different societies, regions and countries of the world might have consciously chosen not to follow the English example of capital-intensive industrialisation, and why that choice made sense.

In a broader context, there is merit to the question of whether the outsourcing of time-consuming activities like flax cultivation, yarn spinning and the weaving of linen fabrics from countries with high wages to regions like Silesia supported the employment of high-value labour in specific other branches of the economy in those countries.[64] That would explain why they were free to invest financial resources in technical equipment to reduce labour costs. In future research, it would be interesting to probe the resulting hypothesis that the labour-intensive orientation of economies in Eastern European regions might have favoured capital-intensive development in the western parts of the continent. Or, to put it differently, one could ask how great the role of the Eastern European provinces had been in the economic development of Western Europe.

Notes

1. Eric Williams, *Capitalism and Slavery* (Chapel Hill: University of North Carolina Press, 1944). See also Patrick O'Brien, 'European Economic Development: The Contribution of the Periphery', *The Economic History Review* 35, no. 1 (1982): 1–18; Pieter C. Emmer, Olivier Pétré-Grenouilleau, and Jessica V. Roitman, eds., *A Deus ex Machina Revisited: Atlantic Colonial Trade and European Development* (Leiden: Brill, 2006). More recently, Pepijn Brandon, and Aditya Sarkar, 'Labour History and the Case against Colonialism', *International Review of Social History* 64, no. 1 (2019): 73–109.
2. Joseph E. Inikori, *Africans and the Industrial Revolution in England: A Study in International Trade and Economic Development* (Cambridge: Cambridge University Press, 2002), 486.

3. Marian Małowist, 'The Economic and Social Development of the Baltic Countries from the Fifteenth to the Seventeenth Centuries', *The Economic History Review* 12, no. 2 (1959): 177. Witold Kula, *An Economic Theory of the Feudal System: Towards a Model of the Polish Economy 1500–1800* (Bristol: Western Printing Service, 1976). See also Marian Małowist, 'Poland, Russia and Western Trade in the 15th and 16th Centuries', *Past and Present* 13, no. 1 (1958): 26–41; Marian Małowist, 'Ekspansja portugalska w Afryce a ekonomika Europy na przełomie XV i XVI w.', *Przegląd Historyczny* 59 (1968): 227–44; Marian Małowist, *Wschód a Zachód Europy w XIII–XVI wieku: Konfrontacja struktur społeczno-gospodarczych* (Warsaw: Państwowe Wydawnictwo Naukowe, 1973); Marian Małowist, 'East and West Europe in the 13th–16th Centuries: Confrontation of Social and Economic Structures', and 'Eastern Europe and the Countries of the Eastern Peninsula: Parallels and Contrasts', in *Western Europe, Eastern Europe, and World Development: 13th–18th Centuries. Collection of Essays by Marian Małowist*, eds. Jean Batou and Henryk Szlajfer (Chicago: Haymarket Books, 2012), 215–2 and 247–58.
4. Zsigmond Pál Pach, 'The East-Central European Aspect of the Overseas Discoveries and Colonization', in *The European Discovery of the World and its Economic Effects on Pre-Industrial Society, 1500–1800: Papers of the Tenth International Economic History Congress*, ed. Hans Pohl (Stuttgart: Franz Steiner Verlag, 1990), 179.
5. Currently a research project on the Baltic timber trade to Spain is underway: Rafał B. Reichert, 'The Role of Wood Supplies from the Southern Baltic Region and the Viceroyalty of New Spain in the Development of Spanish Seaborne Empire in the Eighteenth Century'.
6. Anka Steffen and Klaus Weber, 'Spinning and Weaving for the Slave Trade: Proto-Industry in Eighteenth-Century Silesia', in *Slavery Hinterland: Transatlantic Slavery and Continental Europe, 1680–1850*, eds. Felix Brahm and Eve Rosenhaft (Woodbridge: Boydell & Brewer, 2016), 88–92. Klaus Weber, 'Deutschland, der atlantische Sklavenhandel und die Plantagenwirtschaft der Neuen Welt (15. bis 19. Jahrhundert)', *Journal of Modern European History* 7, no. 1 (2009): 54–6.
7. The nature of the competition between Silesian linens and English woollens and Indian cottons exported to Atlantic markets, especially in Africa, in the early modern period, and the effect this competition had on prices is discussed in Anka Steffen, 'A Fierce Competition! Silesian Linens and Indian Cottons on the West-African Coast in the Late Seventeenth and Early Eighteenth Centuries', in *Globalized Peripheries: Central Europe and the Atlantic World, 1680–1860*, eds. Jutta Wimmler and Klaus Weber (Woodbridge: Boydell & Brewer, 2020), 37–56.
8. Jan Peters, ed., *Gutsherrschaftsgesellschaften im europäischen Vergleich* (Berlin: Akademie Verlag, 1997).
9. The National Archives (TNA), London (Kew), C 104/128.
10. TNA, C 104/126, 129.
11. Johannes Ziekursch, *Hundert Jahre schlesischer Agrargeschichte. Vom Hubertusburger Frieden bis zum Abschluss der Bauernbefreiung* (Aalen: Scientia Verlag, 1978), 132.
12. For the districts of Leobschütz, Neisse and Neustadt, see Friedrich Albert Zimmermann, *Beyträge zur Beschreibung von Schlesien*, vol. 3 (Brieg: Johann Ernst Tramp, 1784), 91–7, 201–5, 253–60, 338–78. For the districts of Bolkenhain-Landeshut, Reichenbach and Schweidnitz, see Friedrich Albert Zimmermann, *Beyträge zur Beschreibung von Schlesien*, vol. 5 (Brieg: Johann Ernst Tramp, 1785), 34–43, 127–31, 241–58. For the districts of Löwenberg-Bunzlau and Hirschberg, see Friedrich Albert Zimmermann, *Beyträge zur Beschreibung von Schlesien*, vol. 6 (Brieg: Johann Ernst Tramp, 1786), 87–107, 303–23. For the district of Goldberg-Hainau, see

Friedrich Albert Zimmermann, *Beyträge zur Beschreibung von Schlesien*, vol. 8 (Brieg: Johann Ernst Tramp, 1789), 247–57. For the county of Glatz, see Friedrich Albert Zimmermann, *Beyträge zur Beschreibung von Schlesien*, vol. 9 (Brieg: Johann Ernst Tramp, 1789), 5–32.

13. Dariusz Adamczyk, *Zur Stellung Polens im modernen Weltsystem der Frühen Neuzeit* (Hamburg: Verlag Dr. Kovač, 2001), 162–85. Markus Cerman, 'Gutsherrschaft vor dem "Weißen Berg": Zur Verschärfung der Erbuntertänigkeit in Nordböhmen 1380–1620', in *Gutsherrschaftsgesellschaften im europäischen Vergleich*, ed. Jan Peters, 91–102. Matthias Weber, 'Disziplinierung und Widerstand: Obrigkeit und Bauern in Schlesien 1500–1700', in *Gutsherrschaft als soziales Modell: Vergleichende Betrachtungen zur Funktionsweise frühneuzeitlicher Agrargesellschaften*, ed. Jan Peters (Munich: R. Oldenbourg Verlag, 1995), 425.
14. Marian Małowist, 'Portuguese Expansion in Africa and European Economy at the Turn of the 15th Century', in *Western Europe, Eastern Europe, and World Development*, eds. Batou and Szlajfer, 372–5, 378–81, 385, 389–90. Klaus Weber, 'Linen, Silver, Slaves, and Coffee: A Spatial Approach to Central Europe's Entanglements with the Atlantic Economy', *Culture & History Digital Journal* 4, no. 2 (2015): 3–5. Ralph Davis, 'English Foreign Trade, 1660–1700', *Economic History Review* 7, no. 2 (1954): 150. David Ormrod, *The Rise of Commercial Empires: England and the Netherlands in the Age of Mercantilism, 1650–1770* (Cambridge: Cambridge University Press, 2003), 143.
15. Andrea Reikat, *Handelsstoffe: Grundzüge des europäisch-westafrikanischen Handels vor der industriellen Revolution am Beispiel der Textilien* (Cologne: Rüdiger Köppe Verlag, 1997), 45–50.
16. Michael Diefenbacher, 'Der Handel des Nürnberger Patriziats nach Osten – Das Beispiel der Tucher um 1500', *Mitteilungen des Vereins für Geschichte der Stadt Nürnberg* 94 (2007): 49–80. Siegfried Kühn, *Der Hirschberger Leinwand- und Schleierhandel von 1648–1806* (Aalen: Scientia Verlag, 1982), 44–5. Gerhard Seibold, *Die Viatis und Peller: Beiträge zur Geschichte ihrer Handelsgesellschaft* (Cologne: Böhlau-Verlag, 1977), 138. Marco Veronesi, *Oberdeutsche Kaufleute in Genua, 1350–1490: Instiutionen, Starategien, Kollektive* (Stuttgart: W. Kohlhammer Verlag, 2014), 257.
17. Arnošt Klíma, 'English Merchant Capital in Bohemia in the Eighteenth Century', *The Economic History Review* 12, no. 1 (1959): 34. Gustav Aubin and Arno Kunze, *Leinenerzeugung und Leinenabsatz im östlichen Mitteldeutschland zur Zeit der Zunftkäufe: Ein Beitrag zur industriellen Kolonisation des deutschen Ostens* (Stuttgart: Verlag W. Kohlhammer, 1940), 42–53, 71–83, 92–105. Marcel Boldorf, 'Regulierte Textilmärkte in Niederschlesien und der Nordschweiz des 18. Jahrhunderts', *Schweizerische Gesellschaft für Wirtschafts- und Sozialgeschichte* 26 (2011): 106. Seibold, *Die Viatis und Peller*, 138–40.
18. Christian Adolph, '[…] Zu Christlichem Troste der Leidtragenden, und wolverdientem Nachruhm, Des […] Johann Christians, Gewesenen fürnehmen Rathsverwandtens und Mitbürgers in Greyffenberg/ […], Leipzig, 1644'.
19. Wolfgang Silber, 'Leichbegängnüß deß weylandt Ehrenvesten/ Wolgeachten Herrn Thomae Cheswrights, Engelländischen Kauffherrens von Londen: Welcher nach Gottes schickung zu Greyffenberg in Schlesien selig verstorben/ […], Görlitz, 1616'.
20. Ray A. Kea, *Settlements, Trade, and Polities in the 17th Century Gold Coast* (Baltimore, MD: John Hopkins University Press, 1982), 208.
21. Pieter de Marees, *Beschryvinghe ende historisch verhael vant Gout Koninckrijck van Gunea, anders de Gout-custe de Mina genaemt, liggende in het deel van Africae […]* (Amsterdam: Cornelis Claesz, 1602), 16, 25.

22. Alfred Zimmermann, *Blüthe und Verfall des Leinengewerbes in Schlesien. Gewerbe- und Handelspolitik dreier Jahrhunderte* (Breslau: Verlag von Wilh. Gottl. Korn, 1885), 12. Gertrud-Ottilie Cassel, *Die Hirschberger Kaufmanns-Sozietät (von 1658–1740): Ein Beitrag zur Geschichte der Weberei im Riesengebirge im Rahmen der österreichischen Merkantilpolitik in Schlesien* (Inaugural-dissertation, Hirschberg: Bote aus dem Riesengebirge, 1918), 8. Kühn, *Der Hirschberger Leinwand- und Schleierhandel*, 16.
23. Hajo Holborn, *Deutsche Geschichte in der Neuzeit, vol. 1: Das Zeitalter der Reformation und des Absolutismus (bis 1790)* (Munich: R. Oldenborg, 1970), 368.
24. William W. Hagen, 'Die brandenburgischen und großpolnischen Bauern im Zeitalter der Gutsherrschaft 1400–1800: Ansätze einer vergleichenden Analyse', in *Gutsherrschaftsgesellschaften im europäischen Vergleich*, ed. Jan Peters, 22. René Schiller, *Vom Rittergut zum Grossgrundbesitz: Ökonomische und soziale Transformationsprozesse der ländlichen Eliten in Brandenburg im 19. Jahrhundert* (Berlin: Akademie Verlag, 2003), 37.
25. Kühn, *Der Hirschberger Leinwand- und Schleierhandel*, 1, 16.
26. Kula, *Economic Theory of the Feudal System*, 81–2.
27. Kühn, *Der Hirschberger Leinwand- und Schleierhandel*, 19.
28. Steffen and Weber, 'Spinning and Weaving', 97–100.
29. Kühn, *Der Hirschberger Leinwand- und Schleierhandel*, 23–4, 28–30.
30. Kühn, *Der Hirschberger Leinwand- und Schleierhandel*, 11, 29.
31. Zimmermann, *Blüthe und Verfall*, 24–5. Kühn, *Der Hirschberger Leinwand- und Schleierhandel*, 3–4.
32. Kula, *Economic Theory of the Feudal System*, 49.
33. Ziekursch, *Hundert Jahre schlesischer Agrargeschichte*, 136.
34. Markus Cerman, 'Protoindustrialisierung und Grundherrschaft: Sozialstruktur, Feudalherrschaft und Textilgewerbe in Nordböhmen (15. bis 17. Jahrhundert)', in *Protoindustrie in der Region: Europäische Gewerbelandschaften vom 16. bis zum 19. Jahrhundert*, eds. Dietrich Ebeling and Wolfgang Mager (Bielefeld: Verlag für Regionalgeschichte, 1997), 176.
35. Steffen, 'A Fierce Competition!', 50–5.
36. Archiwum Państwowe we Wrocławiu, oddział w Jeleniej Górze (APJG), zespół 3, jedn. 77.
37. [Anonymous], *Vergnügte und Unvergnügte Reisen auf das Weltberuffene Schlesische Riesen = Gebirge, Welche von 1696 biß 1737: Theils daselbst den Allerhöchsten zu preisen, theils die erstaunenden Wunder der Natur zu betrachten, theils sich eine Gemüthsvergnügung oder Leibesbewegung zu machen, theils den beruffenen Riebezahl auszukundschafften [...], Schneekoppen-Bücher [...]* (Hirschberg: Dietrich Krahn, 1736), 57.
38. Archiwum Archidiecezjalne we Wrocławiu (AAW), sygn. 272n.
39. AAW, sygn. 272n.
40. Ibid.
41. Kühn, *Der Hirschberger Leinwand- und Schleierhandel*, 5.
42. APJG, zespół 102, jedn. 21. Kühn, *Der Hirschberger Leinwand- und Schleierhandel*, 5. Boldorf, 'Regulierte Textilmärkte', 106–7.
43. Biblioteka Uniwersytecka we Wrocławiu (BUW), Oddział Starych Druków, 366 875, 565 108.
44. ZNO, XVIII 45875-IV - XVIII 458. [Freiherr L. v. Zedlitz-Neukirch], *Neues Preussisches Adels-Lexicon oder genealogische und diplomatische Nachrichten von den in der preussischen Monarchie ansässigen oder zu derselben in Beziehung stehenden*

fürstlichen, gräflichen, freiherrlichen und adeligen Häusern [...], vol. 1 (Leipzig: Gebrüder Reichenbach, 1836), 324.

45. BUW, 366 875, 565 108.
46. APJG, zespół 3, jedn. 3621.
47. Zimmermann, *Beyträge* vol. 6, 364, 382–4.
48. APJG, zespół 105, jedn. 412.
49. 'Leinengarn', in J.C. Schedel (ed.), *Vollständiges allgemeines Waaren-Lexikon für Kaufleute, Commissionäre, Fabrikaten, Mäkler und Geschäftsleute, so wie für alle, welche sich in der Waarenkunde unterrichten wollen.* [...] (Leipzig: Verlag der J. S. Hinrichsschen Buchhandlung, 1834), 688.
50. In the mid- eighteenth century it was estimated that only the very best spinners, working from 4 am to 10 pm (18 hours per day), could spin 9,600 ells of yarn per day. A spinner would have had to work at this pace in order to deliver the demanded four pieces of yarn (57,600 ells) within a week (6 working days). Considering all other compulsory services of serfs, and duties like childcare and housekeeping, spinners might have needed more than a months' time to spin the required yarn, though. Johann Samuel Halle, *Die Leinenmanufaktur, oder die vollständige Oekonomie des Flachsbaues, nach allen seinen Zweigen* [...] (Berlin: Joachim Pauli, 1788), 111.
51. Christian Carl André, *Mannigfaltigkeiten zum Nutzen und Vergnügungen für Hausväter und Hausmütter, Jünglinge und Mädchen, Geistliche und Weltliche, Lehrer, Beamte, Bürger und Landsleute faßlich eingerichtet; [...]* (Prague: Friedrich Temsky, 1821), 172. A 'single Silesias' was 1 metre wide and 36 metres long or $^{6}/_{4} \times 60$ ells. Gemeente Amsterdam Stadsarchief (GAS), 88/ 1306A [letter from Gottfried Glafeys Witwe & Söhne (Hirschberg) to Jan Isaac DeNeufville (Amsterdam), dated 3 Oct. 1731]. GAS, 88/ 1306C [Letter from Johann Heinrich Martens (Hirschberg) to Jan Isaac De Neufville & Comp. (Amsterdam), dated 25 Sept. 1740].
52. APJG, zespół 105, jedn. 412.
53. [John Quincy Adams], *Letters on Silesia, Written During a Tour Through that Country in the Years 1800, 1801 [...]* (London: J. Budd, 1804), 28–9, 157.
54. Otto Behre, *Geschichte der Statistik in Brandenburg-Preussen bis zur Gründung des Königlichen Statistischen Bureaus* (Berlin: Carl Heymanns Verlag, 1905). Friedrich Gottlob Leonhardi, *Erdbeschreibung der Preußischen Monarchie*, 5 vols. (Halle: Hemmerde und Schwetschke, 1791–1799). Leopold Krug, *Topographisch-Statistisch-Geographisches Wörterbuch der sämtlichen Preußischen Staaten oder Beschreibung aller Provinzen, kreise, Distrikte, Städte, Aemter, Flecken, Dörfer, Vorwerke, Flüsse, Seen, Berge, u .u. in den Preußischen Staaten*, vol. 10 (Halle: Karl August Kümmel, 1801). Leopold Krug, *Betrachtungen über den National-Reichthum des preußischen Staats, und über den Wohlstand seiner Bewohner*, vol. 1 (Berlin: Johann Friedrich Unger, 1805). Johann Andreas Ortloff, *Handbuch einer allgemeinen Statistik der Königlich Preussischen Staaten*, vol. 1 (Erlangen: Walthersche Buchhandlung, 1798). Johann Emanuel von Küster, *Umriß der preußischen Monarchie nach statistischen, staats- und völkerrechtlichen Beziehungen* (Berlin: Johann Friedrich Unger, 1800). Ludwig Heinrich von Jakob, *Annalen der preussischen Staatswirtschaft und Statistik*, vols. 1–2 (Halle: Russische Verlagshandlung, 1804–1805).
55. Behre, *Geschichte der Statistik*, 139, 158.
56. Burkhard Nolte, *Merkantilismus und Staatsräson in Preußen: Absicht, Praxis und Wirkung der Zollpolitik Friedrichs II. in Schlesien und in den westfälischen Provinzen (1740–1786)* (Marburg: Verlag Herder-Institut, 2004), 49–84.

57. Nolte, *Merkantilismus und Staatsräson*, 143–63.
58. Zimmermann, *Blüthe und Verfall*, 460–7. Originally published as [Anonymous], 'Nachweisung wie viel leinene Waare von 1748 bis 1788 in Schlesien, und zwar in beyden Cammer-Departements außer Landes versandt worden', *Schlesische Provinzialblätter* 31 (1800): [7–12].
59. Ziekursch, *Hundert Jahre schlesischer Agrargeschichte.*
60. Behre, *Geschichte der Statistik*, 102, 348, 350–1.
61. Melle Klinkenborg, 'Untersuchungen zur Geschichte der Staatsverträge Friedrichs des Großen', *Forschungen zur brandenburgischen und preußischen Geschichte* 17 (1904): 143–61. Hugo Rachel, *Acta Borussica: Handels-, Zoll- und Akzisepolitik*, vol. 1, part 2 (Berlin: Verlag von Paul Parey, 1928), 577–80, 589–90. APJG, zespół 102, jedn. 335, Jour. No. 236. Anka Steffen, 'Schlesische Leinwand als Handelsgut im atlantischen Sklavenhandel der frühen Neuzeit: Das Beispiel der Hirschberger Kaufmanns-Societät', in *Themenportal Europäische Geschichte* (5 January 2017), https://www.europa.clio-online.de/essay/id/fdae-1696. Rachel, *Acta Borussica*, 571–2, 582. N.B. Harte, 'The Rise of Protection and the English Linen Trade, 1690–1790', in *Textile History and Economic History: Essays in Honour of Muss Julia de Lacy Mann*, eds. N.B. Harte and K.G. Pontin (Manchester: Manchester University Press, 1973), 98–9. Alex J. Warden, *The Linen Trade: Ancient and Modern* (London: Longman, Green, Longman, Roberts & Green, 1864), 351–465, 663.
62. The figure of 6% was calculated from data for the year 1767 compiled from Behre and Ziekursch. Behre, *Geschichte der Statistik*, 458. Ziekursch, *Hundert Jahre schlesischer Agrargeschichte*, 136.
63. Marcel Boldorf, 'The Rise and Fall of Silesian Merchant Guilds in the International Trade Net (1700–1850)', in *Spinning the Commercial Web: International Trade, Merchants, and Commercial Cities, c. 1640–1939*, eds. Margit Schulte Beerbühl and Jörg Vögele (Frankfurt am Main: Peter Lang, 2004), 90–1.
64. Similar thoughts are explored by John C. Brown, 'Market Organization, Protection, and Vertical Integration: German Cotton Textiles Before 1914', in *Selected Cliometric Studies on German Economic History*, eds. John Komlos and Scott Eddie (Stuttgart: Franz Steiner Verlag, 1997), 101–9.

Acknowledgements

I would like to express my special thanks to Caroline Shaw, Franziska Steffen and Klaus Weber for their critical comments as well as for ironing out my English at the early stage of this article. I am indebted to the anonymous peer reviewer for his or her remarks and suggestions for improvement. The suggestions deserve much more attention than it was possible here. All remaining errors are mine.

Disclosure statement

No potential conflict of interest was reported by the author(s).

Funding

This research was funded by the 'German Research Foundation' (DFG) in the context of the project 'The Globalized Periphery: Atlantic Commerce, Socioeconomic and Cultural Change in Central Europe (1680–1850)' (WE 3613/2-1) at the European University Viadrina in Frankfurt (Oder) (2015–2018).

Reflections

How important was the slavery system to Europe?

Guillaume Daudin

ABSTRACT
After commending the articles in this Special Issue for opening up the study of the slavery system to new locations and positions in the value-added chain, this comment underlines that it is necessary to imagine counterfactuals to find out how important the slavery system was to Europe. It then argues that it is difficult to imagine that the Industrial Revolution depended on slavery. Yet slavery might have played an important role for the prosperity of Early Modern Europe.

'C'est à ce prix que vous mangez du sucre en Europe'
Voltaire, *Candide*, 1759

Elements of Western societies are eager to cast aside the racism that has played such a role in Western history. Casting aside racism is only possible if we fully comprehend its origins, its development and its consequences. For that to take place, a better understanding of slavery and the role it played in the lives of our forefathers is necessary.

Most of the discussion on the subject so far has covered Britain's involvement in the slavery system, the direct involvement of other Europeans in that trade and the 'peculiar institution' of slavery in ante-bellum Southern United States. Most of the articles in this Special Issue enlarge the geographical scope of the debate: Pepijn Brandon, Ulbe Bosma and Tamira Combrink study the importance of slave-based activities in Holland and the United Provinces; Filipa Ribeiro da Silva looks at the importance of the slave trade in the Portuguese and Brazilian economy and Anka Steffen examines the involvement of Silesia in the slave-trade circuits.

Most of the articles also take the focus away from the Middle Passage part of the slavery system value chain. Brandon, Bosma and Combrink examine the whole chain of economic activities linked to the slave trade and show, respectively, the importance of slave-based activities in Holland and the United Provinces and the role of the Dutch in the merchant-capital-led production system of coffee. Steffen looks at an upstream sector furnishing the goods exchanged for slaves in Africa: Silesian linen. Klas Rönnbäck studies the distribution of rents in the sugar value-added chain in the British case, and locates most of them at the other end of the value chain: the transformation of slave-produced goods in Europe by sugar refiners.

By focusing on other links in the value chain and on less-explored places in Europe, these essays provide a stark reminder that the whole of the European economy was tainted by its association with slavery. Slave-based activities were lucrative: 5.2% of Dutch GDP and 10.4% of the GDP of the province of Holland, according to Brandon and Bosma. This is of a similar order of magnitude to the size of the intercontinental sector for the late 1780s in Britain as measured by Patrick O'Brien (between 7% and 8%) and in France as measured by myself (between 4% and 4.75%).[1] These estimates are not directly comparable because of differences in estimation approaches. Asian trade, which is part of the intercontinental sector and included in the British and the French estimates, was not slave-based and thus is not included in the Dutch estimate: it was quantitatively smaller than Atlantic trade. But the magnitude of these numbers is more important than their precision. It suggests that few people in eighteenth-century Europe would never have consumed any slave-produced goods and that few regions would never have produced goods that, one way or another, the slavery system could use.

Yet the most interesting question is not a detached *cui bono*. 'What do we owe to that past?' should interest us more. Do current Western societies still benefit from their ancestors' atrocities? The answer would help us to determine, for example, if Western societies owe something to the descendants of the victims other than hereditary guilt. Are we the receivers of our ancestors' crime? That is obviously the case for some Western crimes, such as the pillaging of art from other continents. At first sight, if their mode of acquisition can be considered beyond doubt as illegitimate, the works of art should be given back. That way, the current descendants of the victims rather than Western citizens would enjoy easy access to the artworks in their museums.[2] The question is more difficult to answer regarding early modern slavery. None of the goods produced by the slavery system are still being enjoyed. Fine private homes in slavery ports such as Bristol or Nantes were certainly not built directly by slave labour. Even if they were built from fortunes made in the Middle Passage, the analysis has to go further. Without the 1860 plunder, the treasures of the Summer Palace in Beijing would not be in Britain and France. Without slavery, it is possible that Bristol and Nantes merchants would have found other ways to make a fortune.

To assess the importance of slavery for early modern European economies, we need to know what these economies would have been like without slavery. Measuring the size of the slavery sector is very useful – and quite delicate – but it is not enough. We need a counterfactual. Fossil fuels currently provide 80% of human energy needs. The share of the economy that depends on them is very large. Many human activities require at least electricity, which is often produced by fossil fuels. Does that mean that the modern economy depends crucially on fossil fuels, and hence that the only way to avoid the continuation of global warming is to downsize the economy? Hardly. From the 2006 Stern report to the 2018 report by the Energy Transitions Commission, studies show that the long-run cost to move to a zero carbon economy would be quite small.[3] Global GDP would only be reduced by 0.5–2 percentage points by the transition to a zero carbon economy. The counterfactual does not seem very dire as long as the transition is well managed. Thus, in a sense, the prosperity of Western societies does not rest on carbon despite the huge share of energy provided by fossil fuels. Our children will be victims rather than receivers of Western over-dependence on fossil fuels. Maybe the models of these reports are over-optimistic, but we can discuss them because they are explicitly written down. Considering the level of prosperity of the late nineteenth- and twentieth-century Atlantic economy, perhaps the cost of the transition out of the slavery economy was not very large either.

All of the articles here seem to discuss how important the slave trade was to Europe. According to this line of reasoning, and despite their undeniable interest, they do not. To answer the 'how important' question, they would need to take a stand on the way the European economies worked. This would allow the construction of a counterfactual that should explore two questions. Did slavery make pre-industrial Europe richer and by how much? And considering the huge importance of the Industrial Revolution for the future of European prosperity, did slavery make the Industrial Revolution more likely or did it bring it forward by an appreciable amount of time? The example of the Netherlands shows that the question of prosperity is quite different from the question of structural change. The Netherlands had the most prosperous economy in Europe even during the eighteenth-century stagnation of its GDP per capita. Yet they did not go through an Industrial Revolution until the 1860s.[4]

The role of slavery in the advent of the Industrial Revolution is not the direct subject of any of these articles, yet they all provide useful pointers towards answering this question. Let us consider a number of classical explanations of the Industrial Revolution and try to find a role for slavery.

Joel Mokyr, in a number of papers and books, places science, technology and high-end human capital squarely in the forefront of the causes of the Industrial Revolution.[5] A new culture of inventiveness linked to the Enlightenment in Europe in general and in Britain in particular was decisive. He finds the root of this culture in cultural changes in sixteenth- and seventeenth-century Europe. These cultural changes, in turn, were made possible by political fragmentation and knowledge market integration.[6] One would be hard pressed to find a role for slavery in this and other cultural processes. The existence of slavery probably did not shape European culture in major ways: it was far too easy to ignore on that side of the Atlantic.

Another strand of explanation for the 'wave of gadgets' provided by the Industrial Revolution is institutional. It would be difficult to find a relationship between slavery and typical English low-level institutions, such as the Poor Laws, weak guilds or efficient apprenticeship markets. The same is true for some high-level institutions, such as the patent system defending intellectual property rights. Some have made the argument that Atlantic trade in general reinforced the power of traders, who then pushed for the transition to a parliamentary regime from 1688.[7] This is problematic on at least two levels. First, slavery-related trading activities were not the only sectors of dynamic long-distance trade in early modern England. The Royal African Company, which played an important role in the English slave trade before the Glorious Revolution, was no friend of Parliament. The reliance on slavery of pro-Parliament mercantilist interests in the politically decisive late seventeenth century has not been proven. Secondly, the link between Parliament and the Industrial Revolution is circuitous at best. The Industrial Revolution, at least up to the 1830s and railways' voracious appetite for capital, did not depend on the well-functioning secondary centralised financial market that developed throughout the eighteenth century. The role of the credit needs of slavery in developing the financial provision of commercial credit might have been more important.[8] That takes us quite a long way from the technological break that allowed the Industrial Revolution.

Perhaps slavery, by making Britain more prosperous, was important in the formation of a high wage economy. Robert Allen has argued that the high price of labour compared with energy and capital induced the extra research and development that gave rise to the major inventions of the Industrial Revolution in textiles, such as the spinning jenny.[9] This seems a more promising channel. We are now at the core of the second question that a counterfactual should explore. Was slavery decisive in increasing the standard of living in Europe, by how much and for whom? Again, this depends on the model of early modern Europe one believes in. The main three possible guides are Malthus, Solow and Smith.

Apart perhaps from Silesia, it would be difficult to argue that the economies studied here were dominated by Malthusian mechanisms. Nevertheless, a decisive role for slavery might have been to relax the Malthusian constraint in Europe thanks to the exploitation of America's land-abundant economy, even if the argument is more convincing with nineteenth-century rather than eighteenth-century levels of trade.[10]

In a Malthusian economy, increasing the supply of food directly (through sugar calories) or indirectly (by providing an outlet for an export industry that would allow imports of other foodstuffs) should increase living standards only in a transitory way. Mortality would react to improved living standards by declining and fertility by increasing. The population would increase to a higher level, bringing back living standards to the equilibrium that equalises mortality and fertility. Except for possible positive demographic checks including later marriage and more time between births, the positive effect should be transitory. So all else being equal, Malthusian mechanisms would suggest that slavery allowed an increase in the European population. Yet it is not certain that slavery was necessary for the exploitation of transatlantic resources. Contrary to what Voltaire wrote, maybe Europe could have consumed sugar without paying that price. The planters and colonial society certainly argued that slavery was necessary during the debates about abolition, but they had so much at stake that their good faith can be questioned. Indentured or free workers could have been brought in from Europe in greater numbers, thus relaxing further the Malthusian constraint there. Slavery could not be central to European prosperity through Malthusian mechanisms.

Solow and the neoclassical growth model can be another guide. In that case, the crucial question is the role of slavery in capital accumulation in eighteenth-century Europe. This is how the debate was framed by Marx, Williams, members of the World System school and the participants in the 'number game' derided by William Darity in 1985.[11] First, it must be noticed that the neoclassical growth model does not see capital accumulation as the motor for long-term growth and even less as the source for structural change. It will have an effect on transitory dynamics and the level of long-term production but not on long-term growth. Secondly, knowing what alternative use capitalists would have found for their wealth is difficult. If the slavery system was very profitable, presumably the alternative uses would have been less profitable. But by how much? My own computations have found that without the outlet of intercontinental trade, French production factors would have yielded 2% less income.[12] British and Dutch numbers were probably higher but have yet to be computed. A final difficulty is that capital as usually understood, in other words machines and fixed capital, was not that important in pre-industrial Europe. Fixed capital goods (except buildings) were so inexpensive and peripheral that workers very often owned them, a sure sign of their unimportance. Circulating capital was much more important. The limiting factor of prosperity was not physical production, but exchange and market participation.

This brings us to our third potential guide in the question of the role of slavery in early modern economies: Smith. What was the role of slavery in the extension of the market economy during the early modern period? I believe that it was important both in encouraging market participation by workers and consumers, and in helping the accumulation of trading capacities.[13] The consumer side of the argument is that the price decline of coffee and sugar (along with other goods from other continents, such as tea) made them available to a larger number of consumers throughout the century, improving their utility.[14] They were also highly addictive. Thus, these goods from the slavery system encouraged an increased participation of workers in wage labour and other market activities so they could afford them. Slavery thus contributed to the industrious revolution.[15] The trader side of the argument starts from the recognition that, if the amount of industrial capital available was not crucial to early modern prosperity, the amount of merchant circulating capital was. This was all the more the case since this capital was a complement to rather than a substitute for the workforce. Profits from intercontinental trade in general and the slave trade in particular were high enough to encourage domestic traders to accumulate enough capital to be able to enter the current high-profit sector. By doing so, they increased the trading capacities of society as a whole and, among other things, were able to integrate the willing consumers of the first part of the argument into a larger market economy. How much of a difference did slavery make to the willingness of consumers to participate in the market and to the trading capacities of society as a whole? Would the industrious revolution have been possible without slavery? These questions warrant future research that will involve deepening our knowledge of the nature of growth in early modern economies, in line with the existing work on British economic growth by Stephen Broadberry.[16]

My point is that models or stories are necessary. Describing the workings of the slavery system and its scope is very useful. But to answer the higher order question of 'did it matter', one must enter the land of counterfactuals. Research on the consequences of the European early modern slavery system is far from being complete.

Notes

1. Patrick O'Brien, 'European Economic Development: The Contribution of the Periphery', *Economic History Review* 35, no. 1 (1982): 1–18; Guillaume Daudin, 'Do Frontiers Give or Do Frontiers Take? The Case of Intercontinental Trade in France at the End of the Ancien Régime', in *A Deus Ex Machina Revisited. Atlantic Colonial Activities and European Economic Development*, eds. Olivier Pétré-Grenouilleau, Pieter Emmer and Jessica Roitman (Leiden: Brill, 2006), 199–224.
2. For a much more sophisticated take on that question, see Felwine Sarr and Bénédicte Savoy *Rapport sur la restitution du patrimoine culturel africain. Vers une nouvelle éthique relationnelle.* (2018) http://restitutionreport2018.com/.
3. Nicholas Herbert Stern, *The Economics of Climate Change: The Stern Review* (Cambridge: Cambridge University Press, 2007); Adair Turner, 'A Zero-Carbon Economy Is Both Feasible and Affordable', *Financial Times* (22 November 2018), https://www.ft.com/content/1b56f762-ec08-11e8-89c8-d36339d835c0.
4. Joel Mokyr, 'The Industrial Revolution and the Netherlands: Why Did It Not Happen?', *The Economist* 148, no. 4 (1 October 2000): 503–20, https://doi.org/10.1023/A:1004134217178.
5. Joel Mokyr, *The Enlightened Economy: Britain and the Industrial Revolution, 1700–1850* (New Haven, CT: Yale University Press, 2009).
6. Joel Mokyr, *A Culture of Growth: The Origins of the Modern Economy* (Princeton, NJ: Princeton University Press, 2017). For another version of the culture argument, see Deirdre N. McCloskey, *The Bourgeois Virtues: Ethics for an Age of Commerce* (Chicago: University of Chicago Press, 2006).

7. Daron Acemoglu, Simon Johnson, and James A. Robinson, 'The Rise of Europe: Atlantic Trade, Institutional Change and Economic Growth,' *American Economic Review* 95, no. 3 (2005): 546–79.
8. Joseph E. Inikori, 'The Credit Needs of the African Trade and the Development of the Credit Economy in England', *Explorations in Economic History* 27, no. 2 (April 1990): 197–231, https://doi.org/10.1016/0014-4983(90)90010-V.
9. R.C. Allen, 'Why the Industrial Revolution Was British: Commerce, Induced Invention, and the Scientific Revolution', *The Economic History Review* 64, no. 2 (1 May 2011): 357–84, https://doi.org/10.1111/j.1468-0289.2010.00532.x.
10. Kenneth Pomeranz, *The Great Divergence: Europe, China, and the Making of the Modern World Economy*, The Princeton Economic History of the Western World (Princeton, NJ: Princeton University Press, 2000).
11. Karl Marx, *Le Capital: Critique de l'économie Politique, Livre Premier* (Paris: Presses Universitaires de France, 1993); Eric Wilson Williams, *Capitalism and Slavery* (New-York: Capricorn, 1944); Immanuel Wallerstein, *The Modern World System III : The Second Era of Great Expansion of the Capitalist World-Economy, 1730s–1840s* (San Diego, CA: Academic Press, 1989); William Jr. Darity, 'The Number Game and the Profitability of the British Trade in Slaves', *Journal of Economic History* 45 (1985): 693–703. For a fuller bibliography, see Daudin, 'Do Frontiers Give?'
12. Daudin, 'Do Frontiers Give?' and G. Daudin, *Commerce et Prospérité: La France Au XVIIIe Siècle* (Paris: Presses Paris Sorbonne, 2005) for more details on the computation.
13. For more details, see Daudin, *Commerce et Prospérité.*
14. Hans-Joachim Voth and Jonathan Hersh, 'Sweet Diversity: Colonial Goods and the Rise of European Living Standards after 1492', CEPR Working Paper, 2009, 1–38.
15. Jan de Vries, 'The Industrial Revolution and the Industrious Revolution', *Journal of Economic History* 54, no. 2 (1994): 249–70.
16. Roger Fouquet and Stephen Broadberry, 'Seven Centuries of European Economic Growth and Decline', *Journal of Economic Perspectives* 29, no. 4 (2015): 227–44, https://doi.org/10.1257/jep.29.4.227; B.M. Campbell, A. Klein, M. Overton and B. van Leeuwen, *British Economic Growth, 1270–1870* (Cambridge: Cambridge University Press, 2015).

Acknowledgements

I thank Tamira Combrink and Matthias van Rossum for organizing the session that was the basis for this Special Issue.

Disclosure statement

No potential conflict of interest was reported by the author(s).

The value of figures

Pepijn Brandon

ABSTRACT
This comment builds on the methodological reflections presented in the joint article by Brandon and Bosma in this issue. It examines three 'demarcation problems' that beset all the articles presented in this issue: where to draw the line between costs and benefits (for whom, at what stage in the process of reaping the gains of the forced labour of the enslaved, and in what link of the global commodity chain?); how to meaningfully translate benefits drawn from imperial and trans-imperial economic activities to a national accounting framework; and how to account for revenues when these were redistributed through schemes of profit sharing and complicated financial arrangements. Thinking through such seemingly technical problems can bring us closer to essential questions concerning the political economy of slavery. Many of the 'new historians' of capitalism and slavery treat national accounting as essentially hostile terrain. However, when not approached as an abstract numbers game, it can be a valuable tool for clarifying the stakes of the many different actors whose business revolved around the commodified lives of the enslaved, help to understand their interrelations and highlight their involvement in organising new relations of exchange, production and power.

The article by Ulbe Bosma and myself that appears in this Special Issue was first published in Dutch in June 2019 as a stand-alone research article in *The Low Countries Journal of Social and Economic History*.[1] The recalculation of the value of Atlantic slave-based activities that it presents raised quite a stir in the Dutch national media, owing to its conclusion that these activities in the year 1770 contributed over 5% of the GDP of the Netherlands as a whole, well over 10% of the GDP of the Dutch Republic's richest province Holland, provided for almost a quarter of all imports and exports in Dutch harbours during that period, and over a period of four decades were responsible for about 40% of the province of Holland's (by then moderate) economic growth. Predictably, much of this revolved around the question whether 5% is a large or a small proportion of GDP. When posed in this abstract and isolated way, detached from all wider economic-historical reasoning presented in our article, this becomes a rather subjective matter. However, behind the arguments over figures lie important interpretive questions involving difficulties that beset all attempts at accounting for the revenues of early modern international and colonial trade, and touching on the more specific problems that come into play when trying to understand the ways in which slavery was embedded in its wider economic context of emerging international capitalism. Since it would be quite inappropriate for one of the authors of this special issue to engage in depth with the arguments of the other contributors, this comment focuses instead on some of the methodological challenges involved in making these calculations, which necessarily resurface in all attempts to account for the importance of slavery to early modern economies.

Demarcation problems

Apart from the overarching question of reliability of pre-modern GDP and national income estimates, the greatest difficulties in our calculations arise from a set of demarcation problems. Such questions of demarcation beset all the contributions in this special issue. First, there is the far from easy matter of how to delineate costs and benefits in the slave trade and the slave-based commodity trade. As Filipa Ribeiro da Silva explains in relation to the Portuguese case, the easiest figures to come by are estimates of the total value of the trade on specific routes. However, as soon as one attempts to get below this level and say something about who gained what and at what price in the slave trade and slave-based commodity trade, problems start to compound owing to the often fragmentary nature of existing sources. Of course, there is nothing new about this. All serious attempts to estimate the economic weight of slave-based activities in the past have generalised from individual business accounts to come to conclusions about the relationship between the total size of trade flows, the actual economic benefits drawn from them and their division between various actors (plantation owners, international merchants, shipping companies, insurers, investors, captains, sailors and so on).[2] The commodity chain approach proposed here by Tamira Combrink and Klas Rönnbäck does not fundamentally depart from this in terms of its calculating method, but only in its vantage point. Rather than starting from the clerk's desk in the offices of the port-based wholesaler of plantation goods or the shipping company launching a slaving voyage, it starts from the transnational journey of the commodities, using accounts or estimates for all the main players through whose hands the sugar, coffee and cotton travelled before they reached the end consumers. Primarily designed for analysing and explaining 'world-economic spatial inequalities in terms of differential access to markets and resources', the approach can also be mobilised to form a better grasp of the distribution of value added among different parties within each of the 'national' economies through which these chains run.[3] From the perspective of national accounting, however, this raises a second difficult demarcation issue, which is where to draw the borders of the national economy. At least before the rise of the Second Slavery in the Southern states of the United States and in Brazil, slavery operated not primarily in a national but in an imperial setting. Ideally, therefore, a nation-based analysis should be complemented by a notion of the weight of slavery within the combined imperial economy. Given the porous nature of many early-modern imperial projects, however, such an attempt could only move the problem of borders across the globe, not solve it.

Finally, and connected to the first two, there is the fundamental definitional question what economic activities can be counted as based on slavery. This question becomes more difficult at each further step taken beyond the immediate point of production where the enslaved toiled and suffered. As the article by Anka Steffen illustrates, when reaching the opposite end in the commodity chain from the plantation (the end consumer of plantation goods or the primary producers of plantation supplies), economic activities aimed at or derived from the Atlantic plantation complex become hard to separate from those that were not. Nonetheless, connections to Atlantic slavery often remained vital even when hidden through many intermediary steps, especially because, in the second half of the eighteenth century, the spectacular growth of Atlantic trade and the European-wide consumption boom connected to it were such dynamic factors in reshaping the entire structure of international trade.

There are many different ways in which to solve these demarcation issues, each with their own advantages and pitfalls. Obviously, where one draws the line in each case has enormous influence on the resulting figures. In general, it seems to me that as long as such choices are made visible, the reliability of one's estimates does not depend on whether one throws the net wider or more narrowly but rather on the conscientiousness with which these choices are followed through. In general, however, given the divergence in accounting choices made even within the confines of this Special Issue, we should be careful in using the resulting figures as the basis for all too direct international comparison. Real robust comparison at the level of GDP, national income shares, capital formation or any other indicator will only be possible on the basis of working out a shared set of assumptions and calculating approaches, and this requires more transnational collaborative work.

Dividing the spoils

It is important to avoid the impression that the accounting problems mentioned here only stem from issues of definition and method although, of course, clear definitions and methods can help avoid some of the basic pitfalls. More fundamentally, they stem from real complexities in the system of slave-based commodity production, in which the brutal systems of forced labour supply of the transatlantic and internal slave trade were directly connected to transnationally linked systems of commodity production and trade, often mediated through intricate financial arrangements that included parties on several continents. While creating untold misery at the bottom of this system, for the beneficiaries this complicated system created long-distance co-dependencies, principal–agent problems of vast proportions and multiple ways to skim each other's margins that business accounts at best capture only in partial ways. This in essence is what makes the seemingly innocuous question about what constituted profit from slavery far from straightforward in practice.[4]

Revenue circulated through the Atlantic system in many forms which were often hard to disentangle. Two examples taken from the Dutch case both applicable more generally can help to clarify this. The first involves the redistribution of the spoils from slavery downwards within slaving firms, the second the upward redistribution of plantation profits through international finance. Like many other forms of long-distance trade during the early modern period, the slave trade included elaborate financial reward systems for the higher echelons to secure loyalty to the shipping companies and minimise the propensity to cheat, smuggle or fiddle the books. From the perspective of the shipping companies, such bonuses formed part of their personnel costs and thus were not part of net profits. However, from the perspective of the captains who were the main beneficiaries of these rewards, they formed a way to share in the profits of a slaving voyage. The commanding officers on board ships sailing for the Netherlands' most important eighteenth-century private slave-trading company, the Middelburgsche Commercie Compagnie (MCC), received bonuses in two forms. The first was *slavengeld* or slave money, consisting of a set amount per captive sold in the Caribbean. The second component was *recognitiegeld* or recognition money, consisting of a percentage of the total profits of a journey, if profits were made.[5] Similar rewards existed for captains on slaving voyages of other companies, such as the Dutch West India Company (WIC), as they did outside the Netherlands.[6]

Gerhard de Kok's painstaking reconstruction of the business accounts for 101 slaving voyages of the MCC, summarised in the annex to our article for different purposes, shows that these bonuses were far from negligible. In total, the net profits from these 101 voyages amounted to fl.376,802, a figure that factors in the net losses made on many of the journeys and amounts to an average net profit rate of 3.9% per voyage. However, for the same journeys, the combined slave money and recognition money amounted to fl.265,261. Except for highly exceptional cases, captains and other officers earned rewards even on slaving voyages that resulted in a net loss for the company. If these bonuses are seen as a redistribution of profits rather than an addition to wages, the average profit rate per voyage would rise to 7.3%.[7] This does not take into account the fact that captains could also make additional profits by participating in permitted or illicit forms of private trade on board their ships, activities that obviously remained off the books of the trading firms.

At the other end of the spectrum, large internationally operating merchant-financiers exploited planters' need for capital to gain leverage over many sides of the Atlantic commodity boom. From the 1750s to the early 1770s, a wave of speculation in plantation mortgages swept the Amsterdam financial market, involving many of the city's leading finance capitalists.[8] Reflecting the high expectations for the performance of the plantation economy, investors in these funds usually obtained interest rates of 5%, about twice the rate for government bonds on the Amsterdam market. The mortgaging contracts also stipulated a variety of types of reward for the directors of these funds, ranging from a 1% interest rate on top of the 5% paid to bond holders, brokerage fees that could amount to 1.5% of the total value of the loan, commission on the sale of the plantation commodities consigned to them as collateral for the interest payments or commission for insuring the plantation, the slave force or the commodities shipped to the Netherlands (or insurance fees if the directors themselves acted as insurers).[9] A crisis in the early 1770s led to severe arrears in interest payments, in many cases causing investors and directors to lose part of their share in the principal while the face value of bonds dropped dramatically. In many cases, fund directors tried to recuperate their losses by taking over ownership of the plantations. Through such complicated financial constructions, financial services, slave ownership and profits from commodity trade remained connected in often quite intractable ways.

Slavery and political economy

The point about the distribution of the spoils of slavery connects the problem of accounting for slavery, which was the starting point of this Special Issue, to the question of slavery's political economy. With the re-emergence of a lively scholarly debate on the relationship between capitalism and slavery, the latter has gained much more prominence than the former. Indeed, much of this literature is primarily concerned with the effects of slavery that go beyond national accounting per se – its impact on institutions, transnational business networks, geopolitics, forms of labour control, the organisation of firms, innovations in finance or accounting techniques, or even, to put it in Sombartian terms, the highly racialised and deeply power-invested 'spirit of capitalism'.[10] More traditional economic historians have frequently bemoaned this move away from more quantitative measures and have criticised it as a retreat. However, it is important to remember that some of the classical formulations of the problem had precisely such a broad-ranging approach in mind. Eric Williams' much cited *Capitalism and Slavery*, to name just the most obvious example, is far less an attempt at systematic accounting for the profits from the Atlantic slave complex than it is an examination of the evolution of various conflicting interest groups within the British capitalist class and their respective relations to the imperial state and its economic policies.[11]

The contributions to this Special Issue illustrate that these more quantitative or more qualitative approaches are not by any means mutually exclusive. Problems encountered by historians at the micro-level when trying to reconstruct the benefits derived from the vast Atlantic slave-based economy prove to be intimately linked to the constellations of power and interests between international merchants, slavers, financiers and the state. These constellations could be very different from country to country and from colony to colony. Reconstructing the weight of slave-based activities in national accounts is no more than one instrument that we can use to gain a better understanding of slavery's political economy in all its complexity. Many of the 'new historians' of capitalism and slavery still treat quantitative history as essentially hostile terrain. However, when not approached as an abstract numbers game, it can be a valuable tool for clarifying the stakes of the many different actors whose business revolved around the commodified lives of the enslaved, help to understand their interrelations and highlight their deep involvement in organising new relations of exchange, production and power.

Notes

1. Pepijn Brandon and Ulbe Bosma, 'De betekenis van de Atlantische slavernij voor de Nederlandse economie in de tweede helft van de achttiende eeuw', *TSEG/Low Countries Journal of Social and Economic History* 16, no. 2 (2019): 5–46.
2. Patrick O'Brien, 'European Economic Development: The Contribution of the Periphery', *The Economic History Review*, New Series 35, no. 1 (1982): 1–18; Guillaume Daudin, *Commerce et prosperité: La France au XVIIe siècle* (Paris: Presses de l'Université Paris-Sorbonne, 2005); Leonor Freire Costa, Nuno Palma, and Jaime Reis, 'The Great Escape? The Contribution of the Empire to Portugal's Economic Growth, 1500–1800', *European Review of Economic History* 19, no. 1 (2015): 1–22.
3. Gary Gereffi, Miguel Korzeniewicz, and Roberto P. Korzeniewicz, 'Introduction: Global Commodity Chains', in *Commodity Chains and Global Capitalism*, ed. Gary Gereffi and Miguel Korzeniewicz (Westport, CT and London: Greenwood Press, 1994), 1–14, 2. Within the larger project of which the contribution of Ulbe Bosma and myself in this Special Issue formed the synthesis, Tamira Combrink's subproject deals with slave-based commodity chains most systematically.
4. As illustrated by the recent exchange in this journal, Karwan Fatah-Black and Matthias van Rossum, 'Beyond Profitability: The Dutch Transatlantic Slave Trade and its Economic Impact', *Slavery & Abolition* 36, no. 1 (2015): 63–83; David Eltis, Pieter C. Emmer, and Frank D. Lewis, 'More than Profits? The Contribution of the Slave Trade to the Dutch Economy: Assessing Fatah-Black and Van Rossum', *Slavery & Abolition* 37, no. 4 (2016): 724–35; Karwan Fatah-Black and Matthias van Rossum, 'A Profitable Debate?', *Slavery & Abolition* 37, no. 4 (2016): 736–43.
5. Corrie Reinders Folmer-Van Prooijen, *Van goederenhandel naar slavenhandel. De Middelburgse Commercie Compagnie 1720–1755* (Middelburg: Koninklijk Zeeuwsch Genootschap der Wetenschappen, 2000).

6. Henk den Heijer, *Geschiedenis van de WIC. Opkomst, Bloei en Ondergang* (Zutphen: Walburg Pers, 2013); Marcus Rediker, *The Slave Ship. A Human History* (New York: Viking, 2007), 193–4; Ofélia Pinto and Brian West, 'Accounting and the History of the Everyday Life of Captains, Sailors and Common Seamen in Eighteenth-century Portuguese Slave Trading', *Accounting History* 22, no. 3 (2017): 320–47, 333.
7. Calculated on the basis of the voyage by voyage database provided as Annex B in Gerhard de Kok, *Walcherse ketens. De trans-Atlantische slavenhandel en de economie van Walcheren, 1755–1780* (unpublished doctoral thesis, Leiden University, 2019), https://openaccess.leidenuniv.nl/handle/1887/73831 (accessed 21 January 2020).
8. The classical account is J.P. van de Voort, *De Westindische Plantages van 1720 tot 1795. Financiën en Handel* (Eindhoven: Drukkerij De Witte, 1973).
9. *Idem*. For an example of a contract combining several of these items, issued in 1769 at the peak of the boom by Harman van de Poll & Co in Amsterdam, see *Conditien van een Negotiatie ten behoeve van eenige Planters in de Colonie van Surinamen* (Amsterdam, 1769).
10. A showcase in this shift in concerns is Sven Beckert and Seth Rockman, eds., *Slavery's Capitalism. A New History of American Economic Development* (Philadelphia: University of Pennsylvania Press, 2016).
11. Eric Williams, *Capitalism & Slavery* (Chapel Hill: University of North Carolina Press, 1944).

Disclosure statement

No potential conflict of interest was reported by the author(s).

Revisiting Europe and slavery

Sven Beckert

ABSTRACT
This comment explores why the debate on slavery and European economic development, which goes back to the early nineteenth century, has become significant again in the past two decades, with many suggesting the need to take a second look at the problem. It reflects on the articles of this special issue. Taking the discussion beyond the usual case of England and the Industrial Revolution, these articles show that we need to bring slavery into the history of European economic development more broadly, and that we need to see the literature on slavery and the literature on early modern Europe as part of a related set of problems and questions. This special issue makes an important contribution to the debate on slavery and European economic development by specifying more precisely how much slavery mattered. Yet none of them even begins to engage with the important '"why?"' question.

A spectre is haunting European history writing and public discourse – the spectre of slavery. For a very long time, most scholarship on European history made little mention of the almost 400-year history of the transport of as many as 12.5 million enslaved Africans across the Atlantic and their exploitation by European entrepreneurs and statesmen in the Americas. Indeed, so apparently unimportant was slavery to European (early) modernity that hundreds of studies dealing with the histories of Spain, Britain, France, Denmark, Sweden, the Netherlands, Germany and Switzerland, among others, omitted it almost entirely from their explorations of the political, social, cultural and economic development of the continent and its parts.[1] No doubt this position was made easier by the fact that enslavement took place on the distant coasts of Africa and enslaved workers laboured on plantations and in mines on equally distant Caribbean islands and in North and South America. European modernity, as described in the works of Max Weber and many others, was rooted in a set of unusually rational religious beliefs, favourable institutions, geographies conducive to economic development, technical inventiveness and a moderate climate, among other factors – among which slavery was conspicuously absent. To be sure, historians located in Europe have written many important studies on the history of slavery, with hundreds of almost always insightful and often brilliant books and articles chronicling the slave trade and slavery itself.[2] Yet all too often they seemed to belong to another realm, another geography and another set of questions.

Of course there were almost always voices pushing against these dichotomies. The earliest and most important stream of research aimed at bringing slavery into the history of European modernity came from Caribbean historians, not their European counterparts. They argued, as Trinidadian historian Eric Williams pointed out, that '[t]he commercial capitalism of the eighteenth century developed the wealth of Europe by means of slavery and monopoly'. His Guyanese counterpart Walter Rodney added that 'the colonisation of Africa and other parts of the world formed an indispensable link in a chain of events which made possible the technological transformation of the base of European capitalism', and, most famously of all, Trinidadian historian C.L.R. James claimed that

> [n]early all the industries which developed in France during the eighteenth century had their origin in goods or commodities destined either for the coast of Guinea or for America. The capital from the slave-trade fertilized them; though the bourgeoisie traded in other things than slaves, upon the success or failure of the traffic everything else depended.

Martinican author Aimé Césaire showed that colonies played a central role in the emergence of the class from whom 'the first modern industrialists were recruited in Nantes, Rouens, and Bordeaux … ', while Surinamese writer Anton de Kom observed that sugar plantations made Europeans 'prosperous through trade and agriculture'.[3]

These arguments echoed in the works of some of the most perceptive European and North American scholars: the U.S. sociologist W.E.B. Du Bois, for example, argued that

> [b]lack labor became the foundation stone not only of the Southern social structure, but of Northern manufacture and commerce, of the English factory system, of European commerce, of buying and selling on a world-wide scale; new cities were built on the results of black labor, and a new labor problem, involving all white labor, arose both in Europe and America.[4]

Anthropologist Sidney Mintz followed suit in his *Sweetness and Power*, showing how the slave-driven sugar plantations of the New World underwrote many aspects of European modernity.[5] American economist Barbara Solow largely agreed, observing that '[t]he slave-sugar complex became the premier institution of European expansion'.[6] '[T]he actual historical origin of American growth in the early period', Solow says, 'lay with slavery, and the Atlantic trading system of the eighteenth century was directly based upon it'.[7] For Solow, slavery and its by-products constituted the foundation of the very Atlantic economy that was at the centre of British economic ascendancy.[8]

Yet the works of Caribbean scholars were all too often greeted with deafening silence and did not for a long time enter the mainstream of European historiography. If they got any traction at all, it was mostly in works that tried to prove their assumptions wrong and thus remarginalise the history of slavery and, with it, colonial expansion. Pieter Emmer in the Netherlands, for example, discounted for several decades the possibility that the slavery complex could have significantly mattered to the Dutch economy and continues to do so.[9] Stanley Engerman, in a more subtle and thoughtful mode, narrowed the question to the slave trade itself and argued in 1972 that profits from that trade could not possibly have played a significant role in British industrialisation.[10] Ten years later, economic historian Patrick O'Brien concluded that 'for the economic growth of the core, the periphery was peripheral' – an argument that included the Atlantic slavery complex.[11] While such readings have increasingly been challenged, they can still be found.[12]

In the past two decades, however, the Pandora's box of slavery and European economic development has snapped open, with many suggesting the need to take a second look at the problem. Empirically, the richest recent intervention into this debate came in 2002 with Joseph Inikori's painstakingly researched *Africans and the Industrial Revolution in England*, which demonstrated that Atlantic markets, most of which were enabled by Atlantic slavery, played a key role during the crucial decades of Britain's early industrialisation in the second half of the eighteenth century.[13] In his later work, O'Brien also reconsidered the role of the Atlantic economy – and slavery – in British ascendancy and began emphasising its importance.[14] Economists Daron Acemoglu, Simon Johnson and James Robinson came to agree, arguing that 'the rise of Atlantic Europe and the rise of Atlantic ports' – and thus also slavery – was crucial to Western European ascendancy.[15] And my own *Empire of Cotton* emphasised the importance of slave-grown cotton to the revolutionary recasting of the world's cotton industry and global capitalism in the late eighteenth and early nineteenth centuries.[16]

Why has a debate that goes back to the early nineteenth century and the battling worldviews of planters and abolitionists become significant again now? There are three important factors: first, descendants of formerly enslaved peoples have settled in much larger numbers in Europe –in the Netherlands, for example, but also in England and France. They have often brought questions of colonialism, and with it the issue of slavery, into public debates and into their political activism, demanding a public reckoning with that part of European history. They have confronted historians with calls for the 'decolonialization of knowledge' and the 'provincialising of Europe', emphasising the urgency to address issues that have been marginalised for all too long. Recently, they have targeted the continued public honouring of former slave traders and slaveowners in European public spaces, tearing down monuments and renaming streets and buildings, in the process encouraging historians, among others, to reconsider central aspects of European history.

Second, a new global orientation has emerged in the past 15 years in the historical profession, a reorientation that has moved questions about the intercontinental connections of European history and the global production of the local to the forefront.[17] This interest in global connections has brought Africa and the Americas into much closer proximity to Europe and with them issues of enslavement, the slave trade, slave-based commodity production in the Americas and their links to Europe's cultural, social, ideological, political and economic history. The old boundaries between European, African and American history have weakened and in many cases come down, as the Atlantic has increasingly come to be considered as one region whose dynamic, including its economic dynamic, can only be understood from a broad perspective.

Third, in the wake of the economic crisis of 2008, historians have once again taken an interest in economic matters, and a new wave of research has tried to come to terms with the history of capitalism. In that debate, one of the issues that quickly rose in importance was slavery, especially in discussions in the United States. In that rediscovery of economic history, historians reconnected to the rich scholarship that historically-oriented economists had been producing for the past few decades, some of which touched on the issue of slavery and much of which had previously been ignored by historians.[18]

The articles assembled in this special issue of *Slavery & Abolition* extend that discussion and will perhaps help to resolve some of its core questions. For all their differences, these articles have much in common: they aim to move the debate on slavery squarely to the centre of European history. They focus on the importance of slavery to European economies rather than on slavery itself. The lively debates of the 1970s and 1980s about the capitalist or non-capitalist character of slavery itself – represented most pre-eminently by the contrasting arguments by Eugene Genovese on the one hand and Robert Fogel and Stanley Engerman on the other – and recently taken up again in insightful ways by Caitlin Rosenthal – are not represented in these articles.[19] Nor do they consider the almost always deleterious economic effects of slavery and its legacy on post-slavery societies. Their focus is instead on the economic impact of slavery on various distinct regional and national European economies. Moreover, the research featured here is just the tip of the iceberg, as the issue of slavery and its economic impact is now animating some of the liveliest debates in the historical profession.[20]

The articles in this issue of *Slavery & Abolition* mostly take a quantitative approach focused on measuring the importance of slavery on European economic development, and we need to acknowledge at the outset that other historians have taken slightly different tracks. Just think of the work of Rosenthal, Seth Rockman, Diana Berry, Craig Wilder and many others who are working on a more qualitative approach to a similar set of questions in the context of the history of the Unites States.[21]

The articles here all make important contributions to the debate. We learn from Anka Stefan's imaginative essay that the most dynamic industry in eighteenth-century Prussia was the linen industry which had very close ties to Atlantic slavery. She reports that Silesian linens found their way into the African slave trade in significant quantities and later became an important presence in the provisioning trade to the Americas. We learn how the intensification of Atlantic trade put new pressures on rural producers in Silesia and led to an intensification of serfdom in the region, with merchants becoming neo-feudal landowners in order to secure forced labour at low costs. We also learn how important this slave-driven sector was to the Prussian economy and the state as a whole: in the mid-1780s, Silesia was Prussia's most important manufacturing region and the most financially significant of its 11 provinces. Its taxes produced 37% of the income of the state and half of all Prussian profits generated in foreign trade came from Silesian linens. In fact, the slave-dependent expansion of linen production in Silesia financed an increasingly powerful state. Stefan estimates that a stunning 15% of the total value of all manufactures produced in Prussia in 1793 were connected to slave-based activities. She shows that this allegedly 'backward' part of Europe was important to the continent's economic development, reminding us that we need to take not just the Atlantic but also the European hinterland into account when explaining the European economic miracle and to keep the role of Atlantic slavery within our lens.

This issue of *Slavery and Abolition* teaches us that new consumer cultures – often considered by scholars to be important to the advent of European modernity – expanded hand-in-hand with plantation slavery in the Americas. Indeed, as Tamira Combrink suggests, a consumer society emerged partly because of the unfolding of 'violent processes' in the Americas. Combrink's carefully researched and deeply insightful work shows that the coffee trade was important to the Dutch trade position in Europe and that slave-grown coffee made up a significant share of that trade. In the 1770s and 1780s, slave-grown coffee accounted for 7.5% of Dutch foreign trade. Although until the early eighteenth century coffee had largely been produced in Yemen by peasant producers, by 1755, 80% of all coffee consumed in Europe came from the West Indies and was grown by enslaved workers. By the late 1780s, some 60% of the world's coffee came from just one slave colony: Saint Domingue, modern-day Haiti. Even after the enslaved cultivators of Saint Domingue staged a successful revolution, coffee remained a largely slave-grown agricultural commodity elsewhere well into the nineteenth century, that is for almost another century. Combrink reminds us that if we want to understand the importance of the plantation economy of the Americas to the European development of trade, industry and wealth, we need to look at commodity chains in their entirety. This type of investigation even reframes the German 'Kaffeekränzchen', seemingly a quintessentially local tradition (and one tied to cosmopolitan consumption habits and the growth of European modernity), as having deep roots in Atlantic slavery.

Klas Rönnbäck, like Combrink, looks at the entire commodity chain – this time of sugar – to find that the governance of that chain had a significant impact on where profits from sugar accumulated. According to him, the 'triangular trade' added about 5% to British GDP in the late eighteenth century. If we add the American plantation complex itself and British industries dependent on it to that equation, about 11.2% of British GDP was slavery-connected – a very significant number that increased rapidly during the last three decades of the eighteenth century. Rönnbäck then shows how combinations among British sugar refiners kept prices high and thus allowed for the refiners to make significant profits – suggesting that we not only need to keep the entire commodity chain in mind to understand the economic importance of the slavery complex to European economies, but also to see how that commodity chain was infused by power and regulated in ways that shaped the distribution of profits within it.

Filipa Ribeiro da Silva follows up on the question of the distribution of profits from slavery, demonstrating that the substantial profits of the Portuguese slavery complex accrued not just in Lisbon and Rio de Janeiro, but in Hamburg, Amsterdam and the United Kingdom, among other places. In fact, two-thirds of slave-produced Brazilian gold in the eighteenth century ended up in Britain as payments for imported British wares. The Portuguese and Brazilian slavery complex thus breathed further life into the British economy, demonstrating that a purely national or imperial perspective fails to capture the full picture of slavery's importance to European economies.

Most ambitious is Pepijn Brandon and Ulbe Bosma's important research. Their carefully conceptualised study finds that 5.2% of Dutch GDP in 1770, and almost double that of its richest province, Holland, derived from slavery-related economic activities. They show that the focus on the profits of the slave trade itself is misguided, as the vast majority of slavery profits came from the trade in and the transport and financing of slave-grown agricultural commodities, not from buying and selling enslaved workers. Their analysis reveals that the slave sector encompassed a range of activities that began with the trade in enslaved Africans and included the provisioning of that trade, the provisioning of Caribbean plantations, the trade of slave-produced agricultural commodities, the processing of such goods, the trade in the processed goods that resulted and, of course, all the financial services that grew up around it. Slavery's capitalism was thus a many-headed hydra. When the Dutch-language version of this article was published in the Netherlands last year, it generated significant public debate, including moves to acknowledge this part of Dutch history more broadly and an effort by the City of Amsterdam to come to terms with its own very significant investments in the slavery complex.

The articles presented here build a strong case for taking slavery's importance in the development of the European economy seriously. They provide vital new data that strengthens the argument of those who follow in the footsteps of Eric Williams and expands on the crucial insight of economists Ronald Findlay and Kevin O'Rourke that '[t]he link between the Industrial Revolution and the extension of the slave plantations in the New World on which the essential raw material was cultivated could not therefore be more obvious'.[22] Patterns of modern-day inequality, French economist Thomas Piketty has shown recently, are also deeply rooted in the slave past of various societies.[23] The articles here show that we need to bring slavery into the history of European economic development and that the literature on slavery and on early modern Europe are part of the same set of problems. These essays are important because they take the discussion beyond the usual suspect, namely England, even bringing Central Europe into the debate; because they go beyond the question of profits from the slave trade alone; and because they emphasise the early history of capitalism prior to the Industrial Revolution.

It would be too much to ask these articles to conclusively resolve the debate on the importance of slavery to European economic development. The authors add empirical depth to the discussion and fill in more parts of the outline on that huge canvas. Their clarity is important, both for the facts they offer and as a model for how we can tackle some of the central questions. But there are other large issues to take into account as we consider how we can further fill that canvas.

First, the authors are still rooted in national historical perspectives. They investigate Prussia, England, Portugal and the Dutch Republic as discreet units with their own quantifiable relationship to slavery. This is understandable, not least because most data relevant to investigating these issues has been produced to capture the economy of distinct states. Yet as the articles themselves show, capital and capitalists operated in economic spaces that often transcended their origin points. Political and economic spaces did not converge, and the full economic impact of slavery can only be understood from a European-wide, if not global, perspective. Dutch capital fuelled Barbados' plantation revolution, the British cotton textile industry drew on Brazilian cotton for a few crucial decades, French-grown coffee arrived in Dutch ports to be consumed in German cities, and a significant share of the Brazilian slave economy fed not so much into Portugal's economic development as into that of north-western Europe. To understand slavery's economic impact on Europe, we need to position both Europe and slavery within the newly emergent world economy and look at the spread of capital, the transformation of production and the thickening of state power as related processes across vast spaces. If we think of slavery as having played a crucial role in generating 'Atlantic capitalism', we can find new ways of thinking about the divergent developmental paths taking by various states on the European continent. The fact that Portugal did not industrialise is thus not an argument discounting the importance of slavery to European economic development.

Second, the articles assembled here strongly suggest the importance of looking beyond the Industrial Revolution, both backward and forward, to fully investigate the importance of slavery to European economic development. We know that a few European economies took on distinct features that set them apart from economies in other parts of the world before the Industrial Revolution, not least because European capital owners constructed trade networks and spatially extended the control of production far beyond that of other capital owners elsewhere in the world. They were linked to novel kinds of states and built new institutions linked to these states and their exceptional trade networks. Slavery played a key role in all these processes, and we need to assess not just the question of how slavery fed directly into the Industrial Revolution but also consider its impact on various European economies throughout the past 500 years.

Third, in the process of quantifying, we need to be clear about what we are arguing. For slavery to matter to the economic history of Europe, do slavery-related economic activities need to amount to 2, 5, 10 or 50% of total economic activity? At what threshold do things become important? In 2018, the automobile industry constituted about 7.7% of the German economy, while the information, communications and technology industry in the United States added 6.8% to the gross value of all American private industry, with the software sector alone adding 3.6%.[24] Are these industries important to their respective national economies? Don't we know from history, but also from chemistry, biology or physics, that numerically small factors can make a huge difference? Do we need to account for that? And do we need to be more cognisant of the fact that what Braudel calls the 'traditional economy' continued throughout most centuries and thus the incremental change made possible by slavery looms much larger in importance than the actual numbers indicate?

Fourth, beyond the quantitative importance of slavery, there is also its institutional impact. New business strategies, new forms of labour control, new financial institutions and new trade networks all emerged out of Atlantic trade, which was fuelled to a very large extent by slavery. Crucially, moreover, new forms of political power emerged from that expansion of European states and economies. These innovations cannot easily be measured, but they are important, as many historians and economists have shown, to early modern European economies and need to become part of this debate. At the same time, slavery and the slave trade weakened African economies and institutions and left an institutional, political and ideological imprint on the slave lands of the world that had grave long-term economic effects.

Fifth, once we acknowledge the importance of slavery to European modernity, we also need to insist on the importance of enslaved people as actors and not just as powerless victims. We know of the importance of skilled rice cultivators to South Carolina's rice revolution; we have learned much about the importance of skilled enslaved sugar workers to the technologies of the sugar revolution; and we know of the importance of enslaved women's reproductive labour. Enslaved Africans need to also figure in this story as political actors: their almost uninterrupted political activities on plantations and in towns and cities reshaped the slavery complex in fundamental ways through rebellions, strikes, day-to-day resistance and revolution. One just needs to think of the freedom struggle of the enslaved workers of Saint Domingue.[25]

Sixth, we need to insist that what needs explaining is what actually happened, not the fantastic counterfactuals some economists like to suggest. Yes, Irish immigrants could have grown cotton in Mississippi, sugar could have been exported from China, coffee production could have expanded in Yemen and peasant producers could have grown tobacco. The fact remains, however, that they did not. It was enslaved workers of African origin who were forced to grow the cotton, sugar, coffee and tobacco that the West so desired to consume. We need to explain why this was so, and we need to do it by looking at the capitalism that actually existed, not some theoretical construct that could have been but was not. In that actually existing capitalism, slavery – as these articles demonstrate – at certain times in certain places played an important role.

There is another, even bigger, question: how is the slavery complex related to all the other significant economic changes occurring between 1500 and 1900? Certainly, the global countryside was transformed in other ways as well. In England, for example, enclosures opened up more fields to commercial cropping; in the Dutch Republic and the Mexican Bajio commercial farming expanded significantly without recourse to enslavement; in Eastern Europe, the so-called second serfdom allowed for a vast expansion of export-oriented agriculture. These transformations were all related to one another, but they were also different. How did they relate to the emergence of new forms of commercial capital, new institutions and new kinds of states?

The articles in this issue make an important contribution to the debate on slavery and European economic development by specifying more precisely how much slavery mattered. Yet none of them even begins to engage with the all-decisive 'why?' question. They observe the significance of slavery to economic development without explaining why it became important. As scholars have pointed out over and over again, labour mobilisation under capitalism can take many forms, with wage labour over the very long run the most important and characteristic form.[26] In most economic theorising beginning with Adam Smith and Karl Marx, capital owners purchase labour power, not labourers. According to these models, there is no need to own the worker, and in many ways – as economists have shown – owning the worker has important drawbacks to capital owners. So why is it that at certain points in time, capital owners decide it is best to invest in an economy based on slavery?

This is not the place to answer this question conclusively. But to begin to form an answer, we must acknowledge that Europeans, despite their long traditions of forging coercive labour relations, were not attached as such to enslaving agricultural cultivators. We also need to acknowledge that much contemporary economic activity was based on very different systems of labour mobilisation that included small proprietorship, debt peonage, sharecropping and wage labour, among others, and was thus different from slavery.[27]

Mobilising workers by enslaving them must have been a historically specific response to a particular set of constraints and opportunities at a particular moment in particular places. Perhaps ironically, the importance of slavery was rooted as much in the relative weakness of European capital owners as in their strength. To be sure, capturing huge territories thousands of miles away from home, shipping millions of workers to these territories, and forcing them to grow agricultural commodities and dig minerals out of the ground was an awe-inspiring sign of the power of these early capitalists. Yet it also signalled that they had failed to mobilise land, labour and commodities in other ways; indeed, it indicated that the market they were beginning to celebrate in the abstract was not working in the ways capital owners and theorists had envisioned. The capitalist transformations they aspired to were a huge and difficult project that inspired tremendous resistance from elites and commoners alike. In most parts of the world, the capitalist revolution remained weak and rather marginal to economic life, including in large swaths of Europe.

Wherever they invested, the biggest problem capital owners faced was dominating production, as artisans and peasant producers had myriad ways to resist their subordination to commercial capital, not just in Europe but also in India, China, Africa and elsewhere. In much of the world, people enjoyed significant rights to the land and the products of their own labour, and often they were embedded in political structures – the Ottoman Empire, for instance – that made difficult or even impossible the revolutionising agenda of commercial capitalists. Yet the expansion of commercial capital rested to a very significant degree on the transformation of that countryside, and this project succeeded first and foremost in the Americas, typically through the embrace of non-market forms of coercion, slavery prominent among them. It was there, for the first time, that commercial capitalists came to dominate production and to control labour on a truly massive scale. It was that transformation of remote countrysides that accelerated trade flows, allowed for capital accumulation, constituted new institutions and allowed Europe to overcome some of its resource constraints.

One of many examples for this contingency was seventeenth-century Virginia. When planters wanted to engage in the commercial production of tobacco for export, they at first began to draw on indentured workers from England at the very moment that plantation slavery expanded in unprecedented ways, especially in Barbados. When these workers rebelled in 1676–1677 in what is known as Bacon's Rebellion, however, planters began employing enslaved African workers on their plantations, solving what had become an explicitly political problem.[28]

The point here is to argue that embracing slavery was a response by European capital owners to the huge problems generated by a project that was close to their heart: transforming the global countryside. Enslaving workers was an indirect testimony to the social, economic and political strengths that allowed Indian, African and Ottoman peasants, among others, to resist this onslaught of capital owners and their revolutionary agenda. It was the unique ability of European states and capitalists to embark upon this project that would eventually allow them to set themselves decisively apart from states and capitalists in other regions of the world. Ironically, it would eventually let them transform peasant agriculture in these regions of the world as well.[29]

These are big issues that cannot be resolved easily. The authors here do something more modest, yet exceedingly important: they demonstrate and start to quantify the importance of the slave sector for a range of European economies. Their evidence makes it clear that slavery was of far greater significance than many scholars have previously been willing to admit. It makes another thing clear as well: that we can no longer talk about European economic development or European history without considering slavery. Slavery was a crucial ingredient of European modernity.

Notes

1. Douglass C. North and Robert Paul Thomas, *The Rise of the Western World: A New Economic History* (Cambridge: Cambridge University Press, 1973) has no mention of slavery; David S. Landes, *The Unbound Prometheus: Technological Change and Industrial Development in Western Europe from 1750 to the Present* (Cambridge: Cambridge University Press, 1969), 36–7, mentions and discounts the importance of slavery; Joel Mokyr, *The Gifts of Athena: Historical Origins of the Knowledge Economy* (Princeton, NJ: Princeton University Press, 2004) is silent on slavery; E.P. Thompson, *The Making of the English Working Class* (London: Victor Gollancz, 1963), 47, has only one passing mention of slavery; Hans-Werner Hahn, *Die Industrielle Revolution in Deutschland* (Munich: Oldenbourg, 1998) does not mention slavery either.
2. Among many others, see Robin Blackburn, *The Making of New World Slavery: From the Baroque to the Modern 1492–1800* (London/New York: Verso, 1997); Robin Blackburn, *The Overthrow of Colonial Slavery: 1776–1848* (London: Verso, 1988); Michael Zeuske, *Sklaverei: Eine M.enschheitsgeschichte* (Stuttgart: Reclam, 2018); Olivier Pétré-Grenouilleau, *Les Traites Négrières: Essai d'Histoire Globale* (Paris: Gallimard, 2004); Guillaume Daudin, 'Profitability of Slave and Long-distance Trading in Context: The Case of Eighteenth-century France', *Journal of Economic History* 64, no. 1 (2004): 144–71; Pepijn Brandon, 'Dutch Capitalism and Slavery: New Perspectives from American Debates', *Tijdschrift voor Sociale en Economische Geschiedenis* 12, no. 4 (2015): 117–37; Guillaume Daudin, *Commerce et Prospérité: La France au XVIIIe Siècle* (Paris: Presses de l'Université Paris-Sorbonne, 2005); and of, course, the essays in this issue.

3. Eric Williams, *Capitalism and Slavery* (London: André Deutsch, 1964 [orig. 1944]); Walter Rodney, *How Europe Underdeveloped Africa* (Washington, DC: Howard University Press, 1982 [orig. 1972]), 174; C.L.R. James, *The Black Jacobins: Toussaint L'Ouverture and the Haitian Revolution* (New York: Vintage Books, 1989 [orig. 1938]), 48; Aimé Césaire, *Toussaint Louverture: La Révolution Française et le Problème Colonial* (Paris: Présence Africaine, 1962), 21; Anton de Kom, *Wij Slaven van Suriname* (Amsterdam: Uitgevers-Maatschappij Contact, 1934), 60. See also Abdoulaye Ly, *Le Compagnie du Sénégal* (Bordeaux, 1955), 62.
4. W.E.B. Du Bois, *Black Reconstruction in America* (New York: Atheneum, 1969 [orig. 1935]), 5.
5. Sidney W. Mintz, *Sweetness and Power: The Place of Sugar in Modern Industry* (New York: Penguin, 1986).
6. Barbara L. Solow, 'Capitalism and Slavery in the Exceedingly Long Run', *The Journal of Interdisciplinary History* 17, no. 4 (Spring 1987): 715.
7. Barbara L. Solow, *The Economic Consequences of the Slave Trade* (Lanham, MD: Lexington Books, 2014), 107.
8. Javier Cuernca Esteban, 'Comparative Patterns of Colonial Trade: Britain and its Rivals', in *Exceptionalism and Industrialisation: Britain and its European Rivals, 1688–1815*, ed. Leandro Prados de la Escosura (Cambridge: Cambridge University Press, 2009), 36; Solow, 'Capitalism and Slavery', 732 and 735.
9. For the latest instance, see David Eltis, Pieter C. Emmer, and Frank D. Lewis, 'More than Profits? The Contribution of the Slave Trade to the Dutch Economy: Assessing Fatah-Black and Van Rossum', *Slavery & Abolition* 37, no. 4 (2016): 724–35. Other authors who make this argument include Patrick O'Brien, 'European Economic Development: The Contribution of the Periphery', *The Economic History Review* New Series, 35, no. 1 (1982): 1–18; Stanley L. Engerman, 'The Slave Trade and British Capital Formation in the Eighteenth Century: A Comment on the Williams Thesis', *The Business History Review* 46, no. 4 (1972): 430–44.
10. Engerman, 'The Slave Trade and British Capital Formation'.
11. O'Brien, 'European Economic Development', 18.
12. Alan L. Olmstead and Paul W. Rhode, 'Cotton, Slavery, and the New History of Capitalism', *Explorations in Economic History* 67 (January 2018): 1–27; Gavin Wright, 'Slavery and Anglo-American Capitalism Revisited', *The Economic History Review* 73 (May 2020): 353–83.
13. Joseph E. Inikori, *Africans and the Industrial Revolution in England: A Study in International Trade and Economic Development* (Cambridge: Cambridge University Press, 2002).
14. Patrick O'Brien, 'A Critical Review of a Tradition of Meta-narratives from Adam Smith to Ken Pomeranz', in *A Deus Ex Machina Revisited: Atlantic Colonial Trade and European Economic Development*, ed. P.C. Emmer, O. Pétré-Grenouilleau and J.V. Roitman (Leiden: Brill, 2006), 5–25.
15. Daron Acemoglu, Simon Johnson, and James Robinson, 'The Rise of Europe: Atlantic Trade, Institutional Change, and Economic Growth', *The American Economic Review* 95, no. 3 (2005): 546–79.
16. Sven Beckert, *Empire of Cotton: A Global History* (New York: Alfred. A. Knopf, 2014).
17. Sven Beckert and Dominic Sachsenmaier, eds., *Global History, Globally* (London: Bloomsbury, 2018).
18. Among the many titles that could be mentioned here, some stand out. Robert Fogel and Stanley Engerman, *Time on the Cross: The Economics of American Negro Slavery* (New York: Norton, 1974) is an important classic. Gavin Wright's *oeuvre* is full of

important interventions, such as Gavin Wright, *Slavery and American Economic Development* (Baton Rouge: Louisiana State University Press, 2006). See also Robert W. Fogel, *The Slavery Debates, 1952–1990: A Retrospective* (Baton Rouge: Louisiana State University Press, 2003). More recent work includes, Daudin, 'Profitability of Slave and Long-distance Trading'; Ellora Derenoncourt, 'Atlantic Slavery's Impact on European and British Economic Development' (unpublished paper, Harvard University, 2018), https://scholar.harvard.edu/files/elloraderenoncourt/files/derenoncourt_atlantic_slavery_europe_2018.pdf (accessed 13 July 2020). For a good summary of some of this literature, see Eric Hilt, 'Revisiting *Time on the Cross* After 45 Years: The Slavery Debates and the New Economic History', *Capitalism* (Spring 2020): 456–83.

19. Eugene Genovese, *The Political Economy of Slavery: Studies in the Economy & Society of the Slave South* (New York: Vintage Books, 1967); Fogel and Engerman, *Time on the Cross*; Caitlin Rosenthal, *Accounting for Slavery: Masters and Management* (Cambridge, MA: Harvard University Press, 2018).
20. See, for example, the recent debate on the *New York Times* 1619 project. For the project itself see https://www.nytimes.com/interactive/2019/08/14/magazine/1619-america-slavery.html (accessed 20 June 2020). For critical commentary on this project see, among many other writings, Sean Wilentz, 'A Matter of Facts', *The Atlantic*, January 22, 2020.
21. Rosenthal, *Accounting for Slavery*; Daina Ramey Berry, *The Price for their Pound of Flesh: The Value of the Enslaved from Womb to Grave in the Building of a Nation* (Boston: Beacon Press, 2017); Seth Rockman, 'Negro Cloth: Mastering the Market for Slave Clothing in Antebellum America', in *American Capitalism: New Histories*, ed. Sven Beckert and Christine Desan (New York: Columbia University Press, 2018), 170–94; Craig Wilder, *Ebony & Ivy: Race, Slavery, and the Troubled History of America's Universities* (New York: Bloomsbury Press, 2013).
22. Ronald Findlay and Kevin O'Rourke, *Power and Plenty: Trade, War, and the World Economy in the Second Millennium* (Princeton, NJ: Princeton University Press, 2007), 334.
23. Thomas Piketty, *Capital and Ideology* (Cambridge, MA: Harvard University Press, 2020).
24. https://www.wiwo.de/unternehmen/auto/diesel-skandal-und-kartellverdacht-so-abhaengig-ist-deutschland-von-der-autoindustrie/20114646.html; https://ftalphaville.ft.com/2016/01/08/2149557/the-us-tech-sector-is-really-small/ (accessed 14 July 2020).
25. Judith Ann Carney, *Black Rice: The African Origins of Rice Cultivation in the Americas* (Cambridge, MA: Harvard University Press, 2001); Daniel Rood, *The Reinvention of Atlantic Slavery: Technology, Labor, Race, and Capitalism in the Greater Caribbean* (New York: Oxford University Press, 2017); Jennifer L. Morgan, *Laboring Women: Reproduction and Gender in New World Slavery* (Philadelphia: University of Pennsylvania Press, 2004); Vincent Brown, *Tacky's Revolt: The Story of an Atlantic Slave War* (Cambridge, MA: Belknap Press of Harvard University Press, 2020); Aisha K. Finch, *Rethinking Slave Rebellion in Cuba: La Escalera and the Insurgencies of 1841–1844* (Chapel Hill: University of North Carolina Press, 2015); Hilary Beckles, *Black Rebellion in Barbados: The Struggle Against Slavery, 1627–1838* (Bridgetown, Barbados: Carib Research & Publications, 1987); James, *The Black Jacobins*.
26. Marcel van der Linden, *Workers of the World: Essays Toward a Global Labor History* (Leiden: Brill, 2008).

27. Of course, there were connections between various labour regimes, and coercion, even in wage labour, remained widespread long into the nineteenth century and beyond. However, plantation slavery as it emerged in the Americas was a very particular form of labour regime and a particular form of coercion. See Robert Steinfeld, *Coercion, Contract and Free Labor in the Nineteenth Century* (New York: Cambridge University Press, 2001).
28. Edmund S. Morgan, *American Slavery, American Freedom: The Ordeal of Colonial Virginia* (New York: W.W. Norton, 2003).
29. Beckert, *Empire of Cotton.*

Disclosure statement

No potential conflict of interest was reported by the author(s).

Index

Note: Bold page numbers refer to tables; *italic* page numbers refer to figures.

For Product Safety Concerns and Information please contact our EU representative GPSR@taylorandfrancis.com Taylor & Francis Verlag GmbH, Kaufingerstraße 24, 80331 München, Germany